Early Praise for *Modern Systems Programming with Scala Native*

If you're interested in writing more performant, low-level code in a JVM environment, look no further than Scala Native. This book will show you how to harness its power to create lightning-fast software.

➤ **Andy Keffalas**
Lead Software Engineer

If you think the only way to do systems programming is with C, think again! Scala Native is full of comparable features that enable us to implement the same applications C is known for, but in a modern way. Reading this book is really an eye opener that systems programming is not really a thing of the past, but is something that is actually cool.

➤ **Zulfikar Dharmawan**
Software Engineer

Modern Systems Programming with Scala Native is a gentle but thorough introduction to systems programming. Even if you are new to Scala Native, you can benefit from reading this book.

➤ **Gábor László Hajba**
Senior Consultant

This book provides a great (re)introduction to the fundamental, close-to-the-metal programming concepts in a way that those of us using higher-level languages don't deal with directly.

➤ **Justin Nauman**
Senior Systems Engineer

Modern Systems Programming with Scala Native is an excellent guide to applying modern systems' technologies and functional programming to service development. Richard clearly demonstrates how Scala Native effectively models the concepts and supports a high-quality implementation.

➤ **Corey O'Connor**
Founder, GLNGN, LLC

Modern Systems Programming with Scala Native

Write Lean, High-Performance Code without the JVM

Richard Whaling

The Pragmatic Bookshelf

Raleigh, North Carolina

Many of the designations used by manufacturers and sellers to distinguish their products are claimed as trademarks. Where those designations appear in this book, and The Pragmatic Programmers, LLC was aware of a trademark claim, the designations have been printed in initial capital letters or in all capitals. The Pragmatic Starter Kit, The Pragmatic Programmer, Pragmatic Programming, Pragmatic Bookshelf, PragProg and the linking g device are trademarks of The Pragmatic Programmers, LLC.

Every precaution was taken in the preparation of this book. However, the publisher assumes no responsibility for errors or omissions, or for damages that may result from the use of information (including program listings) contained herein.

Our Pragmatic books, screencasts, and audio books can help you and your team create better software and have more fun. Visit us at *https://pragprog.com*.

The team that produced this book includes:

Publisher: Andy Hunt
VP of Operations: Janet Furlow
Executive Editor: Dave Rankin
Development Editor: Katharine Dvorak
Copy Editor: L. Sakhi MacMillan
Indexing: Potomac Indexing, LLC
Layout: Gilson Graphics

For sales, volume licensing, and support, please contact *support@pragprog.com*.

For international rights, please contact *rights@pragprog.com*.

ISBN-13: 978-1-68050-622-8
Book version: P1.0—January 2020

Contents

Part II — Modern Systems Programming

Acknowledgments

This book is only possible because of the people who've helped me along the way:

My friends and my family, who have graciously allowed this project to consume my spare hours and attention over the last two years.

My employers at Spantree Technology Group and M1 Finance, who have supported my writing and speaking generously and cheerfully, despite all the disruptions it has caused.

Brian MacDonald at The Pragmatic Bookshelf, who approached me out of the blue with this opportunity and coached me through the proposal process that made this book happen.

My editor, Katharine Dvorak, who has been a constant cheerleader through all of the ups and downs of taking this book from an idea to a finished thing. Without her support and hard work, this book could never have been finished.

My thoughtful and attentive technical reviewers:

Hillel Wayne, Jan Goyvaerts, Zulfikar Dharmawan, Andy Keffalas, Rod Hilton, Justin Nauman, Eric Richardson, Corey O'Connor, and Gábor László Hajba.

Writing a book about systems programming with correct, tested, portable code is an immense challenge, and it wouldn't be possible without their time, care, and attention to detail.

The beta readers of this book, who have likewise provided a wealth of detailed feedback.

Scala Native's tight-knit community of open-source contributors: David Bouyssié, Mike Samsonov, Eric K. Richardson and Lee Tibbert, who have done so much work on Scala Native's standard library, and beyond, to support this community; Lorenzo Gabriele, who has done so much for the async ecosystem in Scala Native, and made critical insights that improved the second half of this book; and Paweł Cejrowski, whose work on libcurl far outpaces my own.

The broader Scala community, and especially the friends I've found there: I can't name them all here, but Jorge Vicente Cantero, Andy Hamilton, Heather Miller, Lars Hupel, Seth Tisue, Travis Brown, Natan Silnitsky, and Ólafur Páll Geirsson have all been a huge part of my journey with Scala, and I couldn't have gotten here without them.

My good friends in other technical communities, who have provided a perspective and sounding board as I have developed all of this material, especially Hillel Wayne, Alex Koppel, and Bryan Vanderhoof.

And finally, I have to give my thanks to Denys. Scala Native has been a huge and positive part of my life for the last two years, and I am endlessly grateful to him for everything he has done to make this all possible.

Foreword

Systems programming is a broad field that includes topics as diverse as operating systems, memory management, drivers, and direct access to hardware through programming using assembly language.

A key distinguishing characteristic that underlies this domain is the ability to program at the level of abstraction that is most appropriate for the problem at hand. Naturally, some problems require one to intimately understand concepts that are usually hidden by modern languages, such as working with unmanaged memory.

I am excited about *Modern Systems Programming with Scala Native* as it covers modern systems programming through the lens of the Scala programming language. The book builds up from foundational concepts, such as pointers and manual memory management. It walks through direct interoperability with both traditional C APIs and modern native libraries.

As you progress through the book, you are going to dive deeper into the world of lower-level programming. Even though the domain might seem intimidating at first, the gradual delivery of the key insights makes the whole process completely seamless.

Richard Whaling has been at the forefront of building the async I/O story for the Scala Native ecosystem. He is spearheading the adoption of libuv as the avenue for next-generation high-performance async I/O in Scala. In addition to the many great talks he has given on the topic over the years, this book provides another opportunity to learn from his experience.

Denys Shabalin
Author of Scala Native

Preface

If you've ever been frustrated by the many layers of abstraction between your code and the machine it runs on, you're looking at the right book. Over the coming chapters, I'll show you how you can use Scala Native to build efficient, modern programs from the ground up, focusing on practical use cases like REST clients, microservices, and bulk data processing. With Scala Native, you don't have to choose between elegant code and bare-metal performance.

Who This Book Is For

This book is for anyone who wants to learn how to build real software from scratch with a cutting-edge language. Maybe you learned Scala or Clojure on the job, but want to learn more about how to work "close to the metal" in a functional language. Maybe you're an enthusiast and want to write smaller, lightweight Scala programs that perform on tiny, near-embedded Linux systems. Or maybe you're a devops engineer with a strong Java background, who is just learning Scala, and you want to write strongly typed, testable code that doesn't impose the runtime penalties of the JVM. In other words, this book is for the folks who are my peers and colleagues in the Scala and greater JVM-language community.

I've tried my hardest to make this book accessible to folks with no prior systems programming experience—you'll learn about arrays, pointers, and the rest, as we go along.

All the code is in Scala, but we won't be using the advanced Scala techniques you might find in a functional programming text. When we do use intermediate-level techniques like implicits, I'll call them out.

That said, a few days' worth of experience with Scala is highly recommended. If you're totally new to Scala, there are a lot of great resources online. The official Tour of Scala[1] is a great place to start, and if you want to go deeper,

---

1. https://docs.scala-lang.org/tour/tour-of-scala.html

Dave Gurnell's and Noel Welsh's *Creative Scala*[2] or Martin Odersky's Functional Programming Principles in Scala[3] online course are both excellent resources. *Pragmatic Scala*[4] by Venkat Subramaniam offers a great, approachable book-length treatment, as does *Scala for the Impatient*[5] by Cay Horstmann. *Programming in Scala*,[6] by Martin Odersky, Lex Spoon, and Bill Venners, is the official book by the author of the language, and is a great, thorough reference guide, but make sure you get the third edition—the second and first editions are significantly out of date now.

What's In This Book

This book is designed as a series of projects that introduce the fundamental and powerful techniques of systems programming, one by one. Each chapter discusses an important topic in systems programming, and in the spirit of adventure, we may not always take the most direct route to our destination. Sometimes it's best to make a few mistakes, or do things by hand a few times before we skip ahead to the "right answer."

The work will all pay off, though. As you progress and master more and more techniques, you will gradually put the pieces together into something greater than the sum of its parts. And by the end, not only will you have the code for a lightweight, asynchronous microservice framework, you'll also be able to write one yourself if you don't like the way I did it.

The book is divided into two parts:

Part I dives into the fundamental techniques of systems programming using the basic facilities that UNIX-based operating systems have had since the 1980s. Unlike traditional systems programming books, however, networking is introduced early. For a modern programmer, working with remote services over HTTP is more relevant and practical than local file I/O. I then introduce process-based concurrency and parallelism. Although most Scala programmers will be more familiar with threads, processes are a powerful technique that distinguishes Scala Native from most other programming languages, and they're a great, safe introduction to asynchronous programming. We then look at combining these techniques to build a minimalist HTTP server and

---

2. https://www.creativescala.org/creative-scala.html
3. https://www.coursera.org/learn/progfun1
4. https://pragprog.com/book/vsscala2/pragmatic-scala
5. https://horstmann.com/scala
6. https://www.artima.com/shop/programming_in_scala_3ed

measure its performance with a simple stress test. However, we also look at the limits of these traditional techniques.

In Part II, we'll put the "modern" in "modern systems programming." From this point on, all of our code will be fully asynchronous, building upon the capabilities of the event loop library, libuv. Working with an industrial-strength C library like this, we'll introduce new complexities to our code, but it also gives Scala Native a chance to truly shine. With libuv, we'll revisit our HTTP server, introduce idiomatic Scala concurrency techniques, and learn how to work with durable data stores. Then, when we put those components together, we'll have built a framework for solving real-world problems. I'm skeptical of buzzwords, but the low overhead and light footprint of Scala Native code really does put JVM-based "microservices" to shame.

Working with the Code

All the code in this book has been tested with Scala Native 0.4.0-M2, Scala 2.11.12, and sbt 0.13.15 on Mac OS X and Linux (via Docker). You can get detailed instructions on how to set up a Scala Native development environment for Mac, Windows, or Linux in Appendix 1, Setting Up the Environment, on page 211. Since slight environment differences can be disruptive to low-level programs, I recommend using Docker on your preferred development machine, and the examples in the text reflect that.

A Note on Versions

Scala Native is rapidly evolving. The example code in this chapter, as well as all other code in this book, is written for the most recent version of Scala Native available, 0.4.0-M2. To ensure forward compatibility, all of the sbt projects include a compatibility shim file; to use with a newer version, just remove the shim!

You may also notice all the code is for Scala 2.11. When Scala 2.12 and 2.13 become available for Scala Native, I'll update the code files as well. You can download the latest version of the sample code on the pragprog.com website (https://pragprog.com/book/rwscala).

How the Code Is Organized

You can download the source code used in this book from the book's web page at pragprog.com.[7] If you're reading the electronic version of this book,

---

7.   https://pragprog.com/titles/rwscala/source_code

you can click the box above the code excerpts to download that source code directly. Or, if you use the Docker environment, you've already got it.

The code is organized by chapter, and within each chapter, the code is organized into individual projects, each with its own folder. Each project is a self-contained codebase, designed to be built by sbt,[8] the standard Scala build tool.

One important note if you're trying to modify the code: sometimes, for concise presentation, I will not show import statements and outer object Main wrappers in the code printed in the book. For example, have a look at this snippet:

```
import scalanative.unsafe._

object Main {
  def main(args:Array[String]:Unit = {
    // invoking various functions here
    ???
  }

  def helperFunction(arg1:Int, arg2:String) = ???
}
```

It may be displayed as:

```
def main(args:Array[String]:Unit = {
  // invoking various functions here
  ???
}

def helperFunction(arg1:Int, arg2:String) = ???
```

However, all the code files that you download and use are fully functional and complete. If you're interested in modifying my examples, definitely start with the files.

About Text Editors

Although there's no one standard for text editors when it comes to Scala, there are many options. Because Scala Native is still relatively new, the support for it is imperfect in complex IDEs. I instead recommend a plain text editor with good support for Scala syntax, like VSCode, Atom, emacs, or vi. Part of the beauty of starting from scratch is that we don't have to deal with giant Java dependencies with hundreds of classes—our code will be lean enough to write without sophisticated editor assistance. That said, I've found that the Metals plugin[9] for VSCode offers a good balance of common-sense help in an unobtrusive way.

---

8. https://www.scala-sbt.org
9. https://scalameta.org/metals

Online Resources

You'll definitely want to keep tabs on the book's web page at pragprog.com[10] for all the latest code and updates. And if you find any errata, there's a place to let me know about it.[11] I've also created a dedicated chat room on Gitter.[12] If you have any problems building or running the code in the book, or just want to hang out and chat, come on by! I also highly recommend perusing Scala Native's official site,[13] and referring to the Scala Native source code on Github[14] for the occasional deep dive.

With those resources in hand, it's time to get started!

---

10. https://pragprog.com/book/rwscala
11. https://pragprog.com/titles/rwscala/errata
12. https://gitter.im/scala-native-book/community
13. https://scala-native.readthedocs.io
14. https://github.com/scala-native/scala-native

Systems Programming in the Twenty-First Century

Why learn systems programming in the twenty-first century? It's a fair question. When I learned C at the turn of the century, low-level languages like C and C++ were already falling out of favor and being rapidly supplanted by high-level languages such as Ruby and Java. In the intervening years that trend has only accelerated, with functional programming languages such as Clojure, Elixir, Elm, Haskell, and Scala becoming more prominent, and C receding even further from day-to-day relevance.

And yet, C remains at the heart of modern computing: it's in our operating systems, our network stack, our language implementations, our virtual machines, and our web browsers. When performance is critical and resources are constrained, we still fall back on the techniques of low-level programming.

However, in this book, I'll show you that you don't have to choose between the ergonomics of modern languages and the performance of systems programming. With Scala Native, you get to have both.

What Is Systems Programming?

As a working definition, *systems programming* is the art of writing code while remaining aware of the properties and limitations of the machine that will run it. For all the complexity of modern software, computers are still surprisingly simple devices at the machine-code level.

We can identify *five fundamental data structures* for working on bare metal:

- *Primitive* data types—integers, floating-point numbers, and raw bytes that can be directly represented in machine code.

- Low-level *byte strings*—a way of representing textual data of variable length directly in a computer's memory.

- *Structs*—a compound data type that arranges named fields in memory in a fixed way.

- *Array* layout—data of the same type that are arranged in a grid-like fashion, one after another.

- *Pointers*—a numeric representation of the location in memory of some other piece of data.

These five data structures are profoundly interrelated. In this book, I'll introduce them gradually through a series of real-world examples. As you attain more proficiency, the deep connections between these concepts will let you write simple, powerful programs that vastly outperform what you can achieve with regular JVM Scala.

Even if you rarely write low-level code, the knowledge and insight you attain from learning systems programming pays dividends; essential everyday tasks, like tuning and debugging systems, interpreting complex error messages, and predicting the performance characteristics of complex systems, become much easier and more accurate when you have a solid knowledge of the fundamental principles by which computers operate.

That said, this isn't an eat-your-vegetables guide to systems programming. I'm excited to write a systems programming book *now*, because of the new possibilities created by recent developments in cloud computing and distributed systems technology.

Moving Toward Modern Systems Programming

The enterprise IT world is prone to buzzwords, but the rapid adoption of Linux container technology in recent years has been genuinely transformative. Having access to a simple format for packaging and deploying applications, containers, and Docker in particular, has radically altered the day-to-day workflow of working developers.

Best of all, the broad adoption of container technology has also eliminated one of the chief pain points of traditional systems programming: portability. Getting a typical C codebase to compile for the first time on a new development machine could often take days, and handling incompatibilities between different UNIX variants such as Mac OS X, Linux, and Solaris littered code with opaque macros and cryptic bugs. In contrast, Docker containers provide a reliable, Linux-flavored execution environment for any programming language that can run on any recent Windows, Mac OS, or Linux development machine. By giving us access to reproducible builds and uniform deployments, containers truly put the "modern" in "modern systems programming."

The other critical change that distinguishes new-style systems programming from what you'd find in a C textbook is the overwhelming emphasis on network programming in a modern cloud environment. Whereas classic systems programming books focus on file input and output (I/O), many programs written for cloud deployment will communicate over one of a few network protocols, and might never write to a file at all. That's why this book puts practical network programming front and center. You'll learn how TCP sockets work and how to write an HTTP client and server from scratch. By the end of the book, you will have designed and built a powerful, lightweight framework for RESTful microservices.

But that's enough hype from me. Before we dive into the foundations of systems programming, let's roll up our sleeves, write some code, and take a look at Scala Native in action.

Why Scala Native?

Scala Native is an ahead-of-time machine code compiler for the Scala programming language. It can take a Scala program, with traits, objects, garbage collection, and other advanced features of Scala, and translate it down to the same kind of executable machine code that a C compiler would output.

But that's not all. On top of Scala's support for object-oriented and functional programming, Scala Native adds powerful capabilities for working much closer to bare metal. In particular, it provides access to OS-level I/O and networking APIs, system-level shared libraries, and C-style memory management. With these techniques, we can often *replace* C code in performance-critical applications. And Scala's capacity for clean abstraction means that we can make low-level programs more elegant and readable than ever before.

At its best, Scala Native can simultaneously exhibit both modern programming techniques and a close affinity for the underlying hardware. This expressive clarity also makes Scala Native a great way to *learn* systems programming for the first time.

To start, let's set up a Scala Native project. We'll do so much as we would set up a simple Scala project: by creating a new folder (let's call ours my_code/hello/) with three files. The first file is a build.sbt file that describes our project:

InputAndOutput/hello/build.sbt
```
name := "hello"
enablePlugins(ScalaNativePlugin)

scalaVersion := "2.11.8"
scalacOptions ++= Seq("-feature")
nativeMode := "debug"
nativeGC := "immix"
```

The second is a hello.scala file that contains our code:

InputAndOutput/hello/hello.scala
```
object main {
  def main(args:Array[String]) {
    println("hello, world!")
  }
}
```

And the third is a project/plugins.sbt file that imports the actual Scala Native plugin:

InputAndOutput/hello/project/plugins.sbt
```
addSbtPlugin("org.scala-native" % "sbt-scala-native"  % "0.4.0-M2")
```

Much like a regular Scala program, when you enter the command, sbt run, the Scala build tool (sbt)[1] builds the project for you. After it's fully compiled, you should see the expected output of the program, like this:

```
$ sbt run
[warn] Executing in batch mode.
[warn]   For better performance, hit [ENTER] to switch to interactive mode,
[warn]   or consider launching sbt without any commands, or explicitly
[warn]   passing 'shell'
[info] Loading project definition from /root/project-build/project
[info] Set current project to sn-mem-hacks
[info]   (in build file:/root/project-build/)
[info] Compiling 1 Scala source to
[info]   /root/project-build/target/scala-2.11/classes...
[info] 'compiler-interface' not yet compiled for Scala 2.11.8. Compiling...
[info]   Compilation completed in 13.051 s
[info] Linking (2352 ms)
[info] Discovered 1267 classes and 9344 methods
[info] Optimizing (5002 ms)
[info] Generating intermediate code (1015 ms)
[info] Produced 39 files
[info] Compiling to native code (2272 ms)
[info] Linking native code (153 ms)
hello, world
[success] Total time: 28 s, completed Mar 13, 2018 5:11:03 PM
```

---

1.   https://www.scala-sbt.org

This is exactly what we would expect from a regular Scala program: the code we used is identical to a Hello, World in standard Scala, and the build configuration has only added a single plugin to support Scala Native. This is good news. Scala Native is 100% Scala—it's not a variant or a new version. It's simply a plugin that gives the language some additional capabilities.

What Makes Scala Native Different

So far, you've seen that Scala Native can be easy to use. In many cases, it works as a drop-in replacement for mainstream JVM Scala. But what can it do for us that JVM Scala can't?

Smaller Footprint

To see some of Scala Native's more exceptional functionality, run sbt nativeLink. You should see output like this:

```
$ sbt nativeLink
[info] Loading project definition from ...
[info] Set current project to sn-word-sorter (in build file:...
[info] Compiling 1 Scala source to ...
[info] Discovered 1279 classes and 9445 methods
[info] Optimizing (4418 ms)
[info] Generating intermediate code (961 ms)
[info] Produced 37 files
[info] Compiling to native code (2072 ms)
[info] Linking native code (308 ms)
[success] Total time: 17 s, completed Jan 21, 2018 4:25:58 PM
```

If you look in your build directory at target/scala-2.11, you'll see a 4.2MB executable file called hello-minimal-out. This file is a *native binary*—it consists of immediately executable CPU instructions plus headers, symbol tables, and other metadata to allow your operating system to load it and run it.

You should also see a 4.2MB file at target/scala-2.11/hello-minimal-out. That's our program! You can run it on its own just by typing ./target/scala-2.11/hello-minimal-out. You can copy it, move it around, and in many cases copy it to another computer intact. This file contains executable machine code: binary CPU instructions that your OS can load into memory and run without a virtual machine or interpreter.

In contrast, if you were to package up a standard JVM Scala Hello, World project, the output is a 5.5MB file called hello-minimal-assembly-0.1-SNAPSHOT.jar. Unlike our native binary, a .jar file cannot be directly executed—instead, it must be executed by a Java Virtual Machine (JVM). Combined, the size of a

JVM and an application JAR is often close to 100MB for a small app, and can rapidly increase for larger projects with complex dependencies.

Faster Startup

There's another, even more important difference. If we time the execution of both versions of our program, we'll see this:

```
$ time java -jar ./target/scala-2.11/hello_jvm-assembly.jar
hello, world!

real    0m0.350s
user    0m0.368s
sys     0m0.038s
```

```
$ time ./target/scala-2.11/hello_out
hello, world!

real    0m0.024s
user    0m0.021s
sys     0m0.003s
```

This is already an exciting result! Scala Native runs our Hello, World program in about 20 milliseconds, while our JVM program takes almost twenty times longer—close to half of a second—to print a string out to the console. Here we're seeing the impact of the JVM. A Java Virtual Machine is itself a large, complex program that takes time to set up and shut down, and we have to go through that process every time our tiny Scala program runs. In contrast, our native binary is a file containing machine code. Our OS can just load it into memory, point the CPU at the main method, and let it run.

Before we go any further, though, it's worth taking a step back and asking, When does performance matter?

For a command-line tool that a developer runs a few times an hour, a difference in startup time is a nice quality-of-life improvement. But when you're dealing with big data, high-throughput networking, or heavy-duty I/O, efficiency is critical; improving performance or reducing resource usage can save serious amounts of money and make it possible to tackle new, harder problem domains. That level of performance isn't always necessary; there are plenty of problems that are easily solved by higher-level programming languages. But throughout this book, we're going to keep our focus on areas where this kind of performance can make a difference. As a result, we're going to rapidly move from Hello, World to seriously big data.

Let's dive in by exploring the foundations of systems programming, starting with input and output.

Part I

Foundations of Systems Programming

CHAPTER 1

The Basics: Input and Output

Lots of ways exist to get data in and out of a program. Files, networks, and databases all serve this purpose in different ways, and you'll learn about all of them later on in the book. In this chapter, we'll look at the *standard input* and *standard output* streams all UNIX processes have. As you gain proficiency in lower-level input and output (I/O), you'll learn to write programs that perform more like a C program than a Scala program. You'll also become acquainted with *pointers* and *strings*, two of the key concepts of systems programming.

Later in this chapter, we'll start to work through a real-world use case that showcases the dramatic performance benefits to be had from taking a bare-metal approach to a seemingly simple problem. Using the Google Books NGrams dataset, we'll implement a variety of simple algorithms that can process this large data file efficiently. In doing so, we'll gain comfort with the essential concepts of systems programming: primitive types, pointers, strings, structs, and arrays.

Working with Output

You may already be familiar with STDOUT, or standard output, if you've worked with scripting languages like Perl, Python, or Ruby. In fact, we've already used it in the Systems Programming in the Twenty-First Century, on page xix. The "system console" that Scala's println writes to is none other than STDOUT. We can access it directly by importing Scala Native's stdio object, which includes the standard file descriptors as well as the C functions that we'll need to make use of them.

Introducing printf

Throughout this book, when I introduce a new function I'll present its signature and then discuss its inputs, outputs, and effects. Most of the functions

I'll present are provided by the operating system or the C standard library. In any modern operating system, access to all hardware functions, including displaying text on a screen, is protected. Because your computer will have many programs running on it all the time, each program is isolated both from the hardware and from all other programs. To have any kind of effect on the outside world, including printing a line of text to the screen, your program has to *ask* the OS to do it for you.

Standard Functions and System Calls

 Modern operating systems expose their capabilities as *system calls*, or *syscalls* for short, but neither C programs nor Scala Native programs can invoke system calls directly. Instead, the C standard library provides wrapper functions that can pass arguments to the OS on our behalf.

Not all stdlib functions invoke system calls, however; I'll make a note of the exceptions as we proceed.

To start, let's take a quick look at the definition of printf, a C function with similar capabilities to println:

```
def printf(format: CString, args: CVararg*): CInt = extern
```

printf can take one or more arguments: the first will always be a *format string*, containing a template with special placeholders, followed by zero or more additional arguments—one argument per placeholder in the format. This is a bit unusual and slightly error-prone. The Scala compiler won't protect you if you give printf the wrong number or type of arguments, but it's a decent replacement for println, and it can be fast.

First, let's quickly rewrite the Hello, World program we wrote in the introductory chapter to see how much it changes when we use printf. With printf, it looks like this:

InputAndOutput/hello_native/hello.scala
```scala
import scala.scalanative.unsafe._
import scala.scalanative.libc._

object Main {
  def main(args:Array[String]):Unit = {
    stdio.printf(c"hello native %s!\n",c"world")
  }
}
```

Notice two differences here. First, we're using the C printf function from the native.stdio package. We aren't passing any arguments yet, so we don't have any additional arguments or placeholders in the format string.

Second, the string itself now looks like this: c"hello, world\n". This is a CString literal. There are some big differences between a CString and the regular Scala String class you may be used to. A CString is better thought of as an *unsafe, mutable byte buffer*, with few frills or methods, which can make CStrings very difficult to work with; however, they also support a few low-level operations that are impossible with Scala-style Strings, which will make some exciting performance gains possible.

Learning More about CStrings

With printf, we can explore some of the properties of a CString. In addition to using the %s format to display the content of a string, we'll also be using %p to display its address, meaning the *location* in memory where the string is stored. Memory addresses are typically represented as hexadecimal numbers, such as 0x12345678. We'll also use the strlen function, which returns the length of a string, and the sizeof function, which returns the number of bytes of memory occupied by a variable of a given type:

```
def strlen(str: CString): CSize = extern
def sizeof[T](implicit tag: Tag[T]): CSize = undefined
```

Both of these are good examples of standard C functions that are not provided as syscalls by the OS—instead, strlen simply examines the contents of memory without help from the OS, whereas sizeof is implemented entirely by the compiler, before our program even runs. You might also notice the implicit tag parameter on sizeof; although Scala's implicit syntax features can have a somewhat intimidating reputation, our use of them in this book will be mostly straightforward. And in this particular case, Tag is actually a special value generated by the Scala Native compiler with type metadata, which means we don't have to instantiate or pass it at all.

With these methods, we can run some experiments on the CString literal that we used before:

InputAndOutput/cstring_experiment_1/cstring_experiment_1.scala
```
import scala.scalanative.unsafe._
import scala.scalanative.libc._
```

```scala
object Main {
  def main(args:Array[String]):Unit = {
    val str:CString = c"hello, world"
    val str_len = string.strlen(str)
    stdio.printf(c"the string '%s' at address %p is %d bytes long\n",
      str, str, str_len)
    stdio.printf(c"the CString value 'str' itself is %d bytes long\n",
      sizeof[CString])

    for (offset <- 0L to str_len) {
      val chr:CChar = str(offset)
      stdio.printf(c"""the character '%c' is %d bytes long and has binary
        value %d\n""", chr, sizeof[CChar], chr)
    }
  }
}
```

And if we run this code, we get this:

```
$ ./target/scala-2.11/cstring_experiment_1-out
the string 'hello, world' at address 0x55e525a2c944 is 12 bytes long
the CString value 'str' itself is 8 bytes long
'h' is 1 bytes long and has binary value 104
'e' is 1 bytes long and has binary value 101
'l' is 1 bytes long and has binary value 108
'l' is 1 bytes long and has binary value 108
'o' is 1 bytes long and has binary value 111
',' is 1 bytes long and has binary value 44
' ' is 1 bytes long and has binary value 32
'w' is 1 bytes long and has binary value 119
'o' is 1 bytes long and has binary value 111
'r' is 1 bytes long and has binary value 114
'l' is 1 bytes long and has binary value 108
'd' is 1 bytes long and has binary value 100
'' is 1 bytes long and has binary value 0
```

We can learn a lot from this program, so it's worth taking a little time to unpack. The most important point to observe is the difference between the length of the string, which is 12 characters long, and the size of the string variable, which is 8 bytes long. So how do we fit a 12-character string in an 8-byte variable?

The answer isn't necessarily obvious, but there's a clue in the address value if you can read hexadecimal numbers. Because the address 0x55e525a2c944 consists of 16 characters in a hexadecimal representation, we know that the address is exactly 8 bytes wide as well. In fact, it's a 64-bit unsigned integer.

This is no coincidence. If you look at the basic type definitions in the scalanative.native package, you'll see that CString is defined as a type alias, like so:

```
type CString = Ptr[CChar]
```

and that CChar itself is defined as this:

```
type CChar = Byte
```

But what about this Ptr[T] type? It's defined in the same package, but the implementation is mostly abstract, so some explanation is in order.

Working with Pointers

A Ptr[T] is a *pointer*, or a reference to a value of some type T. Pointers are variables that contain the *address* of data somewhere else in the computer's memory. In other words, if we have a variable like val char_pointer:Ptr[CChar], we know that char_pointer is the location of a CChar somewhere else in memory. We can retrieve the value of the character itself by *dereferencing* it, or looking up the address. In Scala Native, we dereference a pointer with the ! operator, like val char_value:CChar = !char_pointer. But when we use a pointer on the left-hand side of assignment, like in !char_pointer = char_value, we are instead *storing* a value into the location denoted by the pointer.

Pointers are one of the most fundamental concepts of low-level programming; we'll use them directly to move data around in memory and when designing our own memory-management strategies, but we'll also use them to manipulate other forms of structured data like arrays, structs, and as we've seen, C-style strings. Most important, we can also treat pointers themselves as a primitive data type: in a modern computer with a 64-bit address space, the address of any given byte is a 64-bit unsigned integer.

By exploiting the representation of pointers as integers, we can perform a variety of useful tasks very efficiently; for example, in our previous piece of example code, the string index lookup operation str(offset) is performed with pointer arithmetic, and we can implement it ourselves if we want to have a better idea of how pointers work. Our goal is to calculate the address of any character in a string, as long as we know the address of the first character. To do this, we need to understand a little more about how strings are laid out in memory.

C-style strings are always laid out one byte after another in a single contiguous region of memory. That means if the first byte of the string is at address 0x8880, the second byte is at 0x8881, the third at 0x8882, and so on. To keep overhead low, C doesn't even track the length of the string—instead, it stores a single binary zero byte, commonly written as '\0', at the very end of the string, which tells any algorithm stepping through the string, including our code and the internal strlen itself, "Hey, this is the end of the string, make sure you don't go any further!"

We can visualize a CString by drawing a string as a series of individual bytes one after another, like this:

Offset	0	1	2	3	4	5	6	7	8	9	A	B	C	D
CChar	H	e	l	l	o	,		w	o	r	l	d	!	
Hex	48	65	6C	6C	6F	2C	20	77	6F	62	6C	64	21	00

So, if we want to get the address of the character at offset, and the address of the first character is string, we can compute it as simply as val char_address = string + offset, and then get the value of that character by dereferencing it with val char_value = !char_address.

We can see these techniques at work by slightly modifying the cstring_experiment program we wrote in the previous section. For clarity, I've added a few more type annotations, and it'll now print the address of each character. Here's the modified program:

InputAndOutput/cstring_experiment_2/cstring_experiment_2.scala

```scala
import scala.scalanative.unsafe._
import scala.scalanative.libc._

object Main {
  def main(args:Array[String]):Unit = {
    val str:Ptr[Byte] = c"hello, world"
    val str_len = string.strlen(str)
    stdio.printf(c"the string '%s' at address %p is %d bytes long\n",
        str, str, str_len)
    stdio.printf(c"the Ptr[Byte] value 'str' itself is %d bytes long\n",
        sizeof[CString])

    for (offset <- 0L to str_len) {
      val chr_addr:Ptr[Byte] = str + offset
      val chr:Byte = !chr_addr
      stdio.printf(c"'%c'\t(%d) at address %p is %d bytes long\n",
          chr, chr, chr_addr, sizeof[CChar])
    }
  }
}
```

And here's the output:

```
the string 'hello, world' at address 0x5653b7aa0974 is 12 bytes long
the Ptr[Byte] value 'str' itself is 8 bytes long
'h'     (104) at address 0x5653b7aa0974 is 1 bytes long
'e'     (101) at address 0x5653b7aa0975 is 1 bytes long
'l'     (108) at address 0x5653b7aa0976 is 1 bytes long
'l'     (108) at address 0x5653b7aa0977 is 1 bytes long
'o'     (111) at address 0x5653b7aa0978 is 1 bytes long
','     (44) at address 0x5653b7aa0979 is 1 bytes long
' '     (32) at address 0x5653b7aa097a is 1 bytes long
'w'     (119) at address 0x5653b7aa097b is 1 bytes long
'o'     (111) at address 0x5653b7aa097c is 1 bytes long
'r'     (114) at address 0x5653b7aa097d is 1 bytes long
'l'     (108) at address 0x5653b7aa097e is 1 bytes long
'd'     (100) at address 0x5653b7aa097f is 1 bytes long
' '     (0) at address 0x5653b7aa0980 is 1 bytes long
```

We can make a few observations from this output to confirm what we deduced earlier and pick up a few more nuances as well. First of all, we see that the address of the string is equal to the address of the first character of the string. Both are 0x5653b7aa0974. We can also gather that adding (or subtracting) a Long from a Ptr[Byte] results in another Ptr[Byte].

If we look even more closely at the address of each character, we can indeed see that successive characters are located in successive addresses, one after another, and that the terminating zero byte is at the address str + str_len. But, as counterintuitive as it may seem, this does mean that storing a string of length n, plus its terminating byte, requires n + 1 bytes of memory. This is hard to get right, so I'll call out future examples with the potential for subtle off-by-one errors.

The last observation is the most fundamental one: every single character in the string has both a numerical address and a value of its own. A pointer is just an address, so it can point to data of any size or quantity. The drawback of this streamlined representation is that we can't know from the pointer type or value alone whether we are pointing to one byte, a 20-byte string, or megabytes of bulk data. Instead, all that context must be passed along manually, by the programmer, which creates a profusion of often-tedious bookkeeping tasks.

When performed correctly, however, effective use of pointers gives us the opportunity to dramatically improve the performance of our programs. By exploiting the lifecycle, location, and layout of memory in critical parts of our code, we can get more done in less time in a way that can seem almost magical. But this power does come at a cost. Many clever pointer operations are fundamentally unsafe, and errors on the part of the programmer can crash your program, corrupt data, or even open up serious security vulnerabilities.

Scala Native can't make these inherent risks go away; however, its support for working with ordinary Scala variables with fully managed memory and for isolating unsafe code to a few performance-critical sections is a genuine game-changer for systems programming.

Don't Panic

Pointers have a particular reputation for being hard to work with, in part due to C's quirky syntax and permissive compiler. Although, in my opinion, Scala Native's syntax is far more clear, I don't want to trivialize the subject either. There are still a fair number of subtle concepts and patterns around pointers you have to learn, and even simple programs often exhibit quirky usages of pointers that may not be obvious at first. I've done my best to introduce all the different patterns gradually, and explain them as I go, but don't worry if something isn't 100% clear the first time you encounter it. Once you've seen a few more examples and worked with all the major concepts, the big picture becomes much more clear, and you'll be slinging pointers around like a pro in no time.

Working with Input

So far, all the strings we've used in our programs have come from CString literals in our code such as c"hello, world". But in general, most strings your programs will handle don't come from the code itself; instead, they come from the outside world, either from a file, network, database, or somewhere else. These scenarios all have different nuances, but they have a lot in common, too. But the simplest way to get data into a command-line program is to read data in from the console.

How do we represent the stream of input from the console in a Scala Native program? In C, and in Scala Native, the standard input and output streams of a command-line program are represented as objects of the same FILE type as an ordinary file on disk, and for the most part, act like one as well. Unlike an ordinary file, these streams, called standard input and standard output, are created by the operating system when a program starts; they generally are not named or persisted to disk, and they cannot be rewound. Once consumed, a byte read from standard input is gone forever; likewise, a byte written to standard output cannot be un-printed. A third stream is called standard error. Like output, it is write-only, but it's intended for error messages or diagnostics that shouldn't interrupt the usual output of a program.

Reading strings in C has a reputation for being difficult, tedious, and error-prone for a variety of reasons. C's string primitives, as we've seen, are low-level, and the standard library doesn't offer the full complement of utilities provided by a modern language like Scala. The difficulty is compounded by the fact that many of the standard I/O functions like gets and scanf are widely considered to be fundamentally broken and insecure.[1]

That said, with careful attention to detail it's certainly possible to do low-level I/O safely in Scala Native, or in C. A variety of different strategies will achieve this, but for now, we'll rely on two somewhat higher-level functions: fgets and sscanf.

Retrieving Input with fgets

We first need to acquire data from outside of our program and store it in a string. We can do that safely with fgets, which has the following signature:

```
def fgets(str: CString, count: CInt, stream: Ptr[FILE]): CString = extern
```

fgets will read one line of text of no more than n characters from file stream, and store it in the string str. str must already be allocated with at least count + 1 bytes of storage. fgets cannot check the bounds of the buffer for you. If fgets succeeds, it returns the pointer to buffer. If fgets fails, it returns null. Checking for failures is important—null is returned most commonly when fgets reaches the end of a file, or EOF.

For the stream argument to fgets, we'll be using stdin, and we'll use disk files, pipes, sockets, and other data sources over the course of the book.

To use fgets correctly, we'll have to think a little bit about where we want to store the data. As we learned earlier, a pointer is represented by an integer, but that doesn't mean we can just tell fgets to store data *anywhere* in memory. In fact, most of the possible 64-bit address space isn't usable—we'd need 16 exabytes of memory to take up all that space! Instead, there are a few different *segments* of memory, each of which takes up a different range of the possible address space. Different segments will have different rules for working with them; some segments, like the text segment and the data segment, are read-only, usually containing the machine code output by the compiler.

The two segments we'll use for allocating memory are called the *stack* and the *heap*. We'll learn a lot more about both in Chapter 2, Arrays, Structs, and the Heap, on page 25, but for now we'll just use the stack to get some temporary storage and read into it, like this:

---

1. https://stackoverflow.com/questions/2430303/disadvantages-of-scanf

```
val buffer:Ptr[Byte] = stackalloc[Byte](1024)
val fgets_result = fgets(buffer, 1024, stdin)
```

This passage grabs a one-kilobyte block of memory on the stack, and returns a pointer to it, which we then read a line into. As long as the pointer is *valid*, we can write to it, or read from it, as much as we like. However, a stack pointer is only valid *until the function in which it is called returns*—that means that we should *never* return a stack pointer from a function, and instead use them only for temporary storage. Neither C nor Scala Native will prevent us from using an invalid pointer, however, so I'll call out some of the habits for safe pointer usage as we go.

Interpreting Input with sscanf

Once we have a well-formed string in a buffer, we can further parse the input if we like. The sscanf function works something like regular expressions in languages like Perl, Python, Java, or Scala: it accepts a *format string* and an *input string* as well as some *output variables*. The format string describes a pattern to search for, usually a combination of strings, numbers, and whitespace. sscanf checks to see if the input string matches the pattern. To the extent it matches, it assigns the results to the output variables. Note that the output variables are provided as pointers. This allows sscanf to deposit its result into memory controlled by the users code in a flexible manner.

That being said, sscanf is still fiddly, error-prone, and difficult to use. It has the unusual property of "succeeding" on partial matches, returning the number of components that have matched, which means the user must know and check the number of components that should match, and prevents many dynamic usages that would be possible in a higher-level language. On the other hand, sscanf is also fast, and for simple cases, the trade-off is generally worth it, as you'll see shortly.

Let's look at the signature for sscanf:

```
def sscanf(buffer: CString, format: CString, args: CVararg*): CInt = extern
```

sscanf takes a string buffer to scan, and another string containing a format, or pattern, to scan for. The format is similar to the format strings accepted by printf, but as you'll see, sscanf has a few additional capabilities.

Another quirk is that we won't be passing regular variables into the CVarargs to hold the results. Instead, we'll be passing in pointers of addresses where sscanf can *store the results of the scan*, just like we would by assigning into a pointer.

Parsing Numbers

To start, let's write a function that uses sscanf to parse integers from a line of text. The pattern for that is going to be easy: c"%d\n", one integer per line of text. To store the integers we read, we're going to use stackalloc. But, we have a problem: how can we safely return the numbers we've read, if the pointers are invalid once our function returns?

Since we're only going to return a single, primitive value from this function, we can actually dereference our Ptr[Int] to get a raw Int, which is safe to return.

This is much more clear in code than it sounds, but I'm going to add more explicit type annotations than usual to make it extra clear:

```scala
InputAndOutput/sscanf_int_example/sscanf_int_example.scala
import scala.scalanative.unsafe._
import scala.scalanative.libc._

object Main {
  def main(args:Array[String]):Unit = {
    val line_in_buffer = stackalloc[Byte](1024)
    while (stdio.fgets(line_in_buffer, 1023, stdio.stdin) != null) {
      parse_int_line(line_in_buffer)
    }
    println("done")
  }

  def parse_int_line(line:CString):Int = {
    val int_pointer:Ptr[Int] = stackalloc[Int]
    val scan_result = stdio.sscanf(line, c"%d\n", int_pointer)
    if (scan_result == 0) {
      throw new Exception("parse error in sscanf")
    }
    stdio.printf(c"read value %d into address %p\n",
      !int_pointer, int_pointer)
    val int_value:Int = !int_pointer

    return int_value
  }
}
```

If you run this and type a few numbers in, you'll see output like this:

```
$ ./target/scala-2.11/sscanf_int_example-out
5
read value 5 into address 0x7ffee428d294
10
read value 10 into address 0x7ffee428d294
a
java.lang.Exception: parse error in sscanf
  ...
```

One interesting phenomenon you may note is that we're actually reusing the same memory address for int_pointer over repeated invocations. What this means is that *before* invoking sscanf, the pointer actually contains *the previous value* that we read. This may seem unusual if you're used to working in high-level languages like Scala, which never exposes uninitialized data. But in Scala Native, when we receive a new pointer, it is uninitialized—it could contain all zeros, or it could contain whatever stale or malformed data previously occupied that spot in memory! Instead, it falls upon the programmer to ensure that uninitialized data is never read.

But as long as we use pointers in a disciplined and thoughtful way, we'll be just fine.

Parsing Strings

Now, let's try to modify our code to scan multiple items from the line input. Since we eventually want to parse a file with structured word counts, let's try to scan a line for string contents. This might seem a bit odd, since the line is already a big string, but once we start scanning for more complex structured data, these techniques will suit us well.

One challenge of working with sscanf and its relatives is that because it takes a variable number of arguments of different types, it's easy to make subtle errors.

For example, you learned how to allocate memory for strings for fgets by allocating a Ptr[Byte] up to the maximum size of the line. But with sscanf, you can easily make an error like this:

```
InputAndOutput/bad_sscanf_string_parse/bad_sscanf_string_parse.scala
import scala.scalanative.unsafe._
import scala.scalanative.libc._
import stdio._

object main {
  def parseLine(line:CString):Unit = {
    var string_pointer:Ptr[CString] = stackalloc[CString]
    stdio.printf(c"allocated %d bytes for a string at %p\n",
                 sizeof[CString], string_pointer)
    val scanResult = stdio.sscanf(line, c"%s\n", string_pointer)
    if (scanResult < 1) {
      throw new Exception(s"insufficient matches in sscanf: $scanResult")
    }
    stdio.printf(c"scan results: '%s'\n", string_pointer)
  }
```

```scala
  def main(args:Array[String]):Unit = {
    val line_in_buffer = stackalloc[Byte](1024)
    val word_out_buffer = stackalloc[Byte](32)
    while (fgets(line_in_buffer, 1023, stdin) != null) {
      parseLine(line_in_buffer)
    }
  }
}
```

This compiles, but if we run it we get this:

```
$ ./target/scala-2.11/bad_sscanf_string_parse-out
foo
allocated 8 bytes for a string at 0x7ffeef500280
scan results: 'foo'
bar
allocated 8 bytes for a string at 0x7ffeef500280
scan results: 'bar'
baz
allocated 8 bytes for a string at 0x7ffeef500280
scan results: 'baz'
foobarbaz
allocated 8 bytes for a string at 0x7ffeef500280
scan results: 'foobarbaz'
Segmentation fault: 11
```

What does this mean, and what did we do wrong?

A *segmentation fault* occurs when a program accesses a numeric memory address that it isn't supposed to. This is an immediate and fatal error, enforced by the operating system. In a memory-safe language like Python, Java, or ordinary Scala, this will never happen—memory addresses cannot be manipulated directly, so a programming error cannot cause an incorrect access. On the other hand, in unsafe languages like C, you, the programmer, can try to access any address you wish, without guarantees of safety. But, an incorrect memory access doesn't *guarantee* a segmentation fault—if the access falls in the wrong place, within memory otherwise controlled by your program, you're more likely to get strange, hard-to-reproduce behaviors than immediate errors.

As for the problem with our program, there's a clue to what went wrong in the output: allocated 8 bytes for a string at 0x7ffe53bd4ad0. We know that we need 8 bytes to hold any pointer, but we don't know anything about the size of the actual string to read. If we were to replace CString with the equivalent Ptr[Byte] in our code, we'd see that when we invoke stackalloc[Ptr[Byte]], we should expect to get a Ptr[Ptr[Byte]]—in other words, a pointer to a pointer to a character. Although that's a perfectly valid type, that's not what we want here at all!

What we want to do, instead, is create space to hold the string data itself. What we can do is stackalloc[Byte](1024), which still returns a Ptr[Byte], pointing at the first of 1024 contiguous, properly allocated Bytes for us to store our strings into.

Pointers and Arrays

 Earlier I said that a pointer is a reference to a value, but in many contexts we treat it as a reference to *one or more* values in contiguous memory. In the next chapter we'll see how to model this kind of memory layout more formally as an *array* and learn more about the close relationship between arrays and pointers. For now, though, it's worth remembering that a type of Ptr[T] can obscure the difference between a reference to a single object and a reference to many objects.

Once we have space allocated, we can start scanning for input. However, even if the code runs, we need to be careful: we've allocated 1024 bytes of storage, which means that we can read a string up to 1023 bytes long. The Ptr[Byte] that we got back from stackalloc can tell sscanf where to store its results, but the pointer variable itself doesn't track the size of the buffer. And because the storage space is uninitialized, strlen can't infer the length of the buffer, either.

Instead, if we want to protect ourselves from overflows, we need to tell sscanf the maximum string length *in its format string*, like this: sscanf(buffer, c"%1023s\n", result), which tells sscanf to read at most 1023 characters of data from buffer into result, or until it reaches a new line. This fragment exhibits most of the techniques necessary to read a string safely:

```
var string_pointer:Ptr[CString] = stackalloc[Byte](1024)
val scanResult = stdio.sscanf(line, c"%1023s %d\n", string_pointer)
```

This technique has downsides, though. For example, we've hard-coded a buffer size of 1024 into our stackalloc call, and a string-length of 1023 into our sscanf call; ideally, a single, configurable parameter would control both. Traditionally, this is challenging to do in C because you have to use C's unwieldy string-manipulation tools to manipulate the format strings, but for now, we'll hard-code our line-parsing function to use properly sized buffers.

There's one more catch: we need some way to *return* a string from a function. In a larger program, all of this stack allocation, error checking, and so on, gets a bit messy, and we'll definitely want to be able to isolate this parsing code and return well-formed, properly initialized data from a nice string-parsing function.

But we can't return a string by dereference like we did with the integers in our last parser; dereferencing a string will return a CChar, the value of only the first character in the string, which isn't what we want! We have a few other options available, though.

If we want a regular String, we could convert our CString into a regular, garbage-collected String, with fromCString(string). If we want to work with CStrings, however, a common pattern is to allocate memory *before* calling a function, pass the resulting pointer in as an argument, and then store the result in the provided pointer. If we do this, though, we'll want to be very careful with the length of the allocated buffer. In general, we want to pass in the length of a string buffer in some way, but then we would need some way to dynamically modify our scanf format string to safely read into these buffers with overflowing.

This isn't a trivial problem to solve, and there are a variety of strategies for us to explore. For now, though, we'll read a string into a stack-allocated temporary buffer, ensure that it doesn't exceed the length of the passed output buffer, and if everything is okay, *copy* the string from the temp buffer to the output buffer. To do this, we'll use the standard library function strncpy, which has the following signature:

```
def strncpy(dest:Ptr[Byte], src:Ptr[Byte], dest_size:Ptr[Byte]):Ptr[Byte]
```

strncpy, as one would expect, copies at most dest_size characters from src to dest; however, there's a subtle catch. As long as src is smaller than dest, everything is fine, and the result in dest will be correctly zero-terminated. If src is greater or equal in length to dest_size, only dest_size characters will be copied over, but the result *will not* be null-terminated. We could write a general-purpose wrapper to ensure null-termination in all cases, but for now we can just ensure that the size of our scanned word is no greater than the size of the output buffer, *minus one* to allow for null-termination. The resulting code, with a short main() function, looks like this:

InputAndOutput/good_sscanf_string_parse/good_sscanf_string_parse.scala
```scala
import scala.scalanative.unsafe._
import scala.scalanative.libc._

object main {
  def parseLine(line:CString, word_out:CString, buffer_size:Int):Unit = {
    val temp_buffer= stackalloc[Byte](1024)
    val max_word_length = buffer_size - 1
    val scanResult = stdio.sscanf(line, c"%1023s\n", temp_buffer)
    if (scanResult < 1) {
      throw new Exception(s"bad scanf result: $scanResult")
    }
```

```
    val word_length = string.strlen(temp_buffer)
    if (word_length >= max_word_length) {
      throw new Exception(
        s"word length $word_length exceeds max buffer size $buffer_size")
    }
    string.strncpy(word_out, temp_buffer, word_length)
  }
  def main(args:Array[String]):Unit = {
    val line_in_buffer = stackalloc[Byte](1024)
    val word_out_buffer = stackalloc[Byte](32)
    while (stdio.fgets(line_in_buffer, 1023, stdio.stdin) != null) {
      parseLine(line_in_buffer, word_out_buffer, 32)
      stdio.printf(c"read word: '%s'\n", word_out_buffer)
    }
  }
}
```

And when we run this, we'll see the following:

```
foo
read word: 'foo'
bar
read word: 'bar'
foobar
read word: 'foobar'
foobarbaz
read word: 'foobarbaz'
```

Looks good! This compact piece of code actually exhibits all the key techniques you learned in this chapter in less than twenty lines of actual code:

- Memory management with pointers.
- Safe I/O with low-level, null-terminated strings.
- File input and output with printf and scanf.

We're now ready to apply these techniques to real data. One of my favorite data sources to work with is the Google Books NGrams dataset. As we apply these techniques, at scale, to a real-world problem, we'll see the dramatic impact that systems programming techniques can have on performance.

Case Study: Google NGrams

The Google Books NGrams dataset is a rich trove of data containing the count of every word that occurs in the millions of books scanned by Google Books since 2005. The dataset is publicly available,[2] quite large, and relatively simple to work with. All the files together consist of hundreds of gigabytes of data,

---

2. http://storage.googleapis.com/books/ngrams/books/datasetsv2.html

and just the counts of individual words take up more than 50GB. Just so we don't get totally overwhelmed, we'll cut it down and only take the 2GB file of words that start with the letter A. In the Docker build environment, you can get it by running the /get_ngram_data.sh script, which will download a file called googlebooks-eng-all-1gram-20120701-a.

(If you're working on your own machine, you can download the data, but if you are using the supplied docker image, it is already there; just run xz -d googlebooks-eng-all-1gram-20120701-a.xz in the /root home directory and wait, patiently, for it to decompress.)

What we want to do is to read through one of these files and find the most frequent word/year combination. Fortunately the file format makes this relatively easy; every line is of this form:

```
ngram TAB year TAB match_count TAB volume_count NEWLINE
```

Such as:

```
A'Aang_NOUN    1879    45    5
```

We're most interested in the word itself, the year, and the match_count (that is, the number of occurrences). The volume_count, indicating the number of books containing the word, is less interesting for our purposes. To find the word/year with the largest count, we don't need to keep all the words in memory—all we need to do is keep track of the word with the largest count we have seen so far, compare each line we read with the current maximum count, and if it's greater, update the maximum and the corresponding word.

Now, if we were to do this in regular, idiomatic Scala, it would look something like this:

```scala
InputAndOutput/max_ngram_naive/main.scala
object main {
  def main(args:Array[String]):Unit = {
    var max = 0
    var max_word = ""
    var max_year = 0

    println("reading from STDIN")
    val read_start = System.currentTimeMillis()
    var lines_read = 0
    for (line <- scala.io.Source.stdin.getLines) {
      val split_fields = line.split("\\s+")

      if (split_fields.size != 4) {
        throw new Exception("Parse Error")
      }
```

```
      val word = split_fields(0)
      val year = split_fields(1).toInt
      val count = split_fields(2).toInt

      if (count > max) {
        println(s"found new max: $word $count $year")
        max = count
        max_word = word
        max_year = year
      }
      lines_read += 1
      if (lines_read % 5000000 == 0) {
        val elapsed_now = System.currentTimeMillis() - read_start
        println(s"read $lines_read lines in $elapsed_now ms")
      }
    }
    val read_done = System.currentTimeMillis() - read_start
    println(s"max count: ${max_word}, ${max_year}; ${max} occurrences")
    println(s"$read_done ms elapsed total.")
  }
}
```

This code is correct, and produces the correct result. But when we're handling
this much data, we also have to worry about how long it takes. With the UNIX
command time we can get the execution time of any program, like this:

```
$ time sbt run < ../../googlebooks-eng-all-1gram-20
120701-a
...
[info] Running main
found new max: A'Aang_NOUN 45 1879
found new max: A.E.U._DET 65 1975
found new max: A.J.B._NOUN 72 1960
found new max: A.J.B._NOUN 300 1963
found new max: A.J.B._NOUN 393 1995
...
found new max: and_CONJ 380846175 2007
found new max: and_CONJ 470334485 2008
found new max: and 470825580 2008
max count: and, 2008; 470825580 occurrences
[success] Total time: 231 s, completed May 2, 2018 7:35:05 PM
real    3m 57.89s
user    1m 32.26s
sys     0m 20.53s
```

As we can see, the code runs and finds that the maximum word is (unsurpris-
ingly) "and." However, it takes about four minutes to complete on my machine.
Just from inspecting the code, we can see a lot of unnecessary allocation. In
particular, we'll allocate a string for every line, then split it into three more
strings, before parsing into ints and updating. All those string allocations add

up and make the JVM garbage collector work pretty hard. So we have every reason to believe that if we can cut out all the allocation and GC overhead, we could improve performance substantially.

Now, let's implement an equivalent program using all of the techniques we've looked at in this chapter. The code will be structurally quite similar to the sscanf example project we just created, but with three major changes:

- We'll use a sscanf format string to parse the tab-separated fields, like so: c"%1023s %d %d %d".

- We'll pass not just a pointer to the current max-word into our line-parsing function, but also the current max count and year.

- We'll only update the current maximum if the count we just read is greater than the maximum.

- To cut down on memory allocation, we'll allocate all of our temporary storage outside of the main loop

By reading directly into temporary storage, we can dramatically reduce the memory usage of our program and eliminate garbage collection overhead entirely, although it becomes a little ungainly. The main() function should look familiar:

InputAndOutput/max_ngram/main.scala

```scala
def main(args:Array[String]):Unit = {
  var max_word:Ptr[Byte] = stackalloc[Byte](1024)
  val max_count = stackalloc[Int]
  val max_year = stackalloc[Int]

  val line_buffer = stackalloc[Byte](1024)
  val temp_word = stackalloc[Byte](1024)
  val temp_count = stackalloc[Int]
  val temp_year = stackalloc[Int]
  val temp_doc_count = stackalloc[Int]

  var lines_read = 0
  !max_count = 0
  !max_year = 0

  while (stdio.fgets(line_buffer, 1024, stdio.stdin) != null) {
    lines_read += 1
    parse_and_compare(line_buffer, max_word, temp_word, 1024,
    max_count, temp_count, max_year, temp_year, temp_doc_count)
  }

  stdio.printf(c"done. read %d lines\n", lines_read)
  stdio.printf(c"maximum word count: %d for '%s' @ %d\n", !max_count,
  max_word, !max_year)
}
```

But the actual parsing code now has more logic in it and takes more arguments:

InputAndOutput/max_ngram/main.scala

```scala
def parse_and_compare(line_buffer:CString, max_word:CString,
                  temp_word:CString, max_word_buffer_size:Int,
                  max_count:Ptr[Int], temp_count:Ptr[Int], max_year:Ptr[Int],
                  temp_year:Ptr[Int], temp_doc_count:Ptr[Int]):Unit = {
  val scan_result = stdio.sscanf(line_buffer, c"%1023s %d %d %d\n",
      temp_word, temp_year, temp_count, temp_doc_count)
  if (scan_result < 4) {
    throw new Exception("bad input")
  }
  if (!temp_count <= !max_count) {
    return
  } else {
    stdio.printf(c"saw new max: %s %d occurences at year %d\n", temp_word,
      !temp_count, !temp_year)
    val word_length = string.strlen(temp_word)
    if (word_length >= (max_word_buffer_size - 1)) {
      throw new Exception(
        s"length $word_length exceeded buffer size $max_word_buffer_size")
    }
    string.strncpy(max_word, temp_word, max_word_buffer_size)
    !max_count = !temp_count
    !max_year = !temp_year
  }
}
```

We'll see the impact of these optimizations when we run the program and collect timing information:

```
$ time ./target/scala-2.11/sort_alphabetically-out < \
  /code/googlebooks-eng-all-1gram-20120701-a
reading from STDIN...
found new max: A'Aang_NOUN 1879 45
found new max: A.E.U._DET 1975 65
found new max: A.J.B._NOUN 1960 72
found new max: A.J.B._NOUN 1963 300
found new max: A.J.B._NOUN 1995 393
...
found new max: and_CONJ 2007 380846175
found new max: and_CONJ 2008 470334485
found new max: and 2008 470825580
done. read 86618505 lines
maximum word count: 470825580 for 'and' @ 2008
real    0m 33.94s
user    0m 30.14s
sys     0m 2.50s
```

Impressive, no?

With a moderate amount of effort, we can improve the performance of our program by a factor of five or more; our JVM version took almost four minutes to complete, whereas Scala Native took *thirty seconds*. We only had to use a few more lines of code than our "vanilla" Scala implementation, and the results are strikingly better. This is a pattern we'll continue to see: Scala Native making high-performance, low-level patterns more concise, legible, and safe than ever before.

What's Next

In this chapter, you progressed from Hello, World in the introductory chapter to slightly more complex programs. You saw how Scala Native's bare-metal techniques for low-level I/O and memory management allow us to substantially outperform equivalent programs on the JVM. In the process, you gained familiarity with strings and pointers, two of the low-level data structures that distinguish systems programming from typical high-level programs. Next, we'll continue our deep dive into the fundamentals of systems programming, learning about arrays and structs as we continue to work through some basic algorithms on our Google NGrams dataset.

CHAPTER 2

Arrays, Structs, and the Heap

In the last chapter, we wrote a program to extract the maximum count from a Google NGrams file in a fraction of the time a traditional Scala program would. Our goal for this chapter is to read the entire NGrams file, aggregate word occurrences by year such that the counts of each word for all years are grouped together, and output the twenty most frequent words in the file. Before we can do that, we'll need to solve a few different subproblems, and we'll need to explore a few more advanced Scala Native techniques, too.

We'll start by looking at heap memory allocation, which offers a good alternative to the stack for bulk, long-term data, like our NGram file. I'll show you how to use *structs* to model the multiple fields of our NGram records in a way that works well with C libraries and data structures. Then we'll design a mechanism based on *arrays* for storing our data into a contiguous, growing region of memory. With those techniques under our belt, we can read and sort our whole data file. We can then add aggregation as a relatively small modification of our previous code, but with a very noticeable impact on performance.

To begin, let's look at how memory works and how we can have different areas of memory with different properties.

The Stack and the Heap

Memory addresses in a process are *virtualized* and *segmented*. A piece of hardware called a *memory management unit* (MMU) translates between the addresses that our program can see and the much more complex hardware devices, all while ensuring isolation as multiple programs run simultaneously. It does this by assigning chunks of memory, called *pages*, to specific positions in the address space of a single program. For example, if there are two programs running at the same time on my computer, they can both have access to totally different objects with the memory address 0x12345678, because the OS has *mapped* different pages of RAM to that address.

A running program with an isolated address space is called a *process*. (You'll learn more about processes in Chapter 4, Managing Processes: A Deconstructed Shell, on page 69.) It's also possible to create concurrent programs where multiple execution contexts occur simultaneously and share a single address space: such execution contexts are called *threads*, and although they're common in JVM programming, we'll make little use of them in this book.

What does this mean for us? As programmers, we see the impact of the OS's memory management practices in the properties of different kinds of memory, which live in different ranges of the address space. Typically, we'll encounter memory addresses in the following three segments:

- The *stack* segment, which holds short-lived local variables that live as long as the function that calls them.

- The *text* segment, which is a read-only segment containing the instructions for the program itself.

- The *data* segment or *heap* segment, which holds everything else.

You'll learn more about how to use the text segment later in this chapter. For now, we need to figure out how to allocate memory on the heap and what constraints we'll need to keep in mind to use it correctly. The most important rule to remember with heap memory is this: once heap memory is allocated, we're *responsible for it* in every sense. (You'll learn more about exactly what that means shortly.)

Heap memory management is one of the fundamental problems of systems programming. You could spend years studying and refining various techniques, and this chapter will only scratch the surface. Errors in memory allocation can also be extremely hard to test, isolate, and debug. For this reason, I strongly advocate the approach of using manual allocation *only where necessary*, and instead relying on higher-level techniques wherever performance constraints aren't extreme.

All that being said, manual memory management allows for a level of cleverness and optimization in program design unmatched by any higher-level language, and a well-designed allocation scheme can be both elegant and highly performant.

malloc

The fundamental function for allocating heap memory is malloc, which has a straightforward signature:

```
def malloc(size:Int):Ptr[Byte]
```

malloc's simple signature hides a great deal of subtlety. First of all, you may notice that unlike stackalloc, malloc doesn't take a type parameter; instead it just takes the number of bytes requested and returns a pointer to an unused region of memory of the requested size. In theory, malloc can fail, but that's essentially impossible on a modern system—your operating system will generally terminate the process before malloc itself returns an error.

Since malloc returns a Ptr[Byte], it's pretty straightforward to apply it to handling the sort of string and buffer data we used in the previous chapter. But what if we want to allocate space for a struct or an array of structs?

To create space for structured data, we can use two techniques in tandem: we can use Scala Native's built-in sizeof[T] function to compute the size, in bytes, of the data type we need, and then multiply that size by the number of elements we wish to store. However, we might request space for ten integers like this:

```
val 10_ints = malloc(10 * sizeof[Int])
```

But the type of 10_ints is still going to be Ptr[Byte], not the Ptr[Int] that we want!

The solution to the problem is a *cast*, an instruction to the compiler to reinterpret the type of a pointer. A *cast* is not the same as a *conversion*—no transformation is applied to the contents of a variable when we cast it. The most common use of a cast is to convert pointer types to and from Ptr[Byte], not only for use with malloc, but also for quasi-generic functions such as malloc (and qsort) in which Ptr[Byte] effectively serves as a catch-all reference type, analogous to Scala's AnyRef.

To cast our 10_ints to our desired type of Ptr[Int], we would do this:

```
val ngram_array = malloc(10 * sizeof[Int]).cast[Ptr[Int]]
```

Whew! But before we can safely use malloc to store our data, we'll need to look at two more functions that are essential for working with heap memory: free and realloc.

free

When we allocate memory with malloc, that block of memory will stay around for as long as we need it; however, we have no garbage collector to rely on with malloc, so if we know we're done with a pointer, we need to call free() to give it back. Failing to call free() in a long-lived program will result in a *memory leak*, in which your program continues to allocate new memory without ever reclaiming unused space until your computer's RAM is totally exhausted.

free works like this:

```
def free(p:Ptr[Byte]):Unit
```

But, there are a few catches that aren't evident in the signature. First of all, the pointer passed to free *must* be a valid pointer created by malloc *that has not been freed previously*. Calling free twice on the same pointer is a severe error, as is calling free on a pointer on the stack, a function pointer, or anything else not managed by malloc.

---

malloc and free: Not System Calls

malloc is another good example of a major C standard library function that isn't a system call. malloc, internally, keeps track of the total size of the heap, plus the size and location of every allocated chunk of memory within it. When we ask for more memory, malloc will either give us an available chunk of memory within the heap or it will *grow* the heap using the more obscure system call, sbrk, to change the size of the heap segment itself.

Likewise, free never makes a system call, but it can still be slow—maintaining malloc's map of allocated memory is expensive in a data-intensive program.

The best way to handle malloc and free is to structure your program so that every pointer created by malloc has a clear lifecycle, such that you can be assured that free will be called in an orderly way for every call to malloc. If it isn't possible to do this, it may be worth either redesigning your program to support this pattern, or else rely on a garbage collector instead.

One edge case can simplify things: if you have a short-lived program, there's relatively little benefit to calling free exhaustively *immediately before your program terminates*. All memory, stack or heap, will be released when your process exits, and it can sometimes be useful to write a short-lived program that simply mallocs until completion.

One more trick we can do: realloc will allow us to *resize* a block of memory returned by malloc. Sort of.

realloc

realloc has the following signature:

```
def realloc(in:Ptr[Byte]):Ptr[Byte]
```

realloc takes a pointer as its sole argument and on success, returns a pointer to a region of memory of the desired size. It may or may not resize the region in-place, depending on whether there is enough space for it in adjacent areas of memory. If realloc returns a pointer to a new address, realloc will internally copy your data from the old space to the new, larger area and free the old pointer. However, this can be dangerous if you have *any* outstanding pointers to the old region somewhere in your program because they have now been invalidated in a nondeterminstic way.

In other words, realloc is powerful, but dangerous, and it can also be expensive. When we use it, we'll want to use it as little as possible.

As you may have observed, all of these heap memory management functions have quirks, caveats, and dangers associated with them. Wherever possible, we'll try to isolate this code, and provide a clean abstraction over it, rather than let our malloc operations and such spread all over our codebase.

Zones

The stack and the heap have been with us for about as long as we've had modern computers; but, Scala Native also provides a newer technique for semiautomatic memory management, in the form of the Zone object. A Zone is an object that can allocate memory and track its usage for us; in other words, it automatically cleans up memory like the stack does, but it can work in the much larger heap segment. It also isn't bound to the scope of a single function —instead, a Zone object can be passed as an implicit argument, which allows many nested functions to share a single Zone, following this sort of pattern:

```
def handler(s:CString):CString = Zone { implicit z =>
  val stringSize = strlen(s) + 1
  val transformed_1 = native.alloc[Byte](stringSize)
  inner_handler(transformed)
}
def inner_handler(s:CString)(implicit z: Zone):CString = {
  // the inner handler can allocate as much as it wants here,
  // and it will all get cleaned up when the outer handler returns.
}
```

Zones are a great alternative to the stack for short-lived objects, and we'll continue to explore ways to use them, especially in the second half of the book.

But for now, let's shift gears and try to plan out *how* to store our data in the big memory chunks that malloc and its friends can give us.

Structs, Arrays, and Sorting

We've already written code in Case Study: Google NGrams, on page 18, that can *read* the contents of the NGrams file, but if we want to *sort* it, we're going to need to store the parsed content of the file in a data structure of some kind. It'll need to track the word, year, and count of each line in the file. But to design this structure, we'll need to have some understanding of the function that will consume it.

That function, qsort, has the following signature:

```
def qsort(data:Ptr[Byte],
          num:Int,
          size:Int,
          comparator:CFunctionPtr2[Ptr[Byte], Ptr[Byte], Int])
```

qsort is powerful, and it can sort almost anything, but it can be a bit cryptic. Like malloc, it uses Ptr[Byte] (or a void pointer in C) as a catch-all generic data type; it can sort anything we can represent as a pointer, and like with malloc, we'll cast the data to Ptr[Byte] to make the types line up. Later on, you'll learn how to properly configure the num, size, and comparator arguments to set up this process.

First, we need to figure out how to represent our NGram records as something that we can fit in a Ptr, and that C APIs will be able to make sense of.

Structs and Strings

If we were working in regular JVM Scala, and we wanted to design a data structure to hold our NGram items, we might use a simple case class like this:

```
case class NGram(word:String, count:Int, year:Int)
```

Or if we wanted to streamline things even further, we could just use a tuple:

```
type NGram = Tuple3[String, Int, Int]
```

Either way, for each line of the file, we're going to need to create a data structure that contains the following:

- The word itself.
- The number of occurrences.
- The year of the occurrences.

In Scala Native, we can, of course, use case classes or tuples in regular code; the trouble is that because those objects are garbage-collected, we can't represent them with pointers or pass them as arguments to C functions.

To model the same data in a C-friendly way, we'll have to use a C-style data structure, called a *struct*. Structs combine many of the properties of strings and tuples with some of the advantages and disadvantages of C-style strings.

Instead, we'll use Scala Native's C interop capabilities to model the data as a struct. A *struct* is a C-style data structure that has some of the properties of a tuple or case class, as well as some of the use and storage characteristics of the CString type that you learned about in Chapter 1, The Basics: Input and Output, on page 3. A struct consists of an ordered series of fields of different types, and all the fields have to be C-friendly Scala Native types like Byte, Int, Ptr, or another struct type.

Because all the fields have known sizes, and every struct instance is laid out the same, structs have the following useful properties:

- The fields of a struct can be stored one after another in memory, just like characters in a string.

- The position of any field is a static byte offset from the beginning of a struct.

- All instances of a struct type have the exact same size, known at compile time.

- A reference to a struct can be represented by a single pointer.

- Structs can be be efficiently allocated in bulk.

Fortunately, Scala Native makes structs just as easy to define as a regular Scala class—we simply define a type alias for CStructN types, that work a lot like tuples. So, we can define a struct type analogous to our NGram type like this:

```
type NGramData = CStruct4[CString, Int, Int, Int]
```

This defines NGramData to be a 16-byte wide region of memory, laid out like this:

Offset	0	1	2	3	4	5	6	7	8	9	A	B	C	D	E	F
Field			Ptr[CString]							Int				Int		

Once we have a struct defined, we can use stackalloc or malloc to allocate space for it and get back a pointer to the uninitialized value, just like with a string.

Scala Native has a bit of syntactic magic for working with the fields of structs; if we have a Ptr to a CStruct value, we can retrieve it's member fields with ._1, ._2, and so on, just like a normal Scala tuple; but if we want the address of a field instead, we can get that with .at1, .at2, and so forth. This allows us to use dereference, assignment, or pointer arithmetic on whole structs or individual fields, but it can look a bit funny at first. To get a sense of it, let's write a modified version of our line-parsing code from Case Study: Google NGrams, on page 18. We'll just pass in a Ptr[NGramData] for it to read into and get rid of the comparison logic, which we don't need any more.

There's one last catch. Because our NGramData struct contains a pointer to the CString, and not the CString content itself, we'll still need to allocate space for the string content and store that Ptr[Byte] value within the struct field. Don't worry; it's easier than it sounds:

```
MemoryManagement/sort_by_count/main.scala
def parseLine(line_buffer:Ptr[Byte], data:Ptr[NGramData]):Unit = {
  val count = data.at2
  val year = data.at3
  val doc_count = data.at4

  val sscanf_result = stdio.sscanf(line_buffer, c"%1023s %d %d %d\n",
                                   temp_word, year, count, doc_count)
  if (sscanf_result < 4) {
    throw new Exception("input error")
  }
  val word_length = strlen(temp_word)
  val new_string = malloc(word_length + 1)
  strncpy(new_string, temp_word, word_length + 1)
  data._1 = new_string
}
```

As you see here, we can store directly into the second, third, and fourth fields of our Ptr[NGramData] by fetching their addresses, and passing them directly into sscanf.

But to assign the string content we have to do things a little differently: we'll read into a temporary buffer, then allocate some dedicated storage for our new string with malloc, and then carefully copy into the newly allocated memory with strncpy. After all that, though, the CString field in our NGramData struct is still uninitialized! Our struct only points to the new memory when we assign to the CString field once we assign into it with data._1 = new_string.

As a rule of thumb, it's much more common to use the ._N form of field accessor than the .atN, for both assignment and dereference. But there will be a few points later in the book when .atN becomes very useful for working with intricate nested data structures. And as we've already seen, it's a great fit for sscanf() in particular.

With this technique in our toolbelt, we're now making serious headway into solving our sorting program. But we still need to devise a strategy for managing and growing our data as we read from our (very large!) input file.

Arrays and Pointers

At this point, introducing arrays feels a bit anticlimactic; we've already seen almost everything one can do with them. How so?

- We've seen strings, which are a special class of byte arrays with unknown length.
- We've used pointer arithmetic to manipulate addresses, which is how array access works.
- We've used malloc and stackalloc to allocate strings and structs, which is how arrays are allocated.

In many ways, we've been working with arrays all along; but we should take this opportunity to review and consolidate what we know, so that we can plan for the amount of data we'll be handling shortly.

An *array* is a data structure consisting of a series of items of the same type. Unlike arrays in higher-level languages, a Scala Native array can't be dynamically resized, and access is unsafe—if you try to read or set an item past the end of the array, you'll get nasty runtime errors. This happens because C and Scala Native represent arrays at runtime by their address only. Despite this, it's generally necessary to track some additional metadata, such as the size of the array.

In addition, if we do need to increase the size of an array with realloc, we must take additional care. Because realloc invalidates pointers passed into it, we must make sure that no stale pointers to discarded memory escape into other data structures. And to reduce the number of expensive realloc calls, we'll want to batch up our allocations periodically, in bulk, which means we'll need to track the *capacity* of the array separately from the size.

To track all this vital data in an organized way, we can design a simple case class, along with some helper methods to streamline the more complex malloc and casting operations—something like this:

```
final case class WrappedArray[T](var data:Ptr[T], var used:Int,
  var capacity:Int)
```

You may note here that I'm using a regular case class, for convenience. The WrappedArray object itself isn't going to require high degrees of performance; rather, its inner data array will be used directly by client code.

Since this component is intended to be used solely for this application, I'm not going to stress about making it fully generic or universal. This also means that the helper functions we write to work with a WrappedArray[NGramData] will belong in the main object declaration of the program, and not in a WrappedArray companion object.

To initialize the array, we can write a helper function like this:

MemoryManagement/sort_by_count/main.scala
```
def makeWrappedArray(size:Int):WrappedArray[NGramData] = {
  val data = malloc(size * sizeof[NGramData]).asInstanceOf[Ptr[NGramData]]
  return WrappedArray[NGramData](data, 0, size)
}
```

And to resize the array, we can just reassign to the inner data field with realloc:

MemoryManagement/sort_by_count/main.scala
```
def growWrappedArray(array:WrappedArray[NGramData], size:Int):Unit = {
  val new_capacity = array.capacity + size
  val new_size = new_capacity * sizeof[NGramData]
  val new_data = realloc(array.data.asInstanceOf[Ptr[Byte]], new_size)
  array.data = new_data.asInstanceOf[Ptr[NGramData]]
  array.capacity = new_capacity
}
```

Best of all, this class is parameterized over the type of the array T, so we could use it to hold anything that we can represent with a pointer: structs, strings, integers, and so on. It should be perfect to hold our big slab of NGramData.

One more thing we should take care of before we move on is when we write a complex data structure like this, it's usually best to also write a utility function to free all of the memory we've allocated when we're done. This might not be strictly necessary for this program, since we are unlikely to have any opportunity to free memory before the program completes, but it could become useful later, and it's not particularly complicated:

MemoryManagement/sort_by_count/main.scala
```
def freeArray(array:Ptr[NGramData], size:Int):Unit = {
  for (i <- 0 until size) {
    val item = array + i
    stdlib.free( item._1 )
  }
  stdlib.free(array.asInstanceOf[Ptr[Byte]])
}
```

The only subtlety here is that since the individual string arrays are stored in the larger array, we have to walk through and free each one before freeing array itself.

Sorting an Array

Now that we know how to structure our data, we can revisit the signature of qsort:

```
def qsort(data:Ptr[Byte],
          num:Int,
          size:Int,
          comparator:CFuncPtr2[Ptr[Byte], Ptr[Byte], Int])
```

We'll pass in an array of NGramData cast to Ptr[Byte], we can get the value of num from the used field of the WrappedArray, and we can get the size of each item just by sizeof[NGgramData]. But for qsort to work, we have to supply the comparator, too; and comparator has a type we haven't seen before, a CFuncPtr, or *function pointer*.

Implementing a Comparator

In a typical systems programming course, abstracting from functions to function pointers is one of the hardest conceptual leaps, and C's syntax certainly doesn't make it any easier. In Scala though, the situation is much easier; Scala developers are used to treating named or anonymous functions as first-class values, and Scala's type system makes it easy to represent the parameter and result types of a function in a straightforward way. However, C functions have some restrictions that Scala functions don't; in particular, for the Scala Native compiler to pass a Scala function into a C function, the Scala function *must not* close over any local variables or state—fortunately, the clean semantics of these comparator functions makes that an easy constraint to obey.

Much like the standard Scala trait Ordered, the comparator function takes two Ptr[Byte]s as arguments, and returns an int depending on the relative position of a and b in the desired sequencing:

- If a should come before b, the comparator should return a value < 0.
- If a is equal to b, the comparator should return 0.
- If a should come after b, the comparator should return a value > 0.

The comparator function is also responsible for casting the input Ptr[Byte] to whatever the correct type of value is, and implementing the comparison as efficiently as possible. For example, we could implement an ascending sort comparator like this:

MemoryManagement/sort_by_count/main.scala

```scala
val by_count_naive = new CFuncPtr2[Ptr[Byte],Ptr[Byte],Int] {
  def apply(p1:Ptr[Byte], p2:Ptr[Byte]):Int = {
    val ngram_ptr_1 = p1.asInstanceOf[Ptr[NGramData]]
    val ngram_ptr_2 = p2.asInstanceOf[Ptr[NGramData]]
    val count_1 = ngram_ptr_1._2
    val count_2 = ngram_ptr_2._2
    if (count_1 > count_2) {
      return -1
    }
    else if (count_1 == count_2) {
      return 0
    }
    else {
      return 1
    }
  }
}
```

It's entirely correct, but a bit inefficient, and since this code will run tens of millions of times, we want to make it as efficient as possible. We can remove all the conditional logic with a clever optimization:

MemoryManagement/sort_by_count/main.scala

```scala
val by_count = new CFuncPtr2[Ptr[Byte],Ptr[Byte],Int] {
  def apply(p1:Ptr[Byte], p2:Ptr[Byte]):Int = {
    val ngram_ptr_1 = p1.asInstanceOf[Ptr[NGramData]]
    val ngram_ptr_2 = p2.asInstanceOf[Ptr[NGramData]]
    val count_1 = ngram_ptr_1._2
    val count_2 = ngram_ptr_2._2
    return count_2 - count_1
  }
}
```

This may seem a bit unintuitive, but every little bit helps when we're working deep inside an inner loop.

Putting It All Together

We're now (finally) ready to sort some NGrams! This doesn't *quite* fulfill the whole exercise that we set out at the start of the chapter, but it's a good intermediate step because it integrates all the techniques we've learned so far. With our resizable array, our comparator, and our parseLine function in hand, the main program loop is quite simple:

1. Initialize the array.

2. While there is input in stdin, resize the array if it is full and then parse the new line of input.

3. Sort the array.

4. Print the top twenty items.

The only thing we have to figure out is our strategy for growing the array. realloc is expensive, which leads us toward infrequent block allocation, but too large of a block size risks over-allocation and consuming unnecessary amounts of memory. In our case, however, we can expect this program to use most (or all) of the available memory on a given system, certainly in the multi-gigabyte range, and from examining the file, we know we have to hold around 80 million items in our array at once!

Based on these factors, I've set a block size of 2^20 or 1048576 items, which will be both the initial size of the array, as well as the amount we grow by when it reaches maximum capacity. Since each NGramData element is exactly 20 bytes long, this means we'll be allocating about 20 megabytes of data at a time; this is a lot, but even in a worst case we can't over-allocate by more than 2% of the total data size. In a more complex program, sizing like this would be a bit aggressive, but it's a good fit for these conditions.

Here's the code:

```scala
MemoryManagement/sort_by_count/main.scala
def main(args:Array[String]):Unit = {
  val block_size = 65536 * 16
  val line_buffer = malloc(1024)

  var array = makeWrappedArray(block_size)

  val read_start = System.currentTimeMillis()
  while (stdio.fgets(line_buffer, 1023, stdin) != null) {
    if (array.used == array.capacity) {
        growWrappedArray(array, block_size)
    }
    parseLine(line_buffer, array.data + array.used)
    array.used += 1
  }
  val read_elapsed = System.currentTimeMillis() - read_start
  stdio.fprintf(stdio.stderr, c"reached EOF after %d lines in %d ms\n",
                array.used, read_elapsed)

  val sort_start = System.currentTimeMillis()
  qsort.qsort(array.data.asInstanceOf[Ptr[Byte]], array.used,
    sizeof[NGramData], by_count)
  val sort_elapsed = System.currentTimeMillis() - sort_start
  stdio.printf(c"sorting done in %d ms\n", sort_elapsed)

  val to_show = if (array.used <= 20) array.used else 20
```

```
  for (i <- 0 until to_show) {
    stdio.printf(c"word %d: %s %d\n", i, (array.data + i)._1,
                    (array.data + i)._2)
  }
  stdio.printf(c"done.\n")
}
```

As you can see, the main function mostly just knits together the pieces we've already constructed, while maintaining control over the sizing and reallocation of the main data array. It runs pretty fast too: on my laptop, it was capable of sorting the full data file in under three minutes, with about 7GB of memory, whereas a JVM Scala implementation wasn't capable of sorting the complete file at all!

```
$ ./target/scala-2.11/sort_by_count-out
< ../../googlebooks-eng-all-1gram-20120701-a
reached EOF after 86618505 lines in 38379 ms
sorting done in 6726 ms
word n: and 470825580
word n: and_CONJ 470334485
word n: and 381273613
word n: and_CONJ 380846175
word n: and 358027403
word n: and_CONJ 357625732
word n: and 341461347
word n: and_CONJ 341045795
word n: and 334803358
word n: and_CONJ 334407859
word n: and 313209351
word n: and_CONJ 312823075
word n: a 303316362
word n: a_DET 302961892
word n: and 285501930
word n: and_CONJ 285145298
word n: and 259728252
word n: and_CONJ 259398607
word n: and 255989520
word n: and_CONJ 255677047
done.
```

Now, we're ready to move on to our final task: implementing aggregation so that we can combine occurrences of the same word across multiple years.

Aggregation at Scale

In a higher-level idiom, without the constraints on scale we could sum up the counts by year easily with a map or dictionary. For example, in more verbose Scala we could do something like this:

```
val data:Seq[NGramData] = ???
val m = mutable.Map[String,Int]
for (d <- data) {
  if (m.containsKey(d.word)) {
    m(d.word) = d.count
  } else {
    m(d.word) += d.count
  }
}
```

Or in an even more functional style, admittedly at the cost of further efficiency, we could do this:

```
val g = l.groupBy(identity).map { i => (i._1,i._2.size) }
```

However, when scale is a concern, planning this sort of bulk data-processing job can be a genuinely hard problem, and Scala frameworks like Spark[1] often do a great job of it. A common technique for large-scale accumulation operations like this is to presort the data first. If the data is already ordered by whatever property one wishes to group by, we can entirely avoid repeated searches of associative data structures, and instead simply buffer a single item in memory at a time.

In our case, we can do even better than this. Upon close inspection, it turns out that the NGrams data files are *already* sorted in this fashion. Although every word-year pair has a separate entry in the file, they all occur one right after another, in ascending chronological order, like so:

```
again_ADV      1505    3         1
again_ADV      1507    20        1
...[lines omitted]...
again_ADV      2006    4833584 139355
again_ADV      2007    5463040 147042
again_ADV      2008    7763389 198434
```

This fortunate property of the data allows us to further optimize our code, and substantially reduce overhead. Instead of reading each line of the file into a separate NGramData instance, we can maintain a single instance of NGramData at a time, and sum all the counts into it until we encounter a new word.

Based on what we've learned so far, how would we plan to cut down our memory overhead, given these constraints? We could go about it in a lot of ways, but what I've chosen is to have parseLine use *two* pointer variables at NGramData instances, called current and next. Most of the time, those will both point at different positions in our array: current will point at the last fully initialized

---

1. https://spark.apache.org

word that we read, whereas next will point at the immediate next item in the array. Here's the trick: we can reuse the same values of current and next over and over, because it's perfectly safe to read into next with sscanf as many times as we want. Combined with a stack-allocated buffer for the temporary word, this strategy should help us cut down memory usage by several orders of magnitude!

Finally, we'll need to use the standard library function strcmp, with the following signature, to check for string equality:

```
def strcmp(left:CString, right:CString):Int
```

Just like our own comparators, strcmp returns -1, 0, or 1 based on the relative ordering of the two strings. Now let's write our modified parseLine, which we'll call parseAndCompare; it has to do a lot more work, but we can break it down further into more helper functions for the following tasks:

1. Scan the input line into a temporary NGramData instance.
2. Compare the temporary data to the top of the buffer.
3. Add the temporary data to the buffer as a new item.
4. Accumulate the count from the temporary data into the current top of the buffer.

By breaking the logic down into small steps, the main loop is clear:

MemoryManagement/aggregate_and_sort/main.scala
```scala
def parseAndCompare(line:CString, array:WrappedArray[NGramData]):Unit = {
  val temp_item = stackalloc[NGramData]
  temp_item._1 = temp_word_buffer
  val next_item = array.data + array.used
  scan_item(line, temp_item)
  if (array.used == 0) {
    add_new_item(temp_item, next_item)
    array.used += 1
  } else {
    val prev_item = array.data + (array.used - 1)
    if (is_item_new(temp_item, prev_item) != 0) {
      add_new_item(temp_item, next_item)
      array.used += 1
    } else {
      accumulate_item(temp_item, prev_item)
    }
  }
}
```

The key change we're making here is passing the WrappedArray itself into parse-AndCompare. With this extra metadata, our code can determine for itself when to increment array.used; however, we won't actually resize the underlying array until later.

Likewise, each of the individual helper functions are straightforward, some of them even one-liners:

MemoryManagement/aggregate_and_sort/main.scala
```scala
def scan_item(line:CString, temp_item:Ptr[NGramData]):Boolean = {
  val temp_word = temp_item._1
  val temp_count = temp_item.at2
  val temp_year = temp_item.at3
  val temp_doc_count = temp_item.at4

  val sscanf_result = stdio.sscanf(line, c"%1023s %d %d %d\n",
    temp_word, temp_year, temp_count, temp_doc_count)
  if (sscanf_result < 4) {
    throw new Exception("input error")
  }

  return true
}

def is_item_new(temp_item:Ptr[NGramData], prev_item:Ptr[NGramData]):Int = {
  strcmp(temp_item._1, prev_item._1)
}

def add_new_item(temp_item:Ptr[NGramData],
                 next_item:Ptr[NGramData]):Unit = {
  val temp_word = temp_item._1
  val new_word_length = strlen(temp_word)
  val new_word_buffer = malloc(new_word_length + 1)

  strncpy(new_word_buffer, temp_word, new_word_length)
  new_word_buffer(new_word_length) = 0

  next_item._1 = new_word_buffer
  next_item._2 = temp_item._2
  next_item._3 = temp_item._3
  next_item._4 = temp_item._4
}

def accumulate_item(temp_item:Ptr[NGramData],
                    prev_item:Ptr[NGramData]):Unit = {
  prev_item._2 = prev_item._2 + temp_item._2
}
}

@extern
object qsort {
  def qsort(data:Ptr[Byte],
        num:Int,
        size:Long,
        comparator:CFuncPtr2[Ptr[Byte], Ptr[Byte], Int]):Unit = extern

}
```

But we still need to handle file I/O in an outer loop, as well as determining when to grow the array itself. Since parseAndCompare() will only ever use one new array cell, all we have to do is make sure that there's just enough space every time we read a new line, like this:

MemoryManagement/aggregate_and_sort/main.scala
```scala
def readAllLines(fd:Ptr[stdio.FILE], array:WrappedArray[NGramData]):Long = {
  var lines_read = 0L
  while (stdio.fgets(line_buffer, 1024, fd) != null) {
    if (array.used >= (array.capacity - 1)) {
      growWrappedArray(array, block_size)
    }
    parseAndCompare(line_buffer, array)
    lines_read += 1
    if (lines_read % 10000000 == 0) {
      stdio.printf(c"read %d lines, %d unique words so far\n", lines_read,
                   array.used)
    }
  }
  return lines_read
}
```

And once that's done, the main loop is even simpler:

MemoryManagement/aggregate_and_sort/main.scala
```scala
def main(args:Array[String]):Unit = {
  val array = makeWrappedArray(block_size)

  val read_start = System.currentTimeMillis()
  val lines_read = readAllLines(stdin,array)
  val read_elapsed = System.currentTimeMillis() - read_start
  println(s"""done. read $lines_read lines, ${array.used} unique words.
         $read_elapsed ms""")

  val sort_start = System.currentTimeMillis()
  qsort.qsort(array.data.asInstanceOf[Ptr[Byte]], array.used,
              sizeof[NGramData], by_count)
  val sort_elapsed = System.currentTimeMillis() - sort_start
  stdio.printf(c"sorting done in %d ms\n", sort_elapsed)

  val to_show = if (array.used <= 20) array.used else 20
  for (i <- 0 until to_show) {
    stdio.printf(c"word n: %s %d\n", (array.data + i)._1, (array.data + i)._2)
  }

  println(c"done")
}
```

Whew! It might have taken a bit of work to get here, but we'll see the benefits of this approach when we run and time the code:

```
read 10000000 lines, 165976 unique words so far
read 20000000 lines, 332408 unique words so far
```

```
...
read 80000000 lines, 1330247 unique words so far
done. read 86618505 lines, 1440378 unique words. 29741 ms
sorting done in 102 ms
word n: are 1826889845
word n: are_VERB 1826888554
word n: at 1562321315
word n: at_ADP 1560015959
word n: an 1266190915
...
done.
```

Not only do we read in the data significantly faster as our previous sorting example—in about 30 seconds, down from 45—but our sort time has improved by two orders of magnitude, from 7 seconds down to about 100 *milliseconds*. And that's just the improvement over our previous Scala Native code. In standard JVM Scala, a Map[String,Int]-based approach couldn't handle the entire file on my machine, and even an ArrayBuffer-based approach takes more than 2 minutes to read in the data and around 4 seconds to sort it. (If you want to look at that code, it's provided in the book's source code available for download on the book's website.[2])

That, in a nutshell, is Scala Native's power: bare-metal performance at the cost of more complexity for certain common tasks. It might not be the right tool to for every problem, but where it fits, the impact is enormous.

All that being said, the code and the techniques that we've explored in this chapter are the hardest in this book, and it isn't necessary to have total fluency or mastery over them to proceed into other topics. Especially if you're encountering these concepts for the first time, the patterns and idioms that may seem opaque right now will make a lot more sense as we see them repeated in the chapters to come.

What's Next

In this chapter, you extended your knowledge of low-level memory management techniques to include compound data structures, as well as pointers, and learned how to cast data back and forth from the generic Ptr[Byte] type to work with C APIs. With these techniques, we extended the Google NGrams code we wrote in the first chapter to handle some real-world sorting and aggregation problems. Next, we're going to shift gears and look at how to communicate over a network in Scala Native using only low-level OS primitives.

---

2. https://pragprog.com/titles/rwscala/source_code

CHAPTER 3

Writing a Simple HTTP Client

Now that we've covered the basics of input and output, we can turn to the most essential domain of modern systems programming: *networking*. Twenty years ago, when most programs still worked with local files or local databases, this wasn't necessarily the case. But, as the internet continues to become pervasive in our daily lives, software that doesn't use a network is almost unheard of.

In this chapter, you'll learn about the fundamental building blocks that allow computers to communicate over the internet and build a working HTTP client from the ground up. After a quick review of the basics of networking, I'll cover all the essential OS facilities and system calls and then I'll show you how to put those pieces together to create a minimal, generic TCP client. Then, you'll learn how other protocols layer on top of TCP; we'll add capabilities until you have a working HTTP client library suitable for interacting with remote APIs.

Defining Terms

Networking is an enormous topic, but we'll focus on clear, practical working definitions. Scala Native does give you the power to go off the beaten path, though. See the Bibliography for some references to less common techniques and protocols.

Networks, Hosts, and Protocols

A *network* is a group of linked computers, all of which may communicate freely with one another.

Each computer on the network is called a *host*. This distinguishes them from other devices on the network, such as routers and switches, which allow the network to function but don't send or receive data on their own behalf.

Computers on a network communicate according to *protocols*: agreed-upon rules and procedures, implemented in software, that allow two machines to understand one another. Without protocols, communication is impossible. Protocols typically define the layout of data at the binary level, and prescribe an order of communication—who sends messages to whom, when to respond, whether to acknowledge receipt, and so on.

Protocols are *layered* on top of one another. The famous Open Systems Interconnection (OSI) model has seven layers, but a working programmer is only likely to encounter four of those layers:

- *Datalink protocols*, such as Ethernet, that control transmission on physical media like fiber optics or electrical wires.

- *Network protocols*, such as IPv4 and IPv6, that allow machines to address one another across one or more networks.

- *Transport protocols*, such as TCP and UDP, which allow individual programs on a machine to access the network, often at the same time.

- *Application protocols*, such as HTTP and FTP, which impose specific rules formatting on the data exchanged between programs.

Typically, datalink and network protocols are entirely handled by the operating system and device drivers. The OS provides the transport protocol, also, but exposes it via an API. By utilizing that API, you can implement an application protocol in *user-space*, outside of the operating system, while still retaining control of the whole stack. But to do that, you'll need to understand how the layers interact.

Addresses

In Internet Protocol (IP) networks, each host has one or more numerical addresses. IPv4 addresses are 4-byte numbers, represented as four dotted numerals between 0 and 255, like 123.220.34.8. IPv6 addresses are 8-byte numbers, represented as groups of 4 hexadecimal digits separated by colons, like 2001:0db8:3c4d:0015:0000:0000:1a2f:1a2b. You might also see leading zeros omitted, and consecutive all-zero bits abbreviated with ::, like in 2001:db8:3c4d:15::1a2f:1a2b.

Both versions of the Internet Protocol allow a host to send a *packet* of data of variable length to any other host of the network. The host is responsible for constructing a packet *header*, which contains the source host's IP address, the destination host's IP address, the length of the data, and a checksum to ensure that the packet is received without error. The data itself is called the packet's *payload*.

Together, the IP header and payload function much like an envelope and a letter in "snail mail" services: I can send a packet onto the network, and the network will make its best effort to deliver it to the correct address. Also, much like standard-class mail, I won't receive notification that my letter is delivered, lost, or delivered out of order.

For all of these reasons, IP is quite hard to work with directly. If we want more than unidirectional, unreliable datagram transmission, we need an additional protocol.

Ports, Sockets, and Connections

All modern operating systems provide implementations of two transport protocols: TCP, the Transmission Control Protocol, and UDP, the User Datagram Protocol. Both are layered on top of IP, so they use IP addresses to reach other machines; however, both transport protocols also provide *ports*, in addition to addresses. Ports allow multiple programs on the same address to send and receive separate streams of data without interfering with one another. Typically, a machine publishes a given service on a well-known port: for example, HTTP usually operates on TCP port 80, and FTP usually operates on TCP port 22.

Operating systems provide these network services in the form of *sockets*: file-like objects that a program can interact with to send and receive data over a network. The most famous and influential implementation is the BSD socket API, or Berkeley Sockets, which has become the standard for all UNIX-based operating systems, and differs only slightly from Windows sockets. Both TCP and UDP-based programs use sockets; but, the two protocols are different enough that the API's aren't quite the same, either.

First, TCP is *connection-based*, whereas UDP is *connectionless*. That means that we have to do some extra work to establish a TCP connection before two computers can communicate. However, TCP gives us some important benefits, as well. TCP is bidirectional, whereas UDP is not. Data transmitted over TCP is *reliable* and *ordered*, which means so long as the connection is intact, the data will eventually be received in the order that it was sent. In contrast, UDP offers only "best effort" delivery, and will frequently deliver messages out of order. Finally, TCP is *stream-oriented*, delivering a continuous sequence of bytes, whereas UDP delivers *datagrams*—whole messages up to a certain limited size.

Because TCP is much more commonly used, I'll only be covering the API for TCP sockets in detail. See the Bibliography for more on working with UDP.

Working with TCP

The good news about TCP, and other low-level network protocols, is that even when we're writing low-level application code, we generally don't need to implement them ourselves. Instead, our OS provides an implementation, and exposes it to us in the form of system calls and their accompanying C library functions. Although we've used syscalls a few times already, this is a good time to discuss some of the technical details.

System Calls and Blocking I/O

When our code invokes a syscall, it hands over execution to the operating system. While the OS is working, it executes its own code, in its own private memory address space, until it has a result to return. Some system calls return almost instantly, although there's still an overhead to switching from our program's memory, to the OS, and then back again. But many other system calls can take long or indeterminate amounts of time to return, and our program can be totally frozen until they do; when this happens, it's referred to as a *blocking* system call, and we'll learn how to work with them effectively over the next several chapters.

In a straightforward, simple-threaded program, however, blocking system calls can be surprisingly intuitive; in fact, you've already used a few in earlier chapters. Although the fgets() and printf() functions I introduced back in Chapter 1, The Basics: Input and Output, on page 3, are not themselves system calls, these C library functions utilize two of the most basic system calls of all: read() and write(). When used with the standard console inputs and outputs, printf() almost always returns nearly instantly, unless your program is producing output too quickly for your terminal to render, but you may have observed that fgets() is different—when we invoke fgets(), our program *waits* for a whole line of text to arrive before it returns and allows our program to proceed.

For now, since we're focused on building an HTTP client for single-threaded applications, we won't have to think too much about it; in many cases, blocking can even provide performance *benefits* to the system as a whole, since the OS can schedule other programs for execution while we wait.

In that spirit, let's look at the system calls we will need to set up a TCP connection.

socket()

Before we establish a connection, we need to create a socket with the socket() function. Its signature and arguments look like this:

```
def socket(domain:Int, socketType:Int, protocol:Int):Int
```

You'll note that socket() doesn't return any sort of Socket struct or object—the Int that is returned is, in this case, a file descriptor. The other three arguments are all enums. Although they are integers from the point of view of the compiler, you'll want to pick one of a few predefined standard values to plug into them. In Scala Native, these are all available if you import the socket bindings. You could write socket(AF_INET, SOCK_STREAM, IPPROTO_TCP) for a TCP socket to an IPv4 address, or socket(AF_INET6, SOCK_DATAGRAM, IPPROTO_UDP) for a UDP socket to an IPv4 address. domain also allows AF_UNIX, which allows you to create objects on the filesystem for local communication over sockets. Likewise, socketType allows you to specify SOCK_RAW for direct access to IP packets, in case you need to implement an alternative transport protocol.

It's important to remember, however, that no communication occurs when we create the socket—all we've done is ask the OS for an object that we can configure for communication. With TCP sockets, the next step is to establish a connection.

connect()

For TCP sockets, connect() is responsible for actually establishing a connection to a remote host. By convention, the host that establishes the connection is typically called a *client*, and the host that receives the connection is called a *server*. Connect has this signature:

```
def connect(socket:Int, serveraddr:Sockaddr, addr_len:socklen_t ):Int
```

The first argument to connect() is the uninitialized socket object that we just created with socket(). The second is a pointer to a Sockaddr data structure that contains the numeric IP address to connect to, and the third argument is the size of the sockaddr struct. This raises a few questions.

First, you might wonder why we need the addr_len at all. After all, you learned in Chapter 2, Arrays, Structs, and the Heap, on page 25, that all CStruct objects have a fixed length and a predetermined memory layout. Why would we need to pass in the length of the address?

We know that connect can take a variety of different kinds of IP addresses. And in the C API's, each address type actually has its own struct type.

They look like this:

```
type in_port_t = uint16_t
type in_addr_t = uint32_t

// IPv6 addresses are a fixed array of 16 bytes
type in6_addr = CStruct1[CArray[uint8_t, _16]]

type sockaddr_in = CStruct3[
  CUnsignedShort,    // sin_family
  in_port_t,         // sin_port
  in_addr_t,         // sin_addr
]

type sockaddr_in6 = CStruct5[
  in6_addr_t, // sin6_addr
  CUnsignedShort, // sin6_family
  in_port_t, // sin6_port
  uint32_t, // sin6_flowinfo
  uint32_t] // sin6_scope_id

type sockaddr = CStruct2[
  sa_family_t,       // sa_family
  CArray[CChar, _14] // sa_data, size = 14 in OS X and Linux
]
```

To make it easier to work with these, Scala Native provides helper methods to address the fields by name. Over the next few major releases, addressing struct fields by name is likely to become the standard practice in Scala Native, but it's limited to these socket-related structs for now.

If you look closely at these structs, though, you'll notice that they're shaped differently, and have totally different sizes. In particular, the in6_addr type is much larger than the abstract sockaddr that connect() is expecting. And there are some internal details that make this even worse. OSs like Mac OS and Linux may have different sizes and layouts for these structs as well. So a reasonable programmer could easily wonder how it's even possible to write safe, portable code with an API like this.

In essence, the way the OS handles this is by taking the addr_len argument that always accompanies a sockaddr, in connect or any other syscall. In other words, the OS function underlying the user-space syscall node *knows* that you can and will pass data that has a different size than what it's nominally expecting from the function definition, which allows it to treat them appropriately. Scala Native can also use this to do some transformation and layout shuffling to smooth out the OS differences. However, one side effect of this design is that Scala Native introduces some additional C code between our invocation and the OS.

So, for us to make use of this facility, we'd just have to do a quick cast of a sockaddr_in struct to sockaddr, while passing the correct sizeof[sockaddr_in as the length, like this:

```
def connect_ip4(socket:Int, addr:Sockaddr_in):Int = {
  val sa = addr.cast[Sockaddr]
  connect(socket, sa, sizeof[Sockaddr_in])
}
```

This technique, sometimes called a type pun, is common in C APIs, since C has no notion of inheritance or interface types, but it feels ugly and unsafe. Although we'll use it a few more times in this book, it's worth avoiding wherever possible. But the good news is that we can avoid performing this cast manually because the standard C library includes address lookup functions that can do most of the hard work for us—and a lot of other chores, too.

getaddrinfo()

So far, we've been working with numeric IP addresses, as represented by the previous structures. But what if we only know the *name* of the host we want to connect to, like www.pragprog.com?

You may be familiar with the Domain Name Service (DNS), which provides a global, distributed, hierarchical registry of host names. You use it every day when you navigate to pages in a web browser. UNIX systems include a few other lookup mechanisms as well.

For example, if you look at the file /etc/hosts in your Docker container, it has a list of hostnames and IP addresses, like this:

```
127.0.0.1 localhost
::1 localhost ip6-localhost ip6-loopback
fe00::0 ip6-localnet
ff00::0 ip6-mcastprefix
ff02::1 ip6-allnodes
ff02::2 ip6-allrouters
172.17.0.2  a970285f20c3
```

So, if we want to look up a hostname, we have a few possible sources. We could have multiple entries in a local file, as well as multiple entries with several remote DNS servers. Rather than implement this logic ourselves, we can rely on our operating system to do the work for us, and combine the results, with the helpful getaddrinfo() function:

```
def getaddrinfo(hostname: CString,
                service: CString,
                hints: Ptr[Addrinfo],
                res: Ptr[Ptr[Addrinfo]] ):Int
```

In the argument list, hostname is a string containing the hostname to look up; service is a string that usually contains the port number, although it can also look up named services like "echo" in some cases; hints can be null, or else it can contain a partially populated Addrinfo object. Finally, we pass it a pointer to a pointer to an addrinfo object that will hold the result. This is the first time we've seen this pattern, so it's worth looking at closely. Why would we need a pointer to a pointer, and how would we create that pointer in our code?

This is a surprisingly common pattern in C APIs. C only allows a function to return a single value, and has no concept of "exceptions" or other language-level error-handling constructs. Instead, many C functions simply return an integer to signal whether an error has occurred or not; by convention, a return of 0 means "no error," and various nonzero values signifies different kinds of errors. But if the function just returns an error/no-error code, how do we get the actual address result that we want?

The answer is in the function signature—the Ptr[Ptr[Addrinfo]] argument is called res for *result*. The outer Ptr is effectively a *mutable cell* that will contain the result if the syscall completes without error; in this case, since the value we receive is itself a Ptr[Addrinfo], we end up with the somewhat dense Ptr[Ptr[Addrinfo]] as the result type. As a side benefit, this also allows the OS to take responsibility for allocating the appropriate amount of memory for an IPv4 or IPv6 address, which simplifies our implementation a bit.

We'll see one more trick at play here—when we look at the actual Addrinfo struct:

```
type addrinfo = CStruct8[
  CInt,                  // ai_flags
  CInt,                  // ai_family
  CInt,                  // ai_socktype
  CInt,                  // ai_protocol
  socklen_t,             // ai_addrlen
  Ptr[sockaddr],         // ai_addr
  Ptr[CChar],            // ai_canonname
  Ptr[addrinfo]          // ai_next
]
```

Fortunately, like with the address types, Scala Native provides field accessors, so we don't have to remember the offset of each field. You may also notice that not only does the struct contain a string form of the address and a bunch of metadata, it also contains a pointer to another addrinfo struct! The key here is that the value of ai_next is permitted to be null, which allows the structure to function as a *linked list* of variable length. This is because in many situations, a name can resolve to multiple addresses. When it does, getaddrinfo() will allocate and return multiple Addrinfo objects. It returns a pointer to the first one, and if we need to find more, we can check if the ai_next pointer is null or not. (We'll always take the first one in this chapter, though.)

Finally, we'll need to free these addrinfo structures, too. Any function you call that allocates memory for you, whether in a library or a system call, should instruct you as to your responsibilities for freeing that memory when you're finished with it. In some cases, you may be responsible for calling free() on the returned pointer, and in other cases, there may be another library call to take care of it for you. In this case, the system also provides a helper function for us:

```
def freeaddrinfo(ai:Ptr[addrinfo]):Unit
```

freeaddrinfo() will also walk through the chain of ai_next values until everything is freed up, so we don't have to deal with it ourselves.

Making a TCP Connection

At last, we're ready to make a TCP connection. To do it, we'll write a helper function that takes a port and an address and performs all the necessary calls to getaddrinfo(), socket(), and connect(), in that order. We'll call the function makeConnection(). If we get errors at any point, we can raise exceptions, just like in an ordinary Scala program, and return the socket as an Int otherwise.

```
HTTPClient/tcpclient/TCPClient.scala
def makeConnection(address:CString, port:CString):Int = {
  val hints = stackalloc[addrinfo]
  string.memset(hints.asInstanceOf[Ptr[Byte]], 0, sizeof[addrinfo])
  hints.ai_family = AF_UNSPEC
  hints.ai_socktype = SOCK_STREAM

  val addrInfo_ptr:Ptr[Ptr[addrinfo]] = stackalloc[Ptr[addrinfo]]
  println("about to perform lookup")
  val lookup_result = getaddrinfo(address, port, hints, addrInfo_ptr)
  println(s"lookup returned ${lookup_result}")
  if (lookup_result != 0) {
    val errString = util.gai_strerror(lookup_result)
    stdio.printf(c"errno: %d %s\n", lookup_result, errString)
    throw new Exception("no address found")
  } else {
    val addrInfo = !addrInfo_ptr
    stdio.printf(c"""got addrinfo: flags %d, family %d, socktype %d,
    protocol %d\n""", addrInfo.ai_family, addrInfo.ai_flags,
    addrInfo.ai_socktype, addrInfo.ai_protocol)
```

```
  println("creating socket")
  val sock = socket(addrInfo.ai_family, addrInfo.ai_socktype,
                    addrInfo.ai_protocol)
  println(s"socket returned fd $sock")
  if (sock < 0) {
    throw new Exception("error in creating socket")
  }

  println("connecting")
  val connect_result = connect(sock, addrInfo.ai_addr, addrInfo.ai_addrlen)
  println(s"connect returned $connect_result")
  if (connect_result != 0) {
    val err = errno.errno
    val errString = string.strerror(err)
    stdio.printf(c"errno: %d %s\n", err, errString)

    throw new Exception("connection failed")
  }
  sock
  }
}
```

Now, we just need to write a simple main method to test it out. For now, we'll just make the connection and write out a short message. But we don't need any special functions for reading and writing; TCP sockets use the same read() and write() system calls that regular files and the STDIN/STDOUT file handles use, which means we can also use fgets, printf(), and so on, safely.

To keep our code nicely compartmentalized, we can write a handleConnection() function to do the actual I/O; this will allow us to easily swap in other implementations later on.

```
// What can we do here?
def handleConnection(sock:Int): Unit = ???
```

However, the open-ended nature of TCP makes this a challenge, since either end of the bidirectional connection can read and write at any time. And since coordinating those patterns of communication is outside the scope of TCP, it falls upon us, as application developers, to add additional protocols, rules, and formats on top of the bare TCP socket.

For our purposes, we can write a reasonably simple, generic structure if we assume that all of our protocols will be text based and that all communication takes a client-initiated request-response pattern, that is, the server cannot "push" data that isn't requested by the client. If we provide an idiomatic, high-level Scala API for this pattern, the signature would look like this:

```
def handleConnection(sock:Int): Unit = ???
def makeRequest(sock:Ptr[File],request:String):String = ???
```

For convenience, we'll also use the fdopen C function to transform the Int socket file descriptors into the same sort of Ptr[File] handles that we use with fgets, fprintf, and other functions; we'll also need fclose() when we're done:

```
def fdopen(fd:Int, mode:CString):Ptr[File] = extern
def fclose(file:Ptr[File]):Int = extern
```

Utilizing these capabilities, the outer handleConnection wrapper looks like this:

HTTPClient/tcpclient/TCPClient.scala
```
def handleConnection(sock:Int): Unit = {
  val resp_buffer = malloc(4096)
  val socket_fd = util.fdopen(sock, c"r+")
  val resp = makeRequest(socket_fd,"hello?  is anybody there?\n")
  println(s"I got a response: ${resp.trim()}")
  fclose(socket_fd)
  println("done")
}
```

But makeRequest will be a bit trickier. In particular, we'll have to convert between the manually managed CString objects and the garbage-collected Scala String objects an application programmer would expect.

To do this, we'll utilize the Zone technique for memory management that we introduced back in Chapter 2, Arrays, Structs, and the Heap, on page 25. Since Zones automatically clean up short-lived memory, they are perfect for temporary string processing, and the Scala Native core provides a helper method toCString for converting Strings to CStrings with the help of an implicit Zone.

Scala's implicit syntax has a reputation for complexity, but in simple cases like this, it just means that functions that run in a certain context have access to special resources, in this case, an allocator that will provide pointers to temporary storage while we're in the block, and then clean them all up afterwards. However, note that this means that if there's no implicit Zone declared, toCString will fail at compile time. On the other hand, the corresponding fromCString method doesn't require a Zone because it only creates true GC'd objects, so we can run it anywhere we want.

To use Zone here, we'll need to do a few things:

1. Create a Zone.
2. Convert the request String to a CString.
3. Send the CString out the socket.

4. Get the response CString.
5. Convert the response CString and return it.

It looks like this:

HTTPClient/tcpclient/TCPClient.scala
```scala
def makeRequest(sock:Ptr[FILE],request:String):String = {
  val resp_buffer = stdlib.malloc(2048)
  val resp = Zone { implicit z =>
    val request_cstring = toCString(request)
    stdio.fprintf(sock, request_cstring)
    val resp_cstring = fgets(resp_buffer, 4095, sock)
    fromCString(resp_buffer)
  }
  stdlib.free(resp_buffer)
  resp
}
```

We can make good use of Zone in our main function as well by converting command-line arguments to CString:

HTTPClient/tcpclient/TCPClient.scala
```scala
def main(args: Array[String]):Unit = {
  if (args.length != 2) {
    println("Usage: ./tcp_test [address] [port]")
    return ()
  }

  val sock = Zone { implicit z =>
    val address = toCString(args(0))
    val port = toCString(args(1))

    stdio.printf(c"looking up address: %s port: %s\n", address, port)

    makeConnection(address, port)
  }
  handleConnection(sock)
}
```

Now, how do we test this out? We won't write a TCP server until later in the book, and although we could test it out on a variety of public internet hosts, like websites, it's usually better to test network code in a controlled environment. On the other hand, I would also argue against a full unit-testing approach to this kind of code: ensuring that network code works on an actual, unsimulated network is absolutely essential.

Fortunately, we have a great tool available for all kinds of network scripting and testing: nc, or netcat, a wonderful general-purpose network utility for the UNIX command line.

Testing Network Code with Netcat

Netcat[1] is most often used to make a TCP connection from a script or a command line, which is great for testing servers; but, it can also *receive* connections from the command line, which is how we'll use it here, to test our client program.

What we want to do is receive a connection on a socket, get a notification when a connection is established, and then write out whatever data we receive. If you're using the Docker container environment, you'll also want to make sure to set up this socket *inside* the same container that contains our Scala Native build environment. If that container isn't running, first boot it back up with `docker run -it -p 8080:8080 --name scala-native rwhaling/scala-native-env`. Then, inside the container, run:

```
$ nc -l -v 127.0.0.1 8080
```

Although this only prints a blank line of output, we're now receiving connections, and the container has mapped to port 8080 on the host.

Now, we should be able to connect to this port/socket combination, either from inside or outside of the container. Finally, run this:

```
$ nc -v 127.0.0.1 8080
Connection to 127.0.0.1 8080 port [tcp/http-alt] succeeded!
```

Now, if you type in a line of text, you should see it copied from one shell session to the other. This works from either the client or the server, reflecting the bidirectional, streaming nature of the TCP protocol.

If you want, take some time to experiment with netcat, or look over the manual page if you want. Once you're comfortable, we can test out our Scala code. Make sure the netcat client session is shut down and the server is listening for a connection. Then, run our program with `./tcpTest 127.0.0.1 8080`. If everything worked well, you should see output like this on the client:

```
$ ./target/scala-2.11/tcpclient-out 127.0.0.1 8081
looking up address: 127.0.0.1 port: 8081
about to perform lookup
lookup returned 0
got addrinfo: flags 2, family 0, socktype 1, protocol 6
creating socket
socket returned fd 3
connecting
connect returned 0
```

---

1. http://netcat.sourceforge.net

And you'll see this on the server:

```
$ nc -v -l 127.0.0.1 8080
hello?  is anybody there?
```

Right now, the client is hanging, waiting for a response from the server. Now, we can actually type a response into the netcat terminal, which will send it back to the client; after that, the client will close the connection, as expected. So we'd see this on the server:

```
$ nc -v -l 127.0.0.1 8081
hello?  is anybody there?
yep!!
```

And here's how the full exchange on the client now looks:

```
$ ./target/scala-2.11/tcpclient-out 127.0.0.1 8081
looking up address: 127.0.0.1 port: 8081
about to perform lookup
lookup returned 0
got addrinfo: flags 2, family 0, socktype 1, protocol 6
creating socket
socket returned fd 3
connecting
connect returned 0
I got a response: yep!!
done
```

So, what have we done so far? We've used UNIX system calls to create a TCP socket, connect to a remote server, send a message, and read a response. Our makeConnection() function can connect to any IP address or hostname, and our handleConnection() function signature can handle any pattern or format of input and output. We could implement just about any TCP client protocol on top of this framework, but for now, we'll focus on HTTP, the protocol that powers the world wide web.

Introducing HTTP

In the last part of this chapter, we're going to implement a usable subset of the Hypertext Transfer Protocol (HTTP). HTTP is indisputably the most important application protocol on the internet. Not only does it power the websites we use every day, but it's rapidly becoming the universal protocol for all kinds of programs to request data from one another, via so-called RESTful APIs.

What does HTTP provide that TCP doesn't? First, it defines a predictable request/response workflow, with well-defined message boundaries. Second, every request must refer to a specific *resource*, or object, named by a Uniform Resource Identifier, or URI. Third, each request must use one of eight methods on the resource, such as GET, POST, PUT, or DELETE, with well-defined semantics. Finally, HTTP transmits all of the above metadata in a message header, but allows any data format to be used for the content of either the request or the response—not just HTML or JSON!

Even though HTTP was originally designed only to deliver hypertext documents to web browsers, its generic and broadly supported capabilities have made it an essential block for all sorts of distributed systems and applications.

The standards body that governs the web, the W3C,[2] continues to promulgate extensions of the basic protocol, and even the giant tech firms that build web browsers can struggle to implement all of the standards correctly. But the core of HTTP is surprisingly simple and straightforward to implement.

An HTTP message contains either a request line or a status line, line-delimited headers, and optionally a body. The newlines are in the carriage-return line-feed style, which is written like \r\n in Scala and C strings. There is a single empty line after the last header. To see this in practice, let's make a simple request. Instead of netcat, we'll use the command-line utility curl:

```
$ curl -v www.example.com
* Rebuilt URL to: www.example.com/
*   Trying 93.184.216.34...
* TCP_NODELAY set
* Connected to www.example.com (93.184.216.34) port 80 (#0)
> GET / HTTP/1.1
> Host: www.example.com
> User-Agent: curl/7.54.0
> Accept: */*
>
< HTTP/1.1 200 OK
< Cache-Control: max-age=604800
< Content-Type: text/html; charset=UTF-8
...
< Content-Length: 1270
<
<!doctype html>
<html>
<head>
  <title>Example Domain</title>
  <meta charset="utf-8" />
  ...
</head>
```

2.   https://www.w3.org

```
<body>
<div>
  <h1>Example Domain</h1>
  <p>This domain is established to be used for illustrative examples ...
  domain in examples without prior coordination or asking for permission.</p>
  <p><a href="http://www.iana.org/domains/example">More information...</a></p>
</div>
</body>
</html>
* Connection #0 to host www.example.com left intact
```

That's a lot of output, but it's a great representation of an actual HTTP exchange. Normally curl just prints out the HTTP response body, which in this case is the HTML content at the bottom, but in -v, or verbose, mode it's also printing out the request headers prefixed by >, the response headers prefixed by <, and TCP connection status prefixed by *. The three headers are Host, indicating the intended recipient of the request; User-Agent, identifying the program making the request; and Accept, indicating the response formats that may be received. */* means any type the server prefers.

The response looks pretty similar, but instead of a request line, it has a status line. The status line consists of the HTTP version again, a response code, and a text description of the response code. You've probably seen response codes before if you've used the web at all: common codes include 200 OK, 301 moved permanently, 404 not found, and the dreaded 500 internal server error. The response has a few more headers; we won't go through them all, but the most important ones are Content-Type, indicating the format of the response body, and Content-Length, indicating the length of the body in bytes. The other interesting header is Connection: keep-alive, which tells us that the client, if it wishes, may keep the TCP connection open and make another request, instead of closing the connection and reconnecting. This can be very helpful for high-performance HTTP clients!

Now, a lot more can go on in an HTTP exchange than what we've seen here, but it all falls within this framework. Most of the subtleties consist of choosing the correct combination of headers and data format for a specific server. The good news for us is that the protocol specifies relatively little of these requirements; for better or for worse, the burden falls on the server provider to document requirements, and client developer to implement them. As we go on, I'll make a note of a few general best-practices that are usually worth following.

Implementing HTTP

How should we go about implementing HTTP on top of our TCP codebase? Although there are a few moving parts, the fundamental requirement is that we need to implement a handleConnection() function that does four things:

- Generate an HTTP request matching the format described in the previous section.

- Transmit the request.

- Receive an HTTP response.

- Decode the HTTP response into a useful form.

Transmitting and receiving the request can be performed with read() and write(), which we looked at in the first chapter. The tricky part is in representing HTTP requests and responses as Scala objects, and in encoding and decoding those to the wire protocol we described in the previous section. If we model the request and response as regular Scala case classes, they could look something like this:

HTTPClient/httpclient/HTTPClient.scala
```scala
case class HttpRequest(
  method:String,
  uri:String,
  headers:collection.Map[String, String],
  body:String)
case class HttpResponse(
  code:Int,
  headers:collection.Map[String, String],
  body:String)
```

First, we'll write out the request in three steps:

1. Write out the header line with the method and the URI.
2. Write out each header line, followed by an empty line.
3. If a body is present, write it out.

We can implement these steps in a few compact bits of Scala code:

HTTPClient/httpclient/HTTPClient.scala
```scala
def writeRequestLine(socket_fd:Ptr[FILE], method:CString,
                     uri:CString):Unit = {
  stdio.fprintf(socket_fd, c"%s %s %s\r\n", method, uri, c"HTTP/1.1")
}

def writeHeader(socket_fd:Ptr[FILE], key:CString, value:CString):Unit = {
  stdio.fprintf(socket_fd, c"%s: %s\r\n", key, value)
}
```

```
def writeBody(socket_fd:Ptr[FILE], body:CString):Unit = {
  stdio.fputs(body, socket_fd)
}
def writeRequest(socket_fd:Ptr[FILE], request:HttpRequest):Unit = {
  Zone { implicit z =>
    writeRequestLine(socket_fd, toCString(request.method),
                     toCString(request.uri))
    for ( (key, value) <- request.headers) {
      writeHeader(socket_fd, toCString(key), toCString(value))
    }
    stdio.fputs(c"\n", socket_fd)
    writeBody(socket_fd, toCString(request.body))
  }
}
```

Reading the response is going to be a bit trickier. As you may remember from Chapter 1, The Basics: Input and Output, on page 3, any time we read data, we need to have space allocated to hold it, whether we use read(), fgets(), fscanf(), or other related I/O function; but in our case, we don't know how big the HTTP response is going to be.

Many binary protocols solve this problem elegantly: they define a message header of a fixed-size number of bytes and store the length of the message body in a header field. With this strategy, a program that wants to read such a message can always read the header into a fixed-size chunk of memory, and each time it gets a header, it knows how many additional bytes to allocate and read for the rest of the message. Lots of protocols use this strategy, including IP itself, UDP, as well as application-level protocols like HTTP/2 and FastCGI.

Unfortunately for us, HTTP1.1 is a text-based protocol; although it has distinct headers and bodies, we cannot know the length of the header ahead of time. Since a header can have any number of key/value pairs, we instead have to scan through the message until we find the empty line that indicates the boundary between the header and the body. We could use a few different strategies, but the simplest is something like this:

1. Read a line of input and validate that it's an HTTP response status line.

2. Read another line of input. If it's not blank, it's a header. Validate it and repeat. If it's blank, we have a complete header. Proceed to step 3.

3. Check whether we have a content-length in the header. If we have a content-length, we can read exactly that number of bytes. Otherwise, raise an error (FN: chunked transfer, http 1.0, and so on).

We can implement this algorithm in Scala step by step, like this:

HTTPClient/httpclient/HTTPClient.scala

```scala
def parseStatusLine(line:CString):Int = {
  println("parsing status")
  val protocol_ptr = stackalloc[Byte](64)
  val code_ptr = stackalloc[Int]
  val desc_ptr = stackalloc[Byte](128)
  val scan_result = stdio.sscanf(line,
                        c"%s %d %s\n",
                        protocol_ptr, code_ptr, desc_ptr)
  if (scan_result < 3) {
    throw new Exception("bad status line")
  } else {
    val code = !code_ptr
    return code
  }
}

def parseHeaderLine(line:CString):(String, String) = {
  val key_buffer = stackalloc[Byte](64)
  val value_buffer = stackalloc[Byte](64)
  stdio.printf(c"about to sscanf line: '%s'\n", line)
  val scan_result = stdio.sscanf(line, c"%s %s\n", key_buffer, value_buffer)
  if (scan_result < 2) {
    throw new Exception("bad header line")
  } else {
    val key_string = fromCString(key_buffer)
    val value_string = fromCString(value_buffer)
    return (key_string, value_string)
  }
}

def readResponse(socket_fd:Ptr[FILE]):HttpResponse = {
  val line_buffer = stdlib.malloc(4096)
  println("reading status line?")
  var read_result = stdio.fgets(line_buffer, 4096, socket_fd)
  val code = parseStatusLine(line_buffer)
  var headers = mutable.Map[String, String]()
  println("reading first response header")
  read_result = stdio.fgets(line_buffer, 4096, socket_fd)
  var line_length = string.strlen(line_buffer)

  while (line_length > 2) {
    val (k,v) = parseHeaderLine(line_buffer)
    println(s"${(k,v)}")
    headers(k) = v
    println("reading header")
    read_result = stdio.fgets(line_buffer, 4096, socket_fd)
    line_length = string.strlen(line_buffer)
  }
```

```scala
    val content_length = if (headers.contains("Content-Length:")) {
                            println("saw content-length")
                            headers("Content-Length:").toInt
                         } else {
                            65535
                         }
    val body_buffer = stdlib.malloc(content_length + 1)
    val body_read_result = stdio.fread(body_buffer, 1, content_length,
                                       socket_fd)
    val body_length = string.strlen(body_buffer)
    if (body_length != content_length) {
      println("""Warning: saw ${body_length} bytes, but expected
                        ${content_length}""")
    }
    val body = fromCString(body_buffer)
    return HttpResponse(code, headers, body)
}
```

For a full implementation of HTTP, we'd want to provide readRequest() and writeResponse() as well; I'll omit the implementation here, but they're present in the code for this chapter, and we'll use them later on when we implement an HTTP server. For now, we can just stitch together our writeRequest() and read-Response() with our makeConnection() and handleConnection() from earlier in this chapter. We'll slightly modify our main() function to take a URL string from the command line, make the request, and print out the response. We'll also supply a few headers in our request. The standard is vague, but most servers require a User-agent header to return a valid response:

HTTPClient/httpclient/HTTPClient.scala

```scala
def main(args: Array[String]):Unit = {
  if (args.length != 3) {
    println(s"${args.length} {args}")
    println("Usage: ./tcp_test [address] [port] [path]")
    return ()
  }

  Zone { implicit z =>
    val address = toCString(args(0))
    val host = args(0)
    val port = toCString(args(1))
    val path = args(2)
    stdio.printf(c"looking up address: %s port: %s\n", address, port)

    val sock = makeConnection(address, port)
    handleConnection(sock,host,path)
  }
}
```

Now, we're ready to test it!

Testing Our Code

Just like with our TCP client earlier in the chapter, we can perform some basic validation of our code with netcat. We'll again open a listening socket with nc -v -l 127.0.0.1 8081, then connect to it with our client like this:

```
$ ./target/scala-2.11/httpclient-out 127.0.0.1 8081 /
looking up address: 127.0.0.1 port: 8081
about to perform lookup
lookup returned 0
got addrinfo: flags 2, family 0, socktype 1, protocol 6
creating socket
socket returned fd 3
connecting
connect returned 0
wrote request
reading status line?
```

It will then hang to await a response. And then on the server we'll see this (as long as we made sure to start the server first):

```
$ nc -v -l 127.0.0.1 8081
GET / HTTP/1.1
Host: 127.0.0.1
```

Because netcat isn't an HTTP server, it won't give any kind of response on its own, and the client should just hang while awaiting an answer to its request. That said, the request itself looks to be formatted correctly. If we were to paste in a placeholder response in the netcat window, we could test out the header and response parsing a bit—but I think we're ready to test this with a real website. Let's try www.example.com again:

```
$ ./target/scala-2.11/httpclient-out www.example.com 80 /
<html>
<head>
  <title>Example Domain</title>
  ...
</head>

<body>
<div>
  <h1>Example Domain</h1>
  <p>This domain is established to be used for illustrative examples ...
  domain in examples without prior coordination or asking for permission.</p>
  <p><a href="http://www.iana.org/domains/example">More information...</a></p>
</div>
</body>
</html>
```

Woohoo! Some celebration is in order. We now have a simple HTTP client that can make requests to many common web servers. But as we noted at the beginning of this section, HTTP is a large specification, and there are some cases we haven't handled:

- Messages using *chunked* transfer, in which the length of the response is included in the body.

- Messages without a content length indication at all.

- Message pipelining, with multiple request/responses on a single persistent connection.

None of these are especially difficult to implement, but they aren't very interesting, either, so I've included them in the code for this chapter. On the other hand, if you try out the client on a few sites in the wild, you're likely to encounter something like this, from http://pragprog.com:

```
HTTP/1.1 302 Found
Content-Type: text/html; charset=utf-8
Date: Sat, 03 Feb 2018 18:44:15 GMT
Location: https://pragprog.com/
Server: nginx + Phusion Passenger 5.0.27
Status: 302 Found
X-Powered-By: Phusion Passenger 5.0.27
X-Request-Id: 810d84407858b4561fc170afd8588aff
X-Runtime: 0.004691
X-UA-Compatible: IE=Edge,chrome=1
Content-Length: 87
Connection: keep-alive
```

This is a valid HTTP response, containing a 302 Found message, which is redirecting us to https://pragprog.com. Note the protocol in the URL: like more and more of the public internet, Pragmatic's main site has switched entirely from HTTP to HTTPS.

In some ways, HTTPS is a misnomer, because it's not a separate application protocol at all. The content and structure of HTTPS is identical to HTTP; the only thing that is different is that a cryptographic protocol, TLS (Transport Layer Security) is inserted seamlessly on top of the TCP transport. TLS encrypts all communication between the client and the server, but it behaves just like a plain TCP socket from the point of view of application code.

As more and more of the business of daily life is conducted over the web, this sort of robust and ubiquitous encryption is essential for privacy and safety. Encryption is notoriously difficult to get right, and even experts may make errors in implementation or specification that can leak sensitive information to attackers; and for that reason I cannot recommend implementing it oneself.

Fortunately, we have many resources at our disposal if we want to support secure communication in our Scala Native programs. As you saw back in Chapter 1, The Basics: Input and Output, on page 3, Scala Native has powerful facilities for invoking external C code, and there are many high-quality libraries available to us. For example, libsodium[3] provides high-quality cryptographic primitives, mbed TLS[4] offers a fully featured TLS connection library, and libcurl[5] provides a full-featured, high-performance HTTP/HTTPS client. Later in this book we'll look at how to work with these C libraries in our Scala Native code. But first, we're going to take a deep dive into Scala Native's memory management and allocation capabilities so that we have the full complement of techniques necessary for working with idiomatic C code.

What's Next

In this chapter, you learned the fundamentals of networking and how our operating system provides network services with sockets. You used the low-level socket APIs to write a simple TCP client, and learned how to test network services with netcat. And you learned all about how HTTP works, how to implement an application protocol on top of the socket API, and implemented a lightweight HTTP client yourself, all in Scala Native. Next, we'll explore more advanced topics in systems programming, starting with fork-based multiprocessing.

---

3. https://libsodium.gitbook.io/doc
4. https://tls.mbed.org
5. https://curl.haxx.se/libcurl

CHAPTER 4

Managing Processes: A Deconstructed Shell

In this chapter, we'll "deconstruct" a UNIX shell. What does that mean? In UNIX, the shell—the command-line interface you use to type commands, move files around, and run programs—is just another user-space program. Although it makes intense use of APIs provided by the OS, the shell itself is not part of the OS, which means we can reverse engineer a shell like bash or zsh and replace it as we please.

Our goal isn't to create a full-featured bash replacement, however. bash and all other descendants of the UNIX sh have a bias toward interactive use—they have a variety of features designed to support a human at a keyboard typing commands in real time.

However, UNIX shells can be surprisingly weak and brittle when used for automation, especially within the sort of large and complex distributed systems in which Scala is often deployed. Thus, our goal is to design the basic components of a Scala library for shell-like automation tasks. Done right, this will let us leverage Scala Native's ahead-of-time compilation to replace bash scripts with compact binaries, and open up our automation tasks to Scala's impressive powers of abstraction.

What are the critical features of a shell for these use cases? Our goal is to:

- Invoke a program with any number of arguments, wait for its completion, and report on its success or failure.

- Execute several programs one after the other, halting in case of error.

- Direct the input and output of one or more programs into files or into one another.

And we'll do all of this in straightforward, idiomatic Scala. However, we'll stay clear of some of the more advanced syntactical features common to DSLs, or domain-specific languages, in Scala, such as implicit conversions, custom string interpolators, and custom symbolic infix operators; instead, our library will be designed for use in straightforward, everyday Scala code.

Let's start by learning more about how a shell invokes a program.

Running a Program

Although most shells have certain built-in capabilities, almost everything they do is done by other programs. That is to say, *a shell is a program that runs other programs.* We've used a shell many times to do this, such as when we first executed our Hello, World program back in Chapter 1, The Basics: Input and Output, on page 3, like this: ./target/scala-2.11/hello-out. We also learned that hello-out is an executable file that contains metadata and machine instructions that the operating system can load and execute.

Binaries and Scripts

 In a UNIX OS, there are two different kinds of executable files: binary files that can be executed directly, and scripts that can be interpreted by another program, like a shell. Plain text files that begin with a special "shebang" line like #!/bin/bash, which means: "interpret the rest of this file with the program at /bin/bash." Scala Native's output, however, isn't interpreted; it's executed directly, just like the output of a C compiler.

In UNIX operating systems, loading and running a program isn't magic, and shells are themselves mostly ordinary programs—everything they do, they do using a few standard system calls. Just as with networking and file I/O, we can break down the functionality of the shell into the underlying system calls and put them back together with idiomatic Scala.

Introducing exec

In Linux and other UNIX-like OSs, a small family of system calls is responsible for loading and executing programs, which is collectively referred to as exec. However, there isn't actually a function named exec. Instead, there are variants for different combinations of arguments. The one we'll be using is called execve, and it has the following signature:

```
def execve(filename:CString, args:Ptr[CString], env:Ptr[CString]):Int
```

execve takes all of its arguments as strings or arrays of strings. The first, path, is a string containing the relative path to the executable. The second, argv, short for *argument vector*, is a Ptr[CString], which is actually an array of strings containing the arguments to the executable as 0-terminated strings. The third, envp, short for *environment pointer*, is also a Ptr[CString], again pointing to an array of 0-terminated strings; however, in this case, each of the strings is of the form key=value. These strings conceptually form a Map[String, String], called the *environment*, which is typically used for passing named parameters and configuration to the program.

These arrays can be a bit tricky to construct, especially from an idiomatic Scala Seq[String], so let's write a utility function to help us out. Two tricky parts can trip us up: one catch is that the the resulting array needs to have space for one more pointer than the number of strings in the Seq, which we'll fill with a null pointer; that's how execve will know it's the end of the array. The other detail is that the first item in the array needs to be the path to the executable, again. But as long as we keep those constraints in mind, it won't be too hard:

```
ForkWaitShell/nativeFork/nativeFork.scala
def makeStringArray(args:Seq[String]):Ptr[CString] = {
  val pid = unistd.getpid()
  val size = sizeof[Ptr[CString]] * args.size + 1
  val dest_array = stdlib.malloc(size).asInstanceOf[Ptr[CString]]
  val count = args.size
  Zone { implicit z =>
    for ( (arg,i) <- args.zipWithIndex) {
      val string_ptr = toCString(arg)
      val string_len = string.strlen(string_ptr)
      val dest_str = stdlib.malloc(string_len + 1).asInstanceOf[Ptr[Byte]]
      string.strncpy(dest_str, string_ptr, arg.size + 1)
      dest_str(string_len) = 0
      dest_array(i) = dest_str
      ()
    }
    ()
  }
  dest_array(count) = null
  for (j <- (0 to count)) {
  }
  dest_array
}
```

With that taken care of, we can wrap it in a more idiomatic Scala Native style by accepting the arguments and environment as a Seq and a Map, respectively. Then we just need to be sure to format the environment variables like KEY=VALUE, and we're good:

ForkWaitShell/nativeFork/nativeFork.scala
```scala
def runCommand(args:Seq[String], env:Map[String,String] = Map.empty):Int = {
  if (args.size == 0) {
    throw new Exception("bad arguments of length 0")
  }
  Zone { implicit z =>
    val fname = toCString(args.head)
    val arg_array = makeStringArray(args)
    val env_strings = env.map { case (k,v) => s"$k=$v" }
    val env_array = makeStringArray(env_strings.toSeq)

    val r = execve(fname, arg_array, env_array)
    if (r != 0) {
      val err = errno.errno
      stdio.printf(c"error: %d %d\n", err, string.strerror(err) )
      throw new Exception(s"bad execve: returned $r")
    }
  }
  ??? // This will never be reached.
}
```

A catch, though, is one you'll see if we write a simple program to try it out. We'll simply run the ls command with no arguments:

ForkWaitShell/bad_exec/bad_exec.scala
```scala
def main(args:Array[String]):Unit = {
  println("about to exec")
  runCommand(Seq("/bin/ls", "-l", "."))
  println("exec returned, we're done!")
}
```

If we run this program, we see the following:

```
$ ./target/scala-2.11/badexec-out
about to exec
total 16
-rw-r--r--  1 rwhaling  staff  2623 Jan 20 10:44 bad_exec.scala
-rw-r--r--  1 rwhaling  staff   156 Jan 20 10:09 build.sbt
drwxr-xr-x  6 rwhaling  staff   192 Jan 20 10:30 project
drwxr-xr-x  5 rwhaling  staff   160 Jan 20 10:36 target
```

Our program appears to successfully run the ls command, but the final println, exec returned, we're done!", never appeared.

What could have gone wrong? The answer is a subtlety of the exec functions, and it's best to reproduce the note from the manual in full:

"execve() does not return on success, and the text, initialized data, uninitialized data (bss), and stack of the calling process are over written according to the contents of the newly loaded program."

What this means is that if execve executes successfully, the state of our program is completely obliterated and replaced with the new program. execve never returns, because once the new program begins running, there's nowhere for it to return to. Our calling program is gone.

What Went Wrong?

You might reasonably be wondering why exec and its brethren are implemented in this counterintuitive way. You might also be wondering how a UNIX shell manages to continue operating during and after it launches a command.

We can start to work toward a solution by more closely parsing two words from the manual excerpt I quoted earlier: *program* and *process*. Although I've tried to use both terms precisely thus far, we don't have a proper working definition of either yet, but now we're ready to take a proper stab at it.

A *program* is a file on disk that can be executed; it's a series of machine instructions loadable by our operating system. A *process* is an *instance* of a program that's in the process of execution (for example, its stack, its heap, and the loaded contents of the program text) and the *instruction pointer*, which is the current position in the program.

What we want to do is run execve in a *new process* so that our code can continue whatever it needs to do. However, since processes are executed separately by the operating system, we also need some way to *wait* for our new process to complete before we continue. In other words, once we're concerned with multiple processes, we have to deal with *concurrency*.

Introducing Concurrency with fork() and wait()

In a UNIX-like OS, processes are traditionally created with the system call fork(). fork() doesn't create a process out of thin air; instead, it creates a copy of the process that calls it, which will have access to all of the calling process's state and code. This is for a good reason: even if we're going to call exec, we need some way to control the behavior of the new process before exec is called. fork() allows us to both *create* a new process and *coordinate* its behavior with the rest of our code.

Its signature is simple:

```
def fork():Int
```

fork() takes no arguments and returns an Int. Unlike every other function we've discussed, and probably unlike every function you've ever written, fork() *returns twice*. It returns exactly once in the calling process, and it returns exactly once in the newly created process.

---

fork vs clone

 Although fork is a low-level concurrency primitive, fork() itself is, surprisingly, not a system call. Just like malloc() wraps the system call sbrk(), fork() likewise wraps a system call named clone() that is similarly unsuited to use by humans. clone() is responsible for creating new processes, as well as new threads, and can control the isolation of units of execution in a more fine-grained fashion than we'll need to.

What is particularly unusual is that it returns different values to the two processes. In the calling process, it returns the *process id* of the newly created process—an integer that uniquely identifies the process for as long as it exists in the system's process table. In the new process, fork() instead returns 0. By inspecting the return value of fork(), we can thus determine which of the two new processes we are in.

To wrap fork() in a way that is suitable to idiomatic Scala, let's just pass it a runnable task, and then return the resulting PID in the parent while ensuring that the child terminates after completing its task:

ForkWaitShell/nativeFork/nativeFork.scala
```
def doFork(task:Function0[Int]):Int = {
  val pid = fork()
  if (pid > 0) {
    pid
  } else {
    val res = task.apply()
    stdlib.exit(res)
    res
  }
}
```

Note, however, that when we execute doFork(), the parent will return immediately, while the child is still running, which means we'll need to be very careful about how we proceed. All modern operating systems take responsibility for deciding *when* processes run, *where* they run, and for how long. We saw this in Chapter 3, Writing a Simple HTTP Client, on page 45, when we observed that other programs would run while ours was blocked waiting for I/O. And in a multicore operating system, not only will both processes proceed with their programs separately, in any order, they may also execute at the same time. This is called *preemptive multitasking*, and it can require a certain amount of defensive coding. For example, could a "race condition" emerge with unintended behaviors if your two processes are executed in a different order than you expected? Fortunately, we have powerful tools to coordinate the work of our processes.

First, there's getpid() and getppid():

```
def getpid():Int
def getppid():Int
```

getpid() simply returns the process id of the process that calls it. This will be useful for understanding the behavior of complex chains of processes.

getppid() returns the pid of the *parent process* when it's called. Because processes are created by fork, every process should have a parent process. In some cases, however, a parent may exit before a child, in which case either the "orphaned" child process may be terminated, or else it will be "adopted" by PID 1, the init process.

Process Groups and Sessions

 In addition to a parent process, UNIX processes also belong to process groups and sessions. Typically, these are used for scenarios such as ensuring that all processes spawned by a terminal session terminate at the same time as the original terminal. This book won't deal with process groups or sessions in depth, but you can refer to the manual for your favorite UNIX OS for more details.

Finally, we must consider wait() and waitpid():

```
def wait(status:Ptr[Int]):Int
def waitpid(pid:Int, status:Ptr[Int], options:Int):Int
def check_status(status:Ptr[Int]):Int
```

wait() is the essential function for synchronizing processes. When called, it blocks until a child of the calling process completes, sets its return code in status, and returns the pid of the completed child process. waitpid simply provides more options: the argument pid can take either the pid of a specific child process, 0 to wait for any child in the same process group, -1 to wait for any child group at all, and -k to wait for any child in process group k. Likewise, options can take several flags, most important of which is WNOHANG, which prevents waitpid() from blocking, and instead returns 0 immediately if no children are exited.

One quirk in the case of certain anomalous exit conditions is that the status return may have multiple values, packed bit-wise into a 4-byte integer address. Although these can be unpacked manually, it's usually best to rely on your OS's facilities for doing so. In Scala Native, these are packaged by the check_status function, which will return the exit code of a terminated process, given a status value. For our purposes, it's sufficient to just check that status is nonzero.

Waiting Is Mandatory

If you're creating processes with fork(), it's essential that you plan to call wait() for each one. Completed child processes keep their exit code in the kernel's process table until wait() is called. These so-called zombie processes can overwhelm and crash a system, even outside of container boundaries, if they're allowed to grow unchecked.

And if we put these together with some boilerplate code to check the different reasons for termination, we get the following:

ForkWaitShell/nativeFork/nativeFork.scala
```scala
def await(pid:Int):Int = {
  val status = stackalloc[Int]
  waitpid(pid, status, 0)
  val statusCode = !status
  if (statusCode != 0) {
    throw new Exception(s"Child process returned error $statusCode")
  }
  !status
}
```

Now we have the basic ingredients in place to launch and monitor commands, just like a shell! All we have to do is stitch runCommand, doFork, and await together, and then it's straightforward to use if we can pass in some string arguments:

ForkWaitShell/nativeFork/nativeFork.scala
```scala
def doAndAwait(task:Function0[Int]):Int = {
  val pid = doFork(task)
  await(pid)
}
```

ForkWaitShell/nativeFork/nativeFork.scala
```scala
def main(args:Array[String]):Unit = {
  if (args.size == 0) {
    println("bye")
    stdlib.exit(1)
  }

  println("about to fork")

  val status = doAndAwait { () =>
    println(s"in child, about to exec command: ${args.toSeq}")
    runCommand(args)
  }
  println(s"wait status ${status}")
}
```

When run, we get the following output:

```
$ ./target/scala-2.11/nativefork-out /bin/ls -l
about to fork
in child, about to exec command: WrappedArray(/bin/ls, -l)
build.sbt              nativeFork.scala        project         target
wait status 0
```

Success! Now we can execute programs, just like a shell. However, a shell can do more than run single programs; some of the most powerful shell capabilities involve running multiple programs in different configurations and routing their inputs and outputs in a controlled fashion. So, how do we implement these patterns in Scala Native?

Supervising Multiple Processes

If we want to run several commands one after another, we can use the code we've already written, like this:

ForkWaitShell/nativeFork/nativeFork.scala
```
def runOneAtATime(commands:Seq[Seq[String]]) = {
  for (command <- commands) {
    doAndAwait { () =>
      runCommand(command)
    }
  }
}
```

That works! But what if we want to run the commands simultaneously? If we don't have other work to do while we wait, we can do something like this:

ForkWaitShell/nativeFork/nativeFork.scala
```
def runSimultaneously(commands:Seq[Seq[String]]) = {
  val pids = for (command <- commands) yield {
    doFork { () =>
      runCommand(command)
    }
  }
  for (pid <- pids) {
    await(pid)
  }
}
```

In this case, it doesn't matter which process we wait for, as long as they all exit eventually. But if we have work to do when a process exits—like launching a new process, or some other task—this approach doesn't work. If process 456 exits while we are blocked waiting for process 123, we'll have *no way* to handle 456's completion until 123 is done. However, if we want to inject custom logic into our loop, we'll have to refactor our approach.

First, we can write a helper function to call waitpid(-1,status,0), to wait for any process from a set of child processes, and return the set remaining:

ForkWaitShell/nativeFork/nativeFork.scala
```scala
def awaitAny(pids:Set[Int]):Set[Int] = {
  val status = stackalloc[Int]
  var running = pids
  !status = 0
  val finished = waitpid(-1, status, 0)
  if (running.contains(finished)) {
    val statusCode = !status
    if (statusCode != 0) {
      throw new Exception(s"Child process returned error $statusCode")
    } else {
      return pids - finished
    }
  } else {
    throw new Exception(s"""error: reaped process ${finished},
                        expected one of $pids""")
  }
}
```

With that in place, we can write a top-level loop that invokes awaitAny() in a loop, while maintaining a list of running processes:

ForkWaitShell/nativeFork/nativeFork.scala
```scala
def awaitAll(pids:Set[Int]):Unit = {
  var running = pids
  while (running.nonEmpty) {
    println(s"waiting for $running")
    running = awaitAny(running)
  }
  println("Done!")
}
```

With this technique, we have much more control over large numbers of child processes; however, we're still blocked entirely while we wait for a child process to exit. It's possible to avoid blocking at all by invoking waitpid() with the WNO-HANG option; but doing so usually requires us to think of *something* else that our program can do while it waits, which is difficult to solve in a general way. We'll explore nonblocking concurrent techniques in the later chapters of this book, starting with Chapter 7, Functions and Futures: Patterns for Distributed Services, on page 131. For now, we'll instead explore ways to coordinate and connect the processes we create.

Working with Pipes

What we've built so far is already sufficient for a lot of automation tasks. For example, with our HTTP client from Chapter 3, Writing a Simple HTTP Client, on page 45, and some JSON parsing, we could easily write a small, safe program that authenticates to an HTTP service and queries another endpoint for service discovery before launching another executable. An equivalent bash program could certainly be written, using tools like curl[1] and jq,[2] but such scripts rapidly grow in complexity and can be painful to maintain. However, there's one more essential shell pattern we've yet to tackle: pipelines.

A *pipeline* is a series of cooperating processes executing simultaneously that communicate over in-memory channels called *pipes*. For example, if we want to list all the files in a directory and then sort them alphabetically, we can do this in bash with ls | sort, which will print out all the filenames.

Pipes work by replacing the standard input and/or standard output of a program. For example, if we run sort on its own, it gets its own stdin and stdout, as in the following diagram:

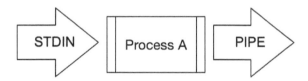

But if we pipe them together, the shell can create a pipe to chain them together without an intermediate file as shown here:

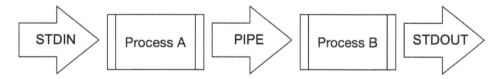

In this case, ls gets the terminal input as STDIN, and sort's output goes to the terminal output. In between, ls's output goes to the write-end of a new, anonymous pipe, whereas sort's input is attached to the read-end of the same pipe. Best of all, if we want to create a larger pipeline, we can chain these pipes one after another.

---

1. https://curl.haxx.se
2. https://stedolan.github.io/jq

The semantics of reading and writing from a pipe can be subtle, but we don't have to worry about them for now; programs written in idiomatic UNIX STDIN/STDOUT patterns should "just work," but in Chapter 8, Streaming with Pipes and Files, on page 155, we'll learn how to work with pipes on a more granular level. All we need to do for now is create a pipe and attach it to both of the new processes we create with fork(). To do this, we'll use two new syscalls: pipe() and dup2().

pipe

Here's the signature for pipe():

```
def pipe(fds:Ptr[Int]):Int
```

pipe takes one argument: an array containing space for exactly two Ints. If pipe succeeds, the two pointers will be filled with file descriptors. The first will contain the write-only side of the pipe, which is suitable for attaching to standard input, and the second will contain the read-only side, which is likewise suitable for standard output.

Here's the riddle though: how do we pass this pipe on so a new process can read or write from it without passing in custom arguments or modified code?

Part of the answer is in a subtlety of the exec functions. Although a successful exec call obliterates the state of the calling program, it *inherits* all open file descriptors. If we want to "trick" a new program into treating the new pipe as though it were the terminal input and output, we can use dup2() to replace the stdin file descriptor with the write end of the pipe.

dup2

dup2() is a more user-friendly variant of another function called dup(), and dup2() has the following signature:

```
def dup2(old_fd:Int, new_fd:Int):Int
```

dup2() is straightforward in terms of signature, but it has some semantic quirks, especially in concert with fork(). Most significantly, when fork, dup2, and pipe are used together, it's common to create situations where multiple processes have the same file open. There are, in fact, good reasons for multiple processes to keep a file descriptor open at once, but it will only cause problems for us. In particular, programs like sort that require their input fd to be closed before completing will hang until *all* processes have closed the file.

Because the file handles created by pipe() are anonymous, it's almost always used in concert with fork(). The general order of system calls is like so:

1. Call pipe.
2. Call fork.
3. In the child, call dup2.
4. In the child, call execve (or do other work).
5. In the parent, call close on the pipe.
6. In the parent, call wait or waitpid.

Implemented in Scala code, we can do this for two processes, like this:

ForkWaitShell/nativePipeTwo/nativePipeTwo.scala

```scala
def runTwoAndPipe(input:Int, output:Int, proc1:Seq[String],
                  proc2:Seq[String]):Int = {
  val pipe_array = stackalloc[Int](2)
  val pipe_ret = util.pipe(pipe_array)
  println(s"pipe() returned ${pipe_ret}")
  val output_pipe = pipe_array(1)
  val input_pipe = pipe_array(0)

  val proc1_pid = doFork { () =>
    if (input != 0) {
      println(s"proc ${unistd.getpid()}: about to dup ${input} to stdin" )
      util.dup2(input, 0)
    }
    println(s"proc 1 about to dup ${output_pipe} to stdout")
    util.dup2(output_pipe, 1)
    stdio.printf(c"process %d about to runCommand\n", unistd.getpid())
    runCommand(proc1)
  }

  val proc2_pid = doFork { () =>
    println(s"proc ${unistd.getpid()}: about to dup")
    util.dup2(input_pipe, 0)
    if (output != 1) {
      util.dup2(output, 1)
    }
    unistd.close(output_pipe)
    stdio.printf(c"process %d about to runCommand\n", unistd.getpid())
    runCommand(proc2)
  }

  unistd.close(input)
  unistd.close(output_pipe)
  unistd.close(input_pipe)
  val waiting_for = Seq(proc1_pid, proc2_pid)
  println(s"waiting for procs: ${waiting_for}")
  val r1 = waitpid(-1, null, 0)
  println(s"proc $r1 returned")
  val r2 = waitpid(-1, null, 0)
  println(s"proc $r2 returned")
  r2
}
```

But in a real shell, we can string together any number of processes into a single pipeline. Generalizing the previous code to take a Seq of commands to run, instead of a pair, actually simplifies the code somewhat and reduces duplication:

ForkWaitShell/nativePipe/nativePipe.scala

```scala
def pipeMany(input:Int, output:Int, procs:Seq[Seq[String]]):Int = {
  val pipe_array = stackalloc[Int](2 * (procs.size - 1))
  var input_fds = mutable.ArrayBuffer[Int](input)
  var output_fds = mutable.ArrayBuffer[Int]()
  // create our array of pipes
  for (i <- 0 until (procs.size - 1)) {
    val array_offset = i * 2
    val pipe_ret = util.pipe(pipe_array + array_offset)
    output_fds += pipe_array(array_offset + 1)
    input_fds += pipe_array(array_offset)
  }
  output_fds += output

  val procsWithFds = (procs, input_fds, output_fds).zipped
  val pids = for ((proc, input_fd, output_fd) <- procsWithFds) yield {
    doFork { () =>
      // close all pipes that this process won't be using.
      for (p <- 0 until (2 * (procs.size - 1))) {
        if (pipe_array(p) != input_fd && pipe_array(p) != output_fd) {
          unistd.close(pipe_array(p))
        }
      }
      // reassign STDIN if we aren't at the front of the pipeline
      if (input_fd != input) {
        unistd.close(unistd.STDIN_FILENO)
        util.dup2(input_fd, unistd.STDIN_FILENO)
      }
      // reassign STDOUT if we aren't at the end of the pipeline
      if (output_fd != output) {
        unistd.close(unistd.STDOUT_FILENO)
        util.dup2(output_fd, unistd.STDOUT_FILENO)
      }
      runCommand(proc)
    }
  }

  for (i <- 0 until (2 * (procs.size - 1))) {
    unistd.close(pipe_array(i))
  }
  unistd.close(input)
```

```
    var waiting_for = pids.toSet
    while (!waiting_for.isEmpty) {
      val wait_result = waitpid(-1,null,0)
      println(s"- waitpid returned ${wait_result}")
      waiting_for = waiting_for - wait_result
    }
    return 0
}
```

Now we're really close to our goal! Let's write a quick main function that strings a few commands together, the equivalent of running this:

```
$ ls -l | sort -R
```

If we wanted to, we could write a small parser for the traditional bash pipe syntax—it's a great, compact notation for interactive shell usage. But as we noted at the start of the chapter, interactive use is just the tip of the iceberg. For contemporary automation tasks, a lean Scala DSL like the one we've started to sketch out has the potential to be more useful; and in particular, Scala Native's small binaries and fast startup time really lend themselves to this sort of use case.

So, for this exercise we'll just bake the command to run into our main function:

ForkWaitShell/nativePipe/nativePipe.scala
```
def main(args:Array[String]):Unit = {
  val status = pipeMany(0,1,Seq(
    Seq("/bin/ls", "."),
    Seq("/usr/bin/sort", "-r")
  ))
  println(s"- wait returned ${status}")
}
```

And when we run it, we'll see this:

```
$ ./target/scala-2.11/nativepipe-out
- proc 1510: running command /usr/bin/sort with args List(/usr/bin/sort, -r)
- waitpid returned 1509
target
project
nativePipe.scala
build.sbt
- proc 1509: running command /bin/ls with args List(/bin/ls, .)
- waitpid returned 1510
- wait returned 0
```

But you may see slightly different results any time you run this program; because we have three processes running in parallel, sharing single terminal output, strange things may happen, as you can see here, where the various output messages can appear interleaved in an unusual order. This is the power and complexity of concurrent programming in a nutshell, and we should take a moment to recognize what we've achieved in this chapter. Orchestrating a nontrivial pipeline of processes isn't easy, and we've done it in a remarkably concise bit of Scala code.

What's Next

In this chapter, you reverse-engineered a UNIX shell to reproduce its signature capability, the pipeline. Along the way, you learned how to write concurrent programs in Scala Native using only UNIX OS primitives. Next, we'll combine these concurrent processing techniques with some of our socket-handling code from Chapter 3, Writing a Simple HTTP Client, on page 45, to construct a working network server.

CHAPTER 5

Writing a Server the Old-Fashioned Way

In the last few chapters, you learned how to apply process-based concurrency to a practical use case. Now, we're ready to take on one of the essential problems of systems programming: writing a server. Servers have a fundamental difference from all the programs we've written so far. Although they provide a variety of capabilities, their behavior is driven not by any preset sequence of commands but instead by reaction to unpredictable external events. Because of this, writing servers isn't easy. However, if you accept the challenge, you'll learn how to write programs that are far more robust in their interactions with the outside world.

In this chapter, and those that follow in Part II, we'll build a usable and performant web server from the ground up. We'll start with a minimal TCP socket server and become familiar with the fundamental OS facilities used by all servers. We'll then reuse our parsing code from Chapter 3, Writing a Simple HTTP Client, on page 45, to construct a working HTTP server and perform a stress test to measure the results. With data in hand, we can then better understand the capabilities and limitations of our code, pointing the way toward the high-performance asynchronous techniques we'll look at in chapters ahead.

Understanding How a Server Works

As you saw in Chapter 3, Writing a Simple HTTP Client, on page 45, writing a simple TCP client is mostly straightforward. We have to jump through a few more hoops to make our server work, though, so before we go into the details, let's take a step back to look at the big picture.

A typical server program does three things:

1. It accepts incoming connections on a known TCP port.
2. It receives requests from clients.
3. It sends back a response to each request.

At first glance this isn't much different from what a TCP client does. The confounding difference is that a server must perform all these actions at the same time, with an unknown number of uncoordinated clients. Later in this chapter, we'll use some of the multiprocessing techniques we looked at in Chapter 4, Managing Processes: A Deconstructed Shell, on page 69, to deal with these concurrent operations.

Although these process-based techniques are not always optimal for a high-performance server, we'll use them, for now, to allow us to focus our attention on the nuances of the socket API, and to serve as a baseline for later improvement. Many successful projects do use this sort of technique, however, including the Postgres database daemon.[1]

So, how does a server function from a systems perspective?

As you learned in Chapter 3, Writing a Simple HTTP Client, on page 45, a TCP client uses the socket() and connect() system calls to establish a connection with a server. The pattern for servers is different. Servers don't initiate TCP connections; they simply wait for inbound connections to arrive and respond appropriately. Thus, implementing the server side requires the use of socket(), but also requires three new system calls: bind(), listen(), and accept().

These calls have to be made in a particular order. A typical flow of a client-server interaction looks similar to the illustration on page 87.

These three new calls are what distinguish a server from a client, so let's take a moment to examine each one.

bind()

```
def bind(socket: CInt,
        address: Ptr[sockaddr],
        address_len: socklen_t
      ): CInt = extern
```

bind() associates a socket file descriptor with an address and port on the host machine. The address is defined as a pointer to the same sockaddr structure that we used with connect() in Chapter 3. The difference is that connect() refers

---

1.   https://www.postgresql.org/docs/8.2/static/connect-estab.html

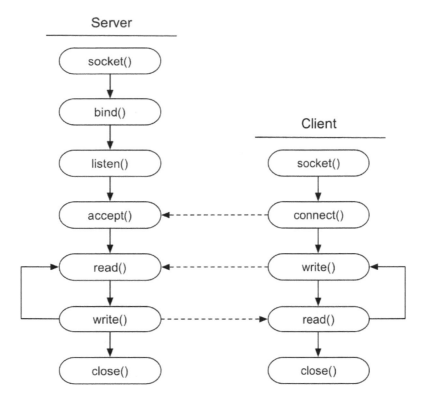

to the address of a remote machine, whereas bind() refers to a port and IP on our own machine.

When we try to bind() to a port and address, our OS performs several checks:

- Is the address valid for this machine?

- Is the address valid for this kind of socket?

- Do we have the permission to bind to this port? (Only root can bind to ports below 1024, typically.)

- Are any other sockets bound to this address and port? (Only one socket can be bound to an address in most protocols.)

If everything is okay, bind() succeeds and returns 0. A simple example looks like this:

```
HTTPServer/bind_example.scala
val server_socket = socket(AF_INET, SOCK_STREAM, 0)

val server_address = stackalloc[sockaddr_in]
!server_address._1 = AF_INET.toUShort  // IP Socket
!server_address._2 = htons(port)       // port
!server_address._3._1 = INADDR_ANY     // bind to 0.0.0.0
val server_sockaddr = server_address.cast[Ptr[sockaddr]]
val addr_size = sizeof[sockaddr_in].toUInt

val bind_result = bind(server_socket, server_sockaddr, addr_size)
println(s"bind returned $bind_result")
```

Note the type pun: our address is a sockaddr_in, and we need to use the fields of that structure to initialize the address, but we'll perform a cast to sockaddr when it's time to pass it to bind().

One interesting technique here is that we're binding to the special address INADDR_ANY, which is equivalent to the IP address 0.0.0.0. This special value binds to every available address of the host. It's especially useful when working in containers, since the internal IP address of a container may not be known until after it is created.

Another useful value for the address is 127.0.0.1, also known as localhost. 127.0.0.1 is also valid on every host, and always refers back to itself; however, that means that if you bind a socket to localhost, you'll only serve requests on the local loopback address, and no remote clients will ever be able to reach you. For now, since we're running in Docker, we'll stick with INADDR_ANY.

listen()

```
def listen(socket: CInt, backlog: CInt): CInt = extern
```

listen() is generally called immediately after bind(), and it only takes two arguments: the socket file descriptor and an integer backlog.

Calling listen() on a bound socket puts it into a listening state. Now our operating system will start to accept and establish incoming connections on the associated address, and then put those connections on an internal queue of size backlog. This will keep happening until we close the bound socket.

listen() is straightforward to invoke:

```
val listen_result = listen(server_socket, 1024)
println(s"listen returned $listen_result")
```

One subtlety is that your operating system will also place limits on the maximum value of backlog. In most Linux environments, including our Docker container, you can see the current setting with cat /proc/sys/net/core/somaxconn.

Although you could traditionally change this with echo or sysctl, Docker actually fixes this value at container initialization; you'll need to pass an argument of the form --sysctl net.core.somaxconn=1024 to docker run. If you're using our Docker build environment, it should already be set to 1024.

accept()

```
def accept(socket: CInt,
           address: Ptr[sockaddr],
           address_len: Ptr[socklen_t]
       ): CInt = extern
```

Once we have a listening socket, we can start accepting incoming connections with our application. But as you can see from the function signature, accept() is a bit trickier to invoke. We'll pass in a pointer to an allocated but initialized sockaddr_in object, again cast to the generic sockaddr type. We'll also pass in a pointer to an integer containing the length of the address.

When accept() returns, it'll set address to the inbound client's IP address and address_len to its length. If we don't care about the client address, we can also pass in NULL and 0 for the address and length:

```
HTTPServer/accept_example.scala
val client_address = stackalloc[sockaddr_in]
val client_sockaddr = client_address.cast[Ptr[sockaddr]]
val client_addr_size = stackalloc[UInt]
!client_addr_size = sizeof[sockaddr_in].toUInt

val connection_socket = accept(server_socket, client_sockaddr,
                                client_addr_size)
println(
  s"""accept returned fd $connection_socket;
     |connected client address is
     |${format_sockaddr_in(client_address)}""".stripMargin
)
```

Upon success, accept() returns a new connected socket file descriptor, which is completely distinct from the listening socket descriptor we passed in.

Once we have a connection, we can read and write to the connected socket much like a pipe or other ordinary file descriptor. accept() will also set the address sockaddr to the address of the client that has connected to us. If we don't care about the incoming address, we can just use NULL for both the sockaddr and the length, which allows us to skip the allocation and the cast. To keep things concise, we'll do just that in our examples to follow; but in a production system, you'd probably want to retain that information for logging, even if your application logic doesn't make use of it directly.

Building Our Server

Now that we know how all the system calls work, let's put them together into working code. Rather than try to deal with concurrency and sockets in one go, we'll first build a nonconcurrent server that we can test for correct implementation of the socket-handling patterns. Then, once we've verified its correctness, we'll modify it to handle multiple concurrent connections.

In the next chunk of code, we'll create the sockaddr_in struct that describes the port and address to bind to. Then, we'll invoke socket() and bind, and check their results, before looping over accept() and handling incoming connections.

```scala
HTTPServer/blocking_server.scala
def serve(port:UShort): Unit = {
    // Allocate and initialize the server address
    val addr_size = sizeof[sockaddr_in]
    val server_address = malloc(addr_size).cast[Ptr[sockaddr_in]]
    !server_address._1 = AF_INET.toUShort  // IP Socket
    !server_address._2 = htons(port)       // port
    !server_address._3._1 = INADDR_ANY     // bind to 0.0.0.0

    // Bind and listen on a socket
    val sock_fd = socket(AF_INET, SOCK_STREAM, 0)
    val server_sockaddr = server_address.cast[Ptr[sockaddr]]
    val bind_result = bind(sock_fd, server_sockaddr, addr_size.toUInt)
    println(s"bind returned $bind_result")
    val listen_result = listen(sock_fd, 128)
    println(s"listen returned $listen_result")
    println(s"accepting connections on port $port")

    // Main accept() loop
    while (true) {
        val conn_fd = accept(sock_fd, null, null)
        println(s"accept returned fd $conn_fd")
        // we will replace handle_connection with fork_and_handle shortly
        handle_connection(conn_fd)
    }
    close(sock_fd)
}
```

We can quickly implement a simple handle_connection() function that just writes back whatever it reads, which is commonly known as an echo server. We'll use read() and write() to actually perform our communication, and we can share the same buffer for each. When it's time to switch to a concurrent architecture, we'll replace handle_connection() with fork_and_handle().

We also have to decide what behavior we'd actually like to implement. For now, we'll do something simple. When a message is received, we'll print a simple message, read a line of text from the client, echo it back out, and have it repeat until the connection is closed:

```
HTTPServer/blocking_server.scala
def handle_connection(conn_socket:Int, max_size:Int = 1024): Unit = {
    val message =
      c"Connection accepted!  Enter a message and it will be echoed back\n"

    val prompt_write = write(conn_socket, message, strlen(message))

    val line_buffer = malloc(max_size)
    while (true) {
        val bytes_read = read(conn_socket, line_buffer, max_size)
        println(s"read $bytes_read bytes")
        if (bytes_read == EOF)
            // This means the connection has been closed by the client
            return
        val bytes_written = write(conn_socket, line_buffer, bytes_read)
        println(s"wrote $bytes_written bytes")
    }
}
```

Now, let's test it out! We can build this just like our other examples by placing sbt nativeLink in the /examples/simple-echo-server directory and executing it with ./target/simple-echo-server-build-out. When you do, you should see a prompt like this:

```
:scala-native:blocking_server $ ./target/simple-echo-server-build-out
bind returned 0
listen returned 0
listening on port 8080
```

So far, so good. It looks like we're blocking at the accept() call, but how do we test the connection-handling logic? We could write a custom client program, but we have a better option: netcat, also known as nc, a multipurpose command-line network utility, which we first used in Chapter 3, Writing a Simple HTTP Client, on page 45. If you're using our Docker-based build environment, netcat is already available—use docker exec -it scala-native-build-env to get another shell into the same container. Then we can connect and interact with the nc address port.

If the echo server is running and you're in the same container, you should see something like this:

```
$ nc localhost 8080
Connection accepted!  Enter a message and it will be echoed back
hello
hello
goodbye
goodbye
```

Our server appears to be echoing correctly. But what happens if we open up a second connection with another new terminal session while keeping both the server and the first connection open?

```
$ nc localhost 8080
```

We get nothing, just a hanging connection. To diagnose this further, let's use nc -v for verbose output:

```
$ nc -v localhost 8080
Connection to localhost 8080 port [tcp/http-alt] succeeded!
```

This is exactly what we would expect. Because our server's socket is in a listening state, the OS will establish the connection for us, send an acknowledgment to the client, and put the connection onto the backlog, where it will remain until we call accept() again. But we won't actually get to call accept() until the first connection terminates.

If we were to fill the backlog up entirely, we'd instead see this:

```
$ nc -v localhost 8080
nc: connect to localhost port 8080 (tcp) failed: Connection refused
```

This is one of the worst failure states for a server program: dropping connections on the floor. We could use many ways to resolve this issue with varying levels of performance and complexity. For now, we'll implement a technique that uses fork() and waitpid(), much like we did in our shell example in Chapter 4.

Creating a Minimum Viable Server

As you'll recall from Chapter 4, Managing Processes: A Deconstructed Shell, on page 69, fork() duplicates a running process in place. It returns different values so that the "parent" and the "child" can take different actions, and it generally requires the parent to call wait() (or one of its variants) to "reap" exited children. How can we use this to improve our server?

The traditional pattern is to call accept() in the parent, and then immediately fork() to create a dedicated child process to handle each incoming connection. From a high level, the flow of system calls follows the order shown in the illustration on page 93.

We can implement this logic in a fork_and_handle() function that calls our previous handle_connection() function for the application behaviors.

We'll also need to provide a cleanup_children() method to clean up the child processes, using the waitpid() function that I described in the previous chapter. In particular, waitpid(-1, NULL, WNOHANG) will allow us to reap any terminated

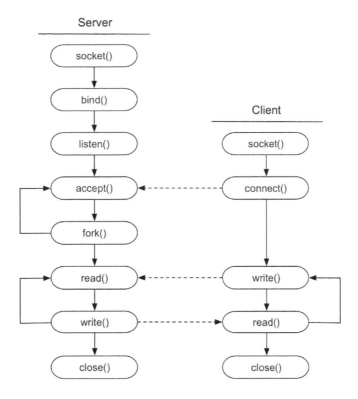

children without blocking, which is exactly what we need for this situation. We'll call it until one of two conditions are reached:

1. No more child processes are running, and waitpid returns -1.
2. Children exist but all are currently running, and waitpid returns 0.

In either case, we're done with cleanup, so we can return immediately:

HTTPServer/fork_server.scala
```scala
def fork_and_handle(conn_fd:Int, max_size:Int = 1024): Unit = {
    val pid = fork()
    if (pid != 0) {
        // In parent process
        println("forked pid $pid to handle connection")
        close(conn_fd)
        cleanup_children()
        return
    } else {
        // In child process
        println("fork returned $pid, in child process")
        handle_connection(conn_fd, max_size)
        sys.exit()
    }
}
```

```scala
def cleanup_children(): Unit = {
  val child_pid = waitpid(-1, NULL, WNOHANG)
  if (child_pid <= 0) {
    return
  } else {
    cleanup_children()
  }
}
```

Now, our server should be able to handle simultaneous connections, and withstand as much load as we can generate with netcat and basic shell scripting. Later in this chapter, we'll subject it to much more rigorous stress tests, but for now, we can consider this to be a minimal TCP server framework to build upon.

Handling HTTP

To make the leap from a generic framework to an actual server, we'll need to implement some sort of behavior or protocol that we can test. Fortunately for us, we already have the tools at hand to implement HTTP.

Beyond TCP's basic streaming capabilities, HTTP adds a request-response messaging pattern, URLs, query parameters, and other useful metadata. HTTP is also universally supported, can pass through most firewall and NAT appliances, and is easy to integrate with browser-based applications.

Much as with our HTTP client code, there are high-quality C libraries available for server-side HTTP parsing;[2] for now, though, we'll stick with our DIY philosophy and repurpose our HTTP parsing code from Chapter 3, Writing a Simple HTTP Client, on page 45.

We can just plug the request-parsing functions into a modified handle_connection() function:

```scala
HTTPServer/httpserver/HTTPServer.scala
import Parsing._
def handle_connection(conn_socket:Int, max_size:Int = 1024): Unit = {
  while(true) {
    parse_request(conn_socket) match {
      case Some(request) =>
        val response = handleRequest(request)
        write_response(conn_socket, response)
        return
```

---

2. https://github.com/nodejs/http-parser

```
        case None =>
            return
    }
  }
}
```

As you see, we reused the parse_request() function intact, as well as the corresponding HttpRequest and HttpResponse types.

Now all we need to do is add some actual application logic: a handle_request() function that transforms a request into a response. We'll simply return a 200 OK code and print out some diagnostics about the request:

HTTPServer/httpserver/HTTPServer.scala
```scala
def handleRequest(request:HttpRequest): HttpResponse = {
  val headers = Map("Content-type" -> "text/html")
  val body = s"received ${request.toString}\n"
  return HttpResponse(200, headers, body)
}
```

Few real-world applications will directly generate a response from only the request parameters; instead, file servers will return a file based on the request URI, model-view-controller applications will query a database, and so-called microservices often query many additional services to collect the data necessary to compose a response.

Likewise, it's common for a routing function to map requests onto more specialized handlers based on the request URL. We'll stick to a single HttpRequest => HttpResponse function for now, but we'll revisit this topic in much more detail later in this book.

Performance Testing with Gatling

Now that we have a working web server, let's test it out. If you've configured the Docker-based environment, port 8080 should be open, and you can run the server like this:

```
:scala-native:httpserver ./target/scala-2.11/httpserver-out
bind returned 0
listen returned 0
listening on port 8080
```

In this way, you should be able to access it at http://localhost:8080. We want to go beyond basic interactive testing, however. We want to stress test our server's performance under realistic load.

Why Measure?

As I noted at the start of the chapter, implementing performant servers is hard. By testing the performance of our server, we can set a baseline for comparison to the more advanced approaches we'll take in Part II of this book. We can also compare our performance to other languages and platforms to better understand how Scala Native sizes up.

That said, many sites now offer "speed tests" of various web servers, often plotted against one another in a giant bar graph. Personally, I am skeptical of this approach; in my experience, web application performance at scale is too complex to reduce to a single variable.

For the purposes of this book, we'll instead focus on characterizing trade-offs between five key criteria:

- Responsiveness—how quickly can the server return a response under light load?

- Throughput—what is the maximum number of requests the server can process in a fixed amount of time?

- Maximum load—under what load does the server produce maximum throughput? Is the error rate tolerable?

- Tail latency—under the same load, what is the response time at the 99th percentile?

- Error handling—under heavy load, are connections dropped promptly, or do they hang or timeout?

Why Gatling?

To perform the stress test, we'll use a Scala-based testing framework called Gatling.[3] Gatling excels at generating large amounts of HTTP traffic; it's also quite good at complex scripting and scenario-based experiments. It doesn't run on Scala Native at this time, but it's the best tool for the job, and so I've included it in the build environment.

Gatling's simulation DSL is mostly self-explanatory, but we'll take a quick look at it here:

---

3. https://gatling.io

HTTPServer/load_simulation.scala
```scala
import io.gatling.core.Predef._
import io.gatling.http.Predef._
import scala.concurrent.duration._

class GenericSimulation extends Simulation {
  val url = System.getenv("GATLING_URL")
  val requests = Integer.parseInt(System.getenv("GATLING_REQUESTS"))
  val users = Integer.parseInt(System.getenv("GATLING_USERS"))
  val reqs_per_user = requests / users
  val rampTime = Integer.parseInt(System.getenv("GATLING_RAMP_TIME"))
  val scn = scenario("Test scenario").repeat(reqs_per_user) {
    exec(
      http("Web Server")
        .get(url)
        .check(status.in(Seq(200,304)))
    )
  }
  setUp(scn.inject(rampUsers(users) over (rampTime seconds)))
}
```

As you can see, it externalizes parameters like the number of requests, number of connections, and URL to request as environment variables.

We'll also need to install Gatling. It's a Scala app, but it has a complex UI and IDE components as well. I've included a helper script in the book's code directory called install_gatling.sh that will install it locally. Once Gatling is installed, we just need to export the environment variables defined earlier and invoke Gatling, like this:

```
$ export GATLING_URL=http://localhost:8080 GATLING_USERS=10
$ export GATLING_REQUESTS=50 GATLING_RAMP_TIME=0
$ gatling.sh http://localhost:8080 10 500
```

This will hit localhost with 500 requests from ten simultaneous connections, and should produce output like this:

```
================================================================================
---- Global Information --------------------------------------------------------
> request count                            500 (OK=500    KO=0    )
> min response time                          6 (OK=6      KO=-    )
> max response time                        266 (OK=84     KO=-    )
> mean response time                        42 (OK=43     KO=-    )
> std deviation                             65 (OK=65     KO=-    )
> response time 50th percentile             35 (OK=3      KO=-    )
> response time 75th percentile            130 (OK=6      KO=-    )
> response time 95th percentile            140 (OK=20     KO=-    )
> response time 99th percentile            171 (OK=170    KO=-    )
> mean requests/sec                        125 (OK=125    KO=-    )
```

```
---- Response Time Distribution -------------------------------------
> t < 800 ms                                        500 (100%)
> 800 ms < t < 1200 ms                                0 (  0%)
> t > 1200 ms                                         0 (  0%)
> failed                                              0 (  0%)
====================================================================
```

All of this is interesting data, but with respect to the five performance qualities that we care about, we only need three: response time 50th percentile, response time 99th percentile, and the error rate by failed at the bottom. Then we can put them in a table like this:

# of users	request count	50th percentile	99th percentile	error rate
10	500	35	171	0

Now, by gradually increasing the number of simulated users and requests, we can collect enough data to see the large-scale trends:

# of users	request count	50th percentile	99th percentile	error rate
10	500	35	171	0
25	1250	71	161	0
50	2500	164	421	0
75	3750	222	641	0
100	5000	228	701	0
150	7500	324	2724	0
200	10000	472	4120	0
250	12500	506	2777	0
300	15000	625	1746	0.4%
350	17500	528	2592	14%
400	20000	545	2661	29%
450	22500	576	2997	29%
500	25000	424	4735	33%
750	37500	536	5137	34%
1000	50000	464	3861	44%
1500	75000	555	4485	44%
2000	100000	559	5484	52%

What can we see here? Real data are always noisy, but there are two clearly visible trends. Our typical performance at the 50th percentile (or median) starts out at 35 milliseconds, but increases almost linearly until it reaches 625ms at 300 users. After 300 users, our median response decreases slightly, and then plateaus around 500ms, but the error rate starts to shoot up very rapidly. If we were optimizing for maximum throughput with minimal errors, we could aim to run this server at a capacity of about 300 users.

However, there's another trend visible in the 99th percentile response, which is relevant to our tail latency criteria. Especially in distributed systems, tail latencies are important—one slow call can have cascading effects in a complex transaction, and an especially long timeout can trigger the termination of an unresponsive server. Even under the lightest load, we have some ugly tail latencies of 171ms, compared to the median at 35ms. With 50 users, the 99th percentile shoots up to 421ms, and at 150 users it goes up to 2724ms.

Thus, we have two different ways we could optimize a deployment of this program at scale. If we were responsible for operating this server in a latency-sensitive situation, we could try to scale it to around 100 users per instance to keep the tail latencies under control. On the other hand, we could instead scale our deployment to about 300 if we needed to maximize throughput.

What's Next

In this chapter, you learned that building a correct, concurrent TCP server is by no means trivial, and there are more than a few tricky parts. Our simple HTTP server can handle a few hundred connections on modest hardware, which is sufficient for a variety of applications. Especially in modern cluster environments, there are many "sidecar services" that play vital roles, despite serving only a few requests per minute. That said, modern frameworks typically perform better than this; a simple node.js application can serve close to a thousand connections comfortably, while frameworks like Akka HTTP[4] and Finagle[5] can easily serve many thousands. The good news is that we can implement many of these same techniques for high-performance servers in Scala Native, either directly, or by using powerful C libraries.

In the remaining chapters of the book, we'll continue to build upon the techniques we've learned, but with a modern twist. In particular, we'll begin to investigate how poll-based techniques could improve the design of our web server, as we come much closer to the domain of heavily asynchronous, massively scalable web services for which Scala is rightly famous.

---

4. https://doc.akka.io/docs/akka-http/current
5. https://twitter.github.io/finagle

Part II

Modern Systems Programming

CHAPTER 6

Doing I/O Right, with Event Loops

In previous chapters, we explored memory management, networking, and concurrency, but with a decidedly retro flavor: we took classic systems programming techniques and updated them with a modern programming language. This chapter, however, marks a turning point. In this chapter and throughout the rest of this book, we'll go deeper and deeper into modern techniques and discover the different capabilities Scala Native gives us for writing state-of-the-art programs. If parts of the previous chapters felt traditional to you, get ready, because we'll soon be going much further off the beaten path.

Blocking and Polling

All the programs we wrote in the first part of the book used blocking I/O operations exclusively; whether we were reading from a file, or writing to a TCP socket, we always stopped the progress of our program until the I/O system call returned. And in the last two chapters, we used multiprocess-based concurrency techniques to allow our programs to keep operating while waiting for an incoming socket, or other long-running system calls. However, the benchmarks for our fork-based web server also pointed at the limitations of this technique, especially for programs that need to handle thousands of simultaneous network connections at once.

Traditional UNIX operating systems provided alternative techniques for *non-blocking I/O* in the form of two system calls: poll() and select(). Both allow a program to *poll*, or check the readiness of, a file handle for reading or writing; thus, instead of starting a call to read or write data and blocking, we can wait until we know that the call can be completed and—if we are entirely disciplined—ensure that our program never blocks.

When properly executed, this pattern can lead to dramatic performance improvements, since all of the time spent waiting on I/O can be spent on other tasks. However, the traditional implementations of poll() and select() also had to deal with some severe bottlenecks: since the set of file handles to poll is kept in the user-space processes' memory, the OS kernel has to walk through and check each handle, one at a time. In other words, the amount of time required to process a call to poll() or select() scales in proportion to the number of file handles. This is fine for programs like our stream-merging code that might have to handle only a few dozen files, but it starts to impose a very noticeable overhead on a busy web server with thousands of simultaneous connections.

The other issue is program complexity. Not only do we have to find something to do while we wait for I/O to happen, but we also have to track all the potential pending I/O requests that have yet to complete and react to them accordingly. These constraints generally lead to an architecture known as an *event loop*, in which a program continuously checks for new things to do, while the programmer defines tasks as *callback functions* that can be executed at some point in the future. Although this is a powerful programming style, it can also be tricky to get right, especially if you have to write everything from scratch.

The good news is that starting in the early 2000s, operating systems began to introduce new interfaces for high-performance asynchronous I/O with the capability to handle tens of thousands of sockets (or more) at once. The bad news is that the major OSs implemented radically different, incompatible interfaces. Linux gave us epoll,[1] FreeBSD and Mac OS X both implemented kqueue,[2] and Windows implemented I/O Completion Ports.[3] Although projects that embrace these capabilities may perform ten times or more better than their predecessors, serious issues with portability and complexity have made them challenging for developers to adopt.

Fortunately, a variety of open-source libraries have emerged to fill the gap, wrapping the complexity and variability of each OS-specific interface behind a consistent (if not necessary simple) surface. Most notably, libuv—extracted from the node.js server-side JavaScript engine—provides an excellent, portable wrapper for all kinds of high-performance I/O tasks, and its C API is exceedingly well documented.[4] To make use of libuv, though, we'll need to

---

1. http://man7.org/linux/man-pages/man7/epoll.7.html
2. https://www.freebsd.org/cgi/man.cgi?kqueue
3. https://docs.microsoft.com/en-us/windows/desktop/fileio/i-o-completion-ports
4. http://docs.libuv.org/en/v1.x

extend Scala Native's capability with C libraries, as well as create function pointers for libuv's celebrated callback programming style.

Introducing libuv

libuv's C API provides a *lot* of functions. In many ways it serves as a replacement for much of the standard library of a traditional UNIX operating system, so that's not too surprising. What's fascinating, though, is how few basic concepts libuv relies upon to provide a consistent programming model over a wide variety of different I/O scenarios: clients and server, sockets and pipes, TCP and UDP. There are three fundamental building blocks to libuv:

- The event loop
- Handles
- Callbacks

They fit together like so: pipes and the like are represented as *handles*, and registered onto the *event loop*. The event loop is responsible for monitoring each handle. When an event occurs, a user-specified *callback function* is invoked with the data received. That's it! The same pattern largely applies to reading and writing to all kinds of sources and destinations, except for files.

To make use of this elegant and consistent model for I/O, we're going to need to look at a lot of different functions from the libuv API. We're also going to need to look at how to work with functions from an external C library like libuv.

Setting Up a Loop

Before we can do anything else, we have to initialize an event loop. Although it's possible to maintain multiple event loops with libuv, I don't recommend it, even for experts—the library was developed for single-threaded programs running a single event loop, and that's where support is strongest. As we'll see, a single thread is capable of serving surprisingly heavy I/O workloads by avoiding blocking and utilizing every CPU cycle available. Since we only need a single loop, then, we can rely on libuv's default loop, which we can retrieve with uv_default_loop:

```
def uv_default_loop():Loop
```

This is probably the simplest function we've seen so far, ironically. The complexity lies in the work we do with the Loop struct it returns. So far, all the structs we've worked with have been relatively simple, with no more than three or four fields. Loop is different. If we look at its definition in the C header file uv.h, we'll see this:

```
struct uv_loop_s {
  /* User data - use this for whatever. */
  void* data;
  /* Loop reference counting. */
  unsigned int active_handles;
  void* handle_queue[2];
  union {
    void* unused[2];
    unsigned int count;
  } active_reqs;
  /* Internal flag to signal loop stop. */
  unsigned int stop_flag;
  UV_LOOP_PRIVATE_FIELDS
};
```

We haven't seen any C code before in this book, and it's not necessary to understand the details of this at all. However, there are two features worth calling out:

- The first field in the struct is an untyped pointer that's free for custom use.

- The end of the struct consists of an unspecified number of nonpublic fields that may vary by OS.

This is a tricky problem. We haven't had to deal with structs that vary their layouts in different environments before, and since Scala Native lacks C's conditional compilation, we don't have an obvious way to represent them. Fortunately, libuv's designers have given us several ways to structure and allocate Loop objects. The basic technique we're going to use is a *type pun*, much like we did with IP address casting in our TCP socket code. Since we never have to allocate a Loop instance ourselves, and we only care about data in its first field, we can represent Loop like this:

```
type Loop = Ptr[Ptr[Byte]]
```

Then we can get at that inner pointer, and its contents, something like this:

```
val loop:Loop
val inner_data_ptr:Ptr[Data] = (!loop).cast[Ptr[Data]]
val inner_data:Data = !inner_data_ptr
```

That's it! And because all pointers are the same size, we can store any kind of data we want; even though the Loop code contains many more fields, our code doesn't need to know about them. This technique *would* cause serious errors if we tried to allocate a Loop and populate it ourselves, but we have no reason to do so. And as you'll see shortly, libuv gives us tools to help with memory allocation as well.

Hello, Asynchronous World!

Once we have a Loop, we can start creating handles and assigning callbacks to them. To start, we'll create something really simple: a Timer handle, which fires an event on the loop after a configurable timeout, with a separately configurable repeat duration. To plug it into our loop, we'll need to do a few different things:

1. Allocate the timer with malloc.
2. Initialize the timer.
3. Start the timer and assign a callback.
4. Run the loop.

We'll do all of these, plus write our callback, step by step. First, though, we have to figure out how to represent the Timer handle as a struct. Unfortunately, the C header definition for uv_timer_t is even gnarlier than uv_loop_t, and we don't have an out—we have to figure out how to allocate it correctly. Fortunately, libuv provides a utility function for this: uv_handle_size, with this signature:

```
def uv_handle_size(uv_handle_t:Int):Int
```

uv_handle_size will tell us, at runtime, exactly how many bytes we need to allocate for any kind of handle, so it's perfect for passing into malloc. The only catch is that we have to look up the uv_handle_t values, which are constants defined in a C header file. I've translated them all from C to Scala:

```
LibUVServer/async_timer/main.scala
val UV_PIPE_T = 7 // Pipes
val UV_POLL_T = 8 // Polling external sockets
val UV_PREPARE_T = 9 // Runs every loop iteration
val UV_PROCESS_T = 10 // Subprocess
val UV_TCP_T = 12 // TCP sockets
val UV_TIMER_T = 13 // Timer
val UV_TTY_T = 14 // Terminal emulator
val UV_UDP_T = 15 // UDP sockets
```

We'll only use a small fraction of these, but they're all extremely well documented on the libuv website.[5] Likewise, the Timer (and all other handles) has a leading data field for application use, so we can structure it exactly the same way as we did Loop:

```
type Timer = Ptr[Ptr[Byte]]
```

---

5.   http://docs.libuv.org/en/v1.x/api.html

Once we have space for a Timer handle allocated, we can initialize it, which associates it with a loop and gives the memory chunk meaningful values. The function to do this, uv_timer_init, is largely self-explanatory:

```
def uv_timer_init(loop:Ptr[Loop], handle:Ptr[Timer]):Int
```

uv_timer_init takes a loop and a handle, initializes the handle, and returns 0 if successful or an error code otherwise. Many libuv functions can return error codes and messages, so it's worth taking a moment to write a small wrapper function to check those errors; it will itself use the helper functions uv_strerr and uv_err_name:

```scala
LibUVServer/async_timer/main.scala
def check_error(v:Int, label:String):Int = {
    if (v == 0) {
      println(s"$label returned $v")
      v
    } else {
      val error = fromCString(uv_err_name(v))
      val message = fromCString(uv_strerror(v))
      println(s"$label returned $v: $error: $message")
      v
    }
}
```

Now we're almost ready to run a function on our event loop. To start the Timer and associate a callback function with it, call uv_timer_start:

```
def uv_timer_start(handle:Timer, callback:uv_timer_cb, timeout:Long, repeat:Long)
```

uv_timer_start takes a Timer handle, a CFunctionPtr callback, and two Long values: timeout, which determines the initial delay before the timer fires, and repeat, which determines the delay for each invocation after the first (both are in milliseconds). The callback is worth special attention. Like we saw with qsort back in Chapter 2, Arrays, Structs, and the Heap, on page 25, the callback function must itself follow a particular signature:

```
type uv_timer_cb = CFunctionPtr1[Timer,Unit]
```

If we pass a function that takes a Timer handle as an argument and returns Unit (in other words, nothing), the event loop will invoke it and pass in our handle every time. Since we can store custom data inside the handle's internal data pointer, we could even keep custom data structures in there if we needed to. We also mustn't forget to use CFunctionPtr.fromFunction1 to convert a regular Scala method into the sort of statically scoped function pointer we can pass to a C API, just like we did with qsort().

Finally, once our loop, its handle, and all of the callbacks are set up, we can run the loop with uv_run:

```
def uv_run(loop:Loop, runMode:Int): Int = extern
```

uv_run takes the loop itself and a runMode—I won't go deep into the details, but each value of runMode determines at what point in the future uv_run will return. In this book, I'll always call it with the constant UV_RUN_DEFAULT, which will run the loop continuously until there are *no outstanding active handles*. In other words, all files are closed, connections are closed, and timers are canceled or completed. (For convenience, I've defined this and other useful constants in a LibUVConstants object that you can see in the accompanying source code.)

With these preliminaries out of the way, we're ready to write a short program to test out libuv. To start, we'll do something really simple: create a short, one-second timer delay, print out a message, complete the loop, and exit. Ironically, we now know that println is itself a blocking, synchronous I/O function, but it remains indispensable for logging, so we'll keep it around a bit longer.

LibUVServer/async_timer/main.scala
```scala
def main(args:Array[String]):Unit = {
  println("hello, world!")
  val loop = uv_default_loop()
  val timer = stdlib.malloc(uv_handle_size(UV_TIMER_T))
  val ret = uv_timer_init(loop, timer)
  println(s"uv_timer_init returned $ret")
  uv_timer_start(timer, timerCB, 1000, 0)
  println("invoking loop")
  uv_run(loop,UV_RUN_DEFAULT)
  println("done")
}

val timerCB = new TimerCB {
  def apply(handle:TimerHandle):Unit = {
    println("timer fired!")
  }
}
```

But there's a catch. This code won't compile yet because we haven't prepared *bindings* for the libuv C API. As far as the Scala compiler is concerned, these functions that we're calling don't exist, just as though we had failed to add a dependency to our build.sbt file. In fact, if we want to use a nonstandard C library in Scala Native, there are two separate steps we need to take. We have to first ensure that the library is compiled and installed on the system, and then we have to supply definitions for all of the functions we need to invoke.

If you're using the Docker-based build environment, libuv is already installed, so you don't have that to worry about it. But if you're working in a noncontainer environment, see Appendix 1, Setting Up the Environment, on page 211, for notes on installing libuv. Writing the bindings themselves will take just a little more work, but we've already done the hard part.

Once a library is installed on our system, we can use its functions by translating their signatures from C into Scala, which is exactly what we've done as we've introduced each function throughout the chapter. Then, we place the function definitions into a special object literal in a Scala file, with three unusual characteristics:

- The object has the @extern annotation, for linking to C functions.
- The object has the @link("uv") function, for linking to the "libuv" library.
- Each function definition has the special term extern assigned as its "implementation"—the Scala Native compiler will do the rest.

All together the bindings for the libuv functions we have used so far look like this:

```scala
LibUVServer/async_timer/main.scala
@link("uv")
@extern
object LibUV {
  type TimerHandle = Ptr[Byte]
  type PipeHandle = Ptr[Ptr[Byte]]

  type Loop = Ptr[Byte]
  type TimerCB = CFuncPtr1[TimerHandle,Unit]

  def uv_default_loop(): Loop = extern
  def uv_loop_size(): CSize = extern
  def uv_is_active(handle:Ptr[Byte]): Int = extern
  def uv_handle_size(h_type:Int): CSize = extern
  def uv_req_size(r_type:Int): CSize = extern

  def uv_timer_init(loop:Loop, handle:TimerHandle):Int = extern
  def uv_timer_start(handle:TimerHandle, cb:TimerCB, timeout:Long,
    repeat:Long):Int = extern
  def uv_timer_stop(handle:TimerHandle):Int = extern

  def uv_run(loop:Loop, runMode:Int): Int = extern

  def uv_strerror(err:Int): CString = extern
  def uv_err_name(err:Int): CString = extern
}
```

Now, our program can run! If you run it from the console, you should see output like this:

```
$ ./target/scala-2.11/async_timer-out
hello, world!
uv_timer_init returned 0
invoking loop
timer fired!
done
```

So far, so good. Next, we'll extend this event-driven programming style to TCP sockets.

Working with Asynchronous TCP Sockets

Just as we did in Chapter 5, Writing a Server the Old-Fashioned Way, on page 85, we're going to write a simple TCP echo server that accepts connections, reads strings from the connected socket, and writes back the same message in response. Although it's about as simple as a network protocol gets, this scenario is enough for us to exercise all the essential API calls we need to make a libuv server work. And as you'll see, there's a close correspondence between these calls and those you learned when we created our blocking server.

Accepting Connections

To receive connections on a server, we have to initialize the socket, bind to a port, listen for incoming connections, and then accept each incoming connection before the connections are usable. We'll do this in much the same way as we did before, but with a different set of API calls and the data structures that we'll need to invoke them. Let's look at all of these definitions at once:

LibUVServer/async_tcp/main.scala

```scala
type Buffer = CStruct2[Ptr[Byte],CSize]
type TCPHandle = Ptr[Ptr[Byte]]
type ConnectionCB = CFuncPtr2[TCPHandle, Int, Unit]
type WriteReq = Ptr[Ptr[Byte]]
type ShutdownReq = Ptr[Ptr[Byte]]

def uv_tcp_init(loop:Loop, tcp_handle:TCPHandle):Int = extern
def uv_tcp_bind(tcp_handle:TCPHandle, address:Ptr[Byte], flags:Int):Int =
  extern
def uv_listen(stream_handle:TCPHandle, backlog:Int,
              uv_connection_cb:ConnectionCB): Int = extern
def uv_accept(server:TCPHandle, client:TCPHandle): Int = extern
def uv_read_start(client:TCPHandle, allocCB:AllocCB, readCB:ReadCB): Int =
  extern
def uv_write(writeReq:WriteReq, client:TCPHandle, bufs: Ptr[Buffer],
             numBufs:Int, writeCB:WriteCB): Int = extern
def uv_shutdown(shutdownReq:ShutdownReq, client:TCPHandle,
                shutdownCB:ShutdownCB): Int = extern
```

```scala
def uv_close(handle:TCPHandle, closeCB: CloseCB): Int = extern

def uv_ip4_addr(address:CString, port:Int, out_addr:Ptr[Byte]):Int = extern
def uv_ip4_name(address:Ptr[Byte], s:CString, size:Int):Int = extern

type AllocCB = CFuncPtr3[TCPHandle,CSize,Ptr[Buffer],Unit]
type ReadCB = CFuncPtr3[TCPHandle,CSSize,Ptr[Buffer],Unit]
type WriteCB = CFuncPtr2[WriteReq,Int,Unit]
type ShutdownCB = CFuncPtr2[ShutdownReq,Int,Unit]
type CloseCB = CFuncPtr1[TCPHandle,Unit]
```

We'll use the type TCPHandle to model a TCP handle in libuv, and we'll use the same technique as we did with Timer to represent it in Scala Native as a Ptr[Ptr[Byte]], ignoring the trailing private fields and internal data structures.

Type Puns and Safety

If we were to inspect the C header, we would see that many of these functions take a stream-type handle, rather than the more specific TCP handle. For example, uv_listen accepts a Stream handle, rather than a TCP instance, because it can handle other socket types (like UDP and named pipes), so that Stream functions like a trait or superclass. However, our bindings don't have to concern themselves, since all handle types in this book will be modeled as opaque Ptr[Ptr[Byte]] aliases.

Note, however, that this means the Scala compiler won't catch certain errors. For example, if we pass a Loop instance to a function that expects a TcpHandle, it won't complain, since both are aliases for Ptr[Ptr[Byte]].

As for the actual functions, they're largely straightforward. uv_tcp_init initializes an allocated TCP handle and returns an error code as an int. uv_tcp_bind binds the initialized handle with a TCP address (which is represented with the same Sockaddr structure we used back in Chapter 3, Writing a Simple HTTP Client, on page 45) and we can use the uv_ip4_addr helper function to populate it. Finally, after we call uv_listen, the event loop will call uv_connection_cb every time there's an incoming connection. The ConnectionCallback itself just gets a reference to the listening TCP socket and a status flag in an int.

In other words, this is the same sequence of fundamental system calls that our blocking server made, but instead of issuing them ourselves, we're setting up handler functions to perform these tasks for us. The complexity introduced by this pattern is that without a top-level outer function to handle a full connection lifecycle, initializing and releasing resources becomes much trickier. In general, we'll want to model all of the state that we need to manage a client connection in a single struct, which we can store via the handle's inner Ptr[Byte] contents. Later on, we'll model more complex structures, but for now we can just store a simple buffer structure with counters for allocated and used data:

```
type ClientState = CStruct3[Ptr[Byte],CSize,CSize]
```

Now we're ready to write a basic main() routine and top-level server logic. We'll abstract over the actual ConnectionCallback implementation, although we'll be getting to that shortly. It's just a few lines of code so far:

LibUVServer/async_tcp/main.scala
```
type ClientState = CStruct3[Ptr[Byte],CSize,CSize]

def main(args:Array[String]):Unit = {
  println("hello!")
  serve_tcp(c"0.0.0.0", 8080, 0, 100, connectionCB)
  println("done?")
}

val loop = uv_default_loop()

def serve_tcp(address:CString, port:Int, flags:Int, backlog:Int,
    callback:ConnectionCB):Unit = {
  val addr = stackalloc[Byte]
  val addr_convert = uv_ip4_addr(address, port, addr)
  println(s"uv_ip4_addr returned $addr_convert")
  val handle = malloc(uv_handle_size(UV_TCP_T)).asInstanceOf[TCPHandle]
  check_error(uv_tcp_init(loop, handle), "uv_tcp_init(server)")
  check_error(uv_tcp_bind(handle, addr, flags), "uv_tcp_bind")
  check_error(uv_listen(handle, backlog, callback), "uv_tcp_listen")
  uv_run(loop, UV_RUN_DEFAULT)
  ()
}
```

Due to libuv's highly consistent programming style, I find this approach much more readable and concise than the traditional UNIX equivalent we wrote before. Next, we have to implement our connection callback.

Handling Connections

When we receive an incoming connection in libuv, we have a few additional problems to concern ourself with. First, we have to accept the connection, which establishes another TCP handle, separate from the one we're listening on, but attached to the same event loop. We'll also need to initialize the ConnectionState struct at this time.

It's also important that we eventually free the memory we allocate for the ConnectionState and other resources; however, we won't be doing that until we're ready to close the connection a little later on. Finally, we'll need to tell libuv what to do when a request arrives. We'll do that with two callbacks, on_alloc and on_read, which we'll be defining in detail in the next section.

As with the previous code sample, libuv's consistent style means that all of this code is remarkably compact:

```
LibUVServer/async_tcp/main.scala
val connectionCB = new ConnectionCB {
  def apply(handle:TCPHandle, status:Int):Unit = {
    println("received connection")

    // initialize the new client tcp handle and its state
    val client = malloc(uv_handle_size(UV_TCP_T)).asInstanceOf[TCPHandle]
    check_error(uv_tcp_init(loop,client), "uv_tcp_init(client)")
    var client_state_ptr = (!client).asInstanceOf[Ptr[ClientState]]
    client_state_ptr = initialize_client_state(client)

    // accept the incoming connection into the new handle
    check_error(uv_accept(handle,client), "uv_accept")
    // set up callbacks for incoming data
    check_error(uv_read_start(client,allocCB,readCB), "uv_read_start")
  }
}

def initialize_client_state(client:TCPHandle):Ptr[ClientState] = {
    val client_state_ptr = stdlib.malloc(sizeof[ClientState]).asInstanceOf
      [Ptr[ClientState]]
    stdio.printf(c"""allocated data at %x; assigning into handle storage at
      %x\n""", client_state_ptr, client)
    val client_state_data = stdlib.malloc(4096)
    client_state_ptr._1 = client_state_data
    client_state_ptr._2 = 4096 // total
    client_state_ptr._3 = 0 // used
    !client = client_state_ptr.asInstanceOf[Ptr[Byte]]
    client_state_ptr
}
```

uv_accept is mostly equivalent to the standard accept function we've already used; however, in this case we need to pass not one, but *two* TCP socket handles into it. And although the type signature indicates any Stream socket will do, we'll only be using TCP. The first handle, server, is the one we created, but we're also guaranteed that it will be passed in to our ConnectionCallback as an argument (and we should always use the handle passed in to the callback, for safety). It's our responsibility to allocate and initialize the handle for the new TCP connection in this ConnectionCallback *before* calling uv_accept. Once we do so, the handle is associated with the event loop; but, it won't receive any data unless we call uv_read_start, which we must also do before we complete our ConnectionCallback.

Receiving Data

Now that our connection is fully established, we can read and write data. When the TCP socket that underlies the TCP handle is ready for reading, the event loop will first invoke the AllocationCallback. In that callback, we're responsible for giving the event loop a Buffer of data that it can safely read into. We haven't seen Buffer before, but libuv uses it ubiquitously for passing binary data around—it's just a simple construct containing two fields: a Ptr[Byte] and a length. In the second Int argument to the callback, libuv passes in a number of bytes to request, but we can basically disregard it. libuv has no idea how much data is going to come in at this point, so it always asks for 65536, which isn't always appropriate—especially for a line-by-line echo server.

To be more conservative, we can implement an AllocationCallback that gives back 4096 bytes instead. Since we indicate the size of the Buffer explicitly in the data structure, the event loop knows not to overflow, and it can always call the AllocationCallback again if it has more data to read. Let's write it quickly:

```
LibUVServer/async_tcp/main.scala
val allocCB = new AllocCB {
  def apply(client:TCPHandle, size:CSize, buffer:Ptr[Buffer]):Unit = {
    println("allocating 4096 bytes")
    val buf = stdlib.malloc(4096)
    buffer._1 = buf
    buffer._2 = 4096
  }
}
```

Once memory has been allocated, the event loop will immediately read data into the buffer and then call the ReadCallback.

In this, and in most libuv programs we'll write, the ReadCallback is the single most complex function we'll write. It has numerous responsibilities in a typical server program:

- It determines whether the client has closed the connection or not.

- It receives data in the form of Buffer and parses or copies it into connection state as needed.

- It determines when and how to send response back to the client.

- Before returning, it frees the memory in the Buffer that we allocated in the AllocationCallback.

Each one of these is complex enough that we'll want to break up our read callback into a top-level function with several helpers.

The most important detail to get right is handling a closed connection. When a client has terminated a connection unprompted, which is normal in a client-server architecture, the read callback will be invoked with a size argument that is less than 0. However, because TCP connections are bidirectional, we can still send a "response" back; many protocols will even use this as a normal indicator of "the request is complete, please send your response." We can take that approach for our echo server. Instead of echoing data back line-by-line, it will read until completion, then echo back everything it has read.

This is enough of a plan for us to fill in the top level of our read callback:

```
LibUVServer/async_tcp/main.scala
val readCB = new ReadCB {
  def apply(client:TCPHandle, size:CSSize, buffer:Ptr[Buffer]):Unit = {
    println(s"read $size bytes")
    var client_state_ptr = (!client).asInstanceOf[Ptr[ClientState]]
    if (size < 0) {
      send_response(client, client_state_ptr)
      println("connection is closed, shutting down")
      shutdown(client)
    } else {
      append_data(client_state_ptr, size, buffer)
      stdlib.free(buffer._1)
    }
  }
}
```

Now we just need to fill in the details. The first thing to get right is storing the data we receive, but that can be tricky. We have no guarantee that on_read will be called with a complete request, or even a complete line, nor do we know that it will be called exactly once. This can create a lot of complications for more complex parsers, but fortunately an echo server is simpler than that. We do, however, need to keep track of how many bytes we've already copied into the ConnectionState, and be sure to always append to the end, like so:

```
LibUVServer/async_tcp/main.scala
def append_data(state:Ptr[ClientState], size:CSSize,
                buffer:Ptr[Buffer]):Unit = {
  val copy_position = state._1 + state._3
  string.strncpy(copy_position, buffer._1, size)
  // be sure to update the length of the data since we have copied into it
  state._3 = state._3 + size
  stdio.printf(c"client %x: %d/%d bytes used\n", state, state._3, state._2)
}
```

Although this pattern is more or less straightforward, the complexity can grow rapidly for more full-featured applications. For example, imagine implementing the pattern of our blocking, fgets-based HTTP parser in this idiom. We would have to handle partial lines, receive multiple lines at once, and maintain huge amounts of dynamic state, all while working with a single data structure. Although it's certainly doable, it can require discipline and planning.

Sending a Response

Once we've read some data, and have decided, one way or another, that we have a complete request, it's time for us to send the client a response. libuv provides us a few functions to help with this, but the pattern is a bit different from reads. Since incoming data is initiated by the client, our program doesn't control when it happens—we just define a handler to invoke when it shows up. Outgoing writes are different. We can decide exactly what gets sent and choose when to initiate the write, but we cannot decide exactly when the client will choose to consume it. As a result, writes are tracked individually, rather than per-connection, which makes things a little more complex to implement, but also simplifies a lot of the harder resource-management problems.

The most important new data structure is the WriteReq, or write request, which looks like this:

```
type WriteReq = Ptr[Ptr[Byte]]
```

Again, it's just another opaque pointer, and we'll initialize it with the uv_req_size helper function. However, the WriteReq doesn't actually contain the response data—that's done with an array of the Buffer objects we've already used for receiving input. (We'll only ever use a single buffer in this book, but it's possible to have larger arrays, which is why uv_write takes a size argument.) I also generally find it convenient to store a pointer to the buffer in the contents of the WriteReq data pointer itself, which will make cleanup easier when we're done, but it's not required, and you could implement much more complex state for write requests if you wished.

Once we have initialized our request and buffer, we can generate our response—I've modeled this as a simple function that takes the ConnectionState and Buffer, but this can, again, be as simple or complex as you wish—and then pass the populated data on to uv_write. uv_write also takes a callback, which will be invoked once the write is completed (has been fully received by the client). That's when we'll be ready to free the write request, buffer, and any other data we've allocated:

```
LibUVServer/async_tcp/main.scala
def send_response(client:TCPHandle,state:Ptr[ClientState]):Unit = {
    val resp = malloc(uv_req_size(UV_WRITE_REQ_T)).asInstanceOf[WriteReq]
    val resp_buffer = malloc(sizeof[Buffer]).asInstanceOf[Ptr[Buffer]]
    resp_buffer._1 = make_response(state)
    resp_buffer._2 = string.strlen(resp_buffer._1)
    !resp = resp_buffer.asInstanceOf[Ptr[Byte]]
    check_error(uv_write(resp,client,resp_buffer,1,writeCB), "uv_write")
}

def make_response(state:Ptr[ClientState]):CString = {
  val response_format = c"received response:\n%s\n"
  val response_data = malloc(string.strlen(response_format) + state._3)
  stdio.sprintf(response_data, response_format, state._1)
  response_data
}

val writeCB = new WriteCB {
  def apply(writeReq:WriteReq, status:Int):Unit = {
    println("write completed")
    val resp_buffer = (!writeReq).asInstanceOf[Ptr[Buffer]]
    stdlib.free(resp_buffer._1)
    stdlib.free(resp_buffer.asInstanceOf[Ptr[Byte]])
    stdlib.free(writeReq.asInstanceOf[Ptr[Byte]])
  }
}
```

Here, our make_response function is about as simple as we can be: we're using snprintf to create a string with a brief message, followed by the data we've consumed so far.

Closing a Connection

We're almost ready to put all the pieces together! We're just missing one last piece: closing a TCP connection, whether initiated by a client, or by our server. TCP sockets make this extra tricky because they are bidirectional, which allows a client to shut down its outgoing writes while still being able to receive a response. We didn't have to deal with this nuance in our blocking HTTP server, since it used sscanf to find request boundaries within a stream of lines. But because our echo server will be reading until the client closes, we have to deal with it.

The good news is that libuv makes this pretty easy for us. It provides two different functions—uv_shutdown and uv_close—with slightly different use cases. uv_close immediately terminates a connection, without waiting for other operations to complete, and shuts down both the read and write side of a socket. uv_shutdown, in contrast, only closes the outgoing (write) side of our connection, and most important, it waits for all pending writes on the connection to complete before doing so.

This means we can invoke uv_shutdown from the on_read callback, right after we invoke uv_write, and be assured that the connection will stay open until the right time. uv_shutdown takes an opaque ShutdownReq, which works exactly like WriteReq, and it also lets us provide another callback, on_shutdown, which is a great place to actually call uv_close. Finally, the on_close callback we provide to uv_close is where we'll free the ConnectionState and related resources. Altogether, these functions look like so:

```
LibUVServer/async_tcp/main.scala
def shutdown(client:TCPHandle):Unit = {
  val shutdown_req = malloc(uv_req_size(UV_SHUTDOWN_REQ_T))
                          .asInstanceOf[ShutdownReq]
  !shutdown_req = client.asInstanceOf[Ptr[Byte]]
  check_error(uv_shutdown(shutdown_req,client,shutdownCB), "uv_shutdown")
}

val shutdownCB = new ShutdownCB {
  def apply(shutdownReq:ShutdownReq, status:Int):Unit = {
    println("all pending writes complete, closing TCP connection")
    val client = (!shutdownReq).asInstanceOf[TCPHandle]
    check_error(uv_close(client,closeCB),"uv_close")
    stdlib.free(shutdownReq.asInstanceOf[Ptr[Byte]])
  }
}

val closeCB = new CloseCB {
  def apply(client:TCPHandle):Unit = {
    println("closed client connection")
    val client_state_ptr = (!client).asInstanceOf[Ptr[ClientState]]
    stdlib.free(client_state_ptr._1)
    stdlib.free(client_state_ptr.asInstanceOf[Ptr[Byte]])
    stdlib.free(client.asInstanceOf[Ptr[Byte]])
  }
}
```

This nicely mirrors the way we allocated resources in our on_connect handler. A general rule of thumb for memory management is to pair every malloc call with a free call, and although it can be a bit tricky to figure out exactly where to do it, it doesn't have to complicate an asynchronous program greatly.

Testing Our Echo Server

With this last bit of code in place, we're ready to run our server! We'll test it out much like we did with our previous TCP echo server—using netcat. First, we'll boot up the server, and we should see a prompt like this:

```
$ ./target/scala-2.11/async_tcp-out
hello!
uv_ip4_addr returned 0
uv_tcp_init(server) returned 0
uv_tcp_bind returned 0
uv_tcp_listen returned 0
```

Now, we can connect to it with netcat, and type in some text:

```
$ nc localhost 8080
foo
bar
```

When we do this, we won't see an immediate response because we still have our connection open. This means the server is still waiting for us to send more data. However, we can see in the server logs that it has consumed the data we sent so far:

```
...
received connection
uv_tcp_init(client) returned 0
allocated data at 6ac02ce0; assigning into handle storage at 6ac02bd0
uv_accept returned 0
uv_read_start returned 0
allocating 4096 bytes
read 4 bytes
client 6ac02ce0: 4/4096 bytes used
allocating 4096 bytes
read 4 bytes
client 6ac02ce0: 8/4096 bytes used
```

To terminate the connection on the client side, type Ctrl + D. We'll then see the client receive a response:

```
...
received response:
foo
bar

$
```

And we can also see the server responding to the connection that just closed:

```
allocating 4096 bytes
read -4095 bytes
uv_write returned 0
connection is closed, shutting down
uv_shutdown returned 0
write completed
all pending writes complete, closing TCP connection
uv_close returned 169822304: Unknown system error 169822304...
closed client connection
```

If you see an error like the uv_close error above, don't panic! It's routine on many operating systems—Mac OS included—when we try to close a socket that has already been shut down on both sides, but otherwise harmless.

After all this, our server is still running and ready to accept more connections. I recommend testing it with multiple simultaneous or sequential connections and seeing how it behaves.

Now that we have a working echo server on a TCP socket, there's one more step left: we still need to adapt our HTTP parsing code from Chapter 3, Writing a Simple HTTP Client, on page 45, to work with our asynchronous server.

Building an Asynchronous HTTP Server

Unfortunately, we can't simply reuse our previous parsing methods. Most important, we can't do blocking socket I/O as we did in Chapter 3, Writing a Simple HTTP Client, on page 45, so we'll need to adapt all the I/O patterns to libuv.

We'll also want to think hard about memory allocation. With the low-overhead, asynchronous architecture we've used in this chapter, our server could potentially be handling thousands of requests per second. At that scale, the overhead of garbage collection, or even manual memory allocation, can have a serious impact on performance.

Designing the API

Before we get into the guts of the implementation, though, let's take a moment to work through the design of an API that we could present to an end user. Since we've already written an HTTP server once before, we can tweak our design based on what we've learned so far. With a design in hand, we can then consider several different strategies for implementation and evaluate the trade-offs of each one.

Back in Chapter 5, Writing a Server the Old-Fashioned Way, on page 85, we defined an HTTP Request and Response with the following case class:

```
case class HttpRequest(
  method:String,
  uri:String,
  headers:collection.Map[String, String],
  body:String)

case class HttpResponse(
  code:Int,
  headers:collection.Map[String, String],
  body:String)
```

We can build on these by defining the fundamental type signatures that define an HTTP server in terms of these fundamentals. The most important signature is this:

```
type RequestHandler = Function1[HttpRequest,HttpResponse]
```

This RequestHandler function can actually define lots of different parts of a server:

- It naturally defines the handling for any particular kind of request.

- It defines the router, which determines which handler to invoke based on the method, uri, headers, and body of the request.

- It defines, in some sense, the server itself, which may just be a trivial wrapper around a router method at this point.

Based on these insights, we could define a simple public API that looks like this:

```
object HttpServer {
  def serve_http(port:Short,router:RequestHandler):Unit
}
```

With an API like this, we could write a clean, simple main function like this:

LibUVServer/async_http/main.scala
```
def main(args:Array[String]):Unit = {
  serve_http(8080, request =>
    HttpResponse(200, Map("Content-Length" -> "12"),"hello world\n"))
}
```

Later on, we'll work on the design of more sophisticated and performant routing logic, but a great benefit of this design is that we can serve a single-route request handler for now, and plug in other designs as we please. Next, we'll proceed with implementing this API from the outside in, reusing as much of our previous work as possible.

Choices for Implementation

To implement this API, we'll need to solve three basic design problems:

1. How to parse incoming data into a HttpRequest object.
2. How to render HttpResponse objects into valid WriteReq structs.
3. How to pass the supplied router function to libuv's event handlers.

All of these will make the code a bit more complicated than the blocking, fork-based HTTP server we wrote before. In particular, since we had a dedicated process for each connection, we could use fgets to read exactly one line at a time from a TCP socket, which made parsing the HTTP headers much easier.

In contrast, libuv will simply give us a chunk of whatever bytes are available, up to the maximum size of the buffer. This opens up a wide range of problematic scenarios, some more likely than others:

- A single onRead call is very likely to receive multiple lines of input at once.
- Depending on the size of the request and the buffer, onRead may or may not be able to receive the whole request in a single call.
- If the request doesn't fit in a single buffer, it most likely doesn't break on a line boundary.
- If the client is especially slow in sending the request, onRead may receive a partial request that's smaller than the buffer.
- If a request is incomplete, the end of the received data may fall in the headers or the body of the request.

Further, all of these scenarios are complicated by the imperative, stateful nature of the HTTP protocol, which changes its behavior depending on what headers are read. In short, asynchronous parsing is a hard problem, and not one we should underestimate. There are good C libraries we could bring in for this; there's even node.js's own HTTP-parser C library, which has a close affinity for libuv, and would be a great option for a server like this.

But we do already have our own parsing code to adapt, and we also have our Gatling stress-testing scenario from before. So, instead of embarking upon a large engineering project and greatly enlarging the scope of this book, I've opted to adapt our existing code in a more straightforward way, while making a few optimistic assumptions. In particular, I found that with reasonably sized buffers and large requests, libuv is unlikely to provide a partial request for processing. And once we've implemented this, we can run our stress test and see how well our assumptions hold up.

There's one more catch, though. We also have to figure out a strategy to connect our user-supplied RequestHandler function with libuv. This is tricky, because Scala Native only allows us to generate a CFunctionPtr for static functions that are fully known at compile time. This means we can't directly convert the router argument into something that we can use as a libuv read handler. Instead, we'll use mutable object state to hold on to our router function, and then bring it back in for our onRead handler a little later on.

Following this pattern, serve_http will look like so:

```
LibUVServer/async_http/main.scala
var router:RequestHandler = (_ => ???)

def serve_http(port:Int, handler:RequestHandler):Unit = {
  println(s"about to serve on port ${port}")
  this.router = handler
  serve_tcp(c"0.0.0.0",port,0,4096,connectionCB)
}
```

Here, we're writing a thin wrapper around our pre-existing serve_tcp and on_connect functions. The next modification we'll make is in our on_read function. In some ways, it'll be simpler than before; since we don't allow client requests to span multiple calls to on_read, we no longer need to maintain a ClientState data structure, for example. If we abstract out the details of parsing requests, the code is straightforward:

```
LibUVServer/async_http/main.scala
val readCB = new ReadCB {
  def apply(client:TCPHandle, size:CSSize, buffer:Ptr[Buffer]):Unit = {
    if (size < 0) {
      shutdown(client)
    } else {
      try {
        val parsed_request = HTTP.parseRequest(buffer._1, size)
        val response = router(parsed_request)
        send_response(client,response)
        shutdown(client)
      } catch {
        case e:Throwable =>
          println(s"error during parsing: ${e}")
          shutdown(client)
      }
    }
  }
}
```

With these relatively thin wrappers in place, we're ready to begin writing our parsing code.

Parsing in libuv

Assuming we'll receive a full request in a single onRead call, we can express our parsing algorithm, in pseudocode, like this:

1. Scan the first line of the request as an HTTP request line and extract the method and URI.

   - If the request line is malformed, raise an exception and kill the connection.

2. Scan additional lines as headers, validating them but not extracting them.

   • If a header is malformed, the request is likely incomplete, and we can raise an exception.

3. When we encounter an empty line, we have reached the end of the headers, and should mark that point.

4. If there is content after the end of the headers, it constitutes the request body.

The trick with this is to minimize the amount of garbage allocation we do in the process, as well as the copying of intermediate values. If we're going to populate a Map of our headers, we won't be able to go for a completely zero-copy implementation style, but even a few considerate gestures will save us a lot of memory churn. In particular, since this is a single-threaded application, we can statically allocate a few buffers for temporary storage of request header lines and their components, and thus cut down on memory allocation during request handling.

For example, the first thing we'll have to do is parse the HTTP request line. We'll malloc buffers outside of the function as top-level fields of the enclosing object. We'll also use a scanf modifier * in our pattern to indicate noncapturing matches—in this case, we don't need to grab the HTTP protocol version—as well as the pseudo-pattern %n, which lets us capture and return the number of bytes read at the end, like this:

```
LibUVServer/async_http/http.scala
val method_buffer = malloc(16)
val uri_buffer = malloc(4096)

def scan_request_line(line:CString):(String,String,Int) = {
  val line_len = stackalloc[Int]
  val scan_result = stdio.sscanf(line, c"%s %s %*s\r\n%n", method_buffer,
    uri_buffer, line_len)
  if (scan_result == 2) {
    (fromCString(method_buffer), fromCString(uri_buffer), !line_len)
  } else {
    throw new Exception("bad request line")
  }
}
```

This method will then return the HTTP method, request URI, as well as the length, in bytes, of the line that it read, so that the enclosing on_read function can know where to start scanning next.

Next, we need to scan headers. These are a little trickier, since there may be whitespace at a few different parts, including within the content of the value portion of the line, as in Accept-Encoding: gzip, deflate, br. To match this, we'll use more constrained character patterns than before, such as %[^\r\n], to match anything but new lines, or %[^:] to match anything but a colon or space, rather than %s. And since we don't want to allocate storage for headers at all, we'll use the %n pseudo-pattern even more liberally, which will allow us to validate the start and end of the key and value portion of the line, without copying them to temporary storage. The resulting pattern string is a bit of a handful: c"%*[^\r\n:]%n: %n%*[^\r\n]%n%*[\r\n]%n"; we'll also be passing in pointers from the outer calling function, since it will need to be able to inspect some of the offsets to determine whether we're at the final header in the request.

All this logic makes things a bit more complicated, but it's not too bad:

```scala
LibUVServer/async_http/http.scala
def scan_header_line(line:CString,
                     out_map:mutable.Map[String,String],key_end:Ptr[Int],
                     value_start:Ptr[Int], value_end:Ptr[Int],
                     line_len:Ptr[Int]):Int = {
  !line_len = -1
  val scan_result = stdio.sscanf(line,
    c"%*[^\r\n:]%n: %n%*[^\r\n]%n%*[\r\n]%n",
    key_end, value_start, value_end, line_len)
  if (!line_len != -1) {
    val start_of_key = line
    val end_of_key = line + !key_end
    !end_of_key = 0
    val start_of_value = line + !value_start
    val end_of_value = line + !value_end
    !end_of_value = 0
    val key = fromCString(start_of_key)
    val value = fromCString(start_of_value)
    out_map(key) = value
    !line_len
  } else {
    throw new Exception("bad header line")
  }
}
```

Now we can stitch these two functions together into a function that will parse and validate requests for us.

Because both scan functions give us back the number of bytes read, we can use that value to maintain a counter of how many total bytes we've read so far. We'll also inspect the trailing whitespace at the end of each header line. If we have 2 bytes trailing, we should expect another header, whereas if there are 4 bytes left, we know this header is the last one. Finally, we'll need to check for the request body after the headers and parse it to a CString as well.

The whole function works like this:

LibUVServer/async_http/http.scala

```scala
val line_buffer = malloc(1024)

def parseRequest(req:CString, size: Long):HttpRequest = {
  req(size) = 0 // ensure null termination
  var req_position = req
  val line_len = stackalloc[Int]
  val key_end = stackalloc[Int]
  val value_start = stackalloc[Int]
  val value_end = stackalloc[Int]
  val headers = mutable.Map[String,String]()

  val (method,uri,request_len) = scan_request_line(req)

  var bytes_read = request_len
  while (bytes_read < size) {
    req_position = req + bytes_read
    val parse_header_result = scan_header_line(req_position, headers,
      key_end, value_start, value_end, line_len)
    if (parse_header_result < 0) {
      throw new Exception("HEADERS INCOMPLETE")
    } else if (!line_len - !value_end == 2) {
      bytes_read += parse_header_result
    } else if (!line_len - !value_end == 4) {
      val remaining = size - bytes_read
      val body = fromCString(req + bytes_read)
      return HttpRequest(method,uri,headers,body)
    } else {
      throw new Exception("malformed header!")
    }
  }
  throw new Exception(s"bad scan, exceeded $size bytes")
}
```

With HTTP parsing taken care of, we've implemented all of the components needed, and our server is done! When we compile and run it, we should see output like this:

```
$ ./target/scala-2.11/async_http-out
about to serve on port 8080
```

If we then navigate to http://localhost:8080/ in a web browser, we should promptly see the Hello, World response.

Measuring Performance

But we're just getting started. Now that we've done the work to create a non-blocking HTTP server, let's compare its performance to the blocking server we created in Chapter 5, Writing a Server the Old-Fashioned Way, on page

85. As a refresher, we used Gatling to measure the response time at the 50th and 99th percentile, as well as the overall throughput and error rate at different levels of concurrency, starting from 10 users and going up to 2000. Our fork-based server performed best with about 250 users, handling about 500 requests per second.

Let's run the exact same script on our new asynchronous server, like so:

```
$ export GATLING_URL=http://localhost:8080 GATLING_USERS=10
$ export GATLING_REQUESTS=50 GATLING_RAMP_TIME=0
$ gatling.sh http://localhost:8080 10 500
```

By running that same command with different user counts, we can tabulate results and compare the performance of the two servers:

# of users	request count	50th %ile	99th %ile	req/second	error rate
10	500	1	18	500	0
25	1250	1	44	625	0
50	2500	2	32	1250	0
75	3750	2	51	1875	0
100	5000	3	62	2500	0
150	7500	4	136	2500	0
200	10000	5	147	3333	0
250	12500	4	151	4166	0.1%
300	15000	5	245	3000	3%
350	17500	8	300	2916	5%
400	20000	8	258	4000	6%
450	22500	6	221	4500	4%
500	25000	11	326	3571	7%
750	37500	16	335	3750	12%
1000	50000	12	326	2380	14%
1500	75000	8	301	1744	15%
2000	100000	8	437	3255	14%

The performance of the asynchronous server is dramatically improved! Median performance is 30 to 50 times faster across the board; 99th percentile response and overall throughput is 10 times better than the blocking implementation; and error rates are much reduced at the highest levels of load, from 52% to 14% at 2000 users. Further, we can also see that although the local Gatling test is excellent at finding the peak throughput of our symptoms, it's also unrealistically harsh at simulating actual users. We'd expect response times and server load to be at least an order of magnitude less in a real-world cloud deployment, which suggests that our server could handle 10,000 users, or more, in many scenarios.

What's Next

In the next chapter, and indeed for the rest of the book, we're going to build upon this simple, robust server infrastructure we've built, as we continue to put the "modern" in "modern systems programming." By adding an asynchronous HTTP client, tightly integrated with the server, you'll gain the ability to interact with the outside world in a general, powerful way. And by adding support for asynchronous router and handler functions in our framework, you'll do all of this while preserving the striking performance characteristics we just examined.

CHAPTER 7

Functions and Futures: Patterns for Distributed Services

At the end of the last chapter, we implemented the core of a fully asynchronous web server based on a C binding for the libuv event loop. In this chapter, we'll extend those techniques and implement a highly capable asynchronous HTTP client based on the celebrated C library, libcurl.[1]

In many ways, we'll be retracing the steps we took in Chapter 3, Writing a Simple HTTP Client, on page 45, where we implemented a blocking HTTP client using just the low-level UNIX socket API and some simple regular expressions with scanf. However, our client had limitations to its efficiency and capabilities: its blocking nature limited its applicability to many highly parallel use cases, and the simple parser couldn't handle more sophisticated protocol variants such as HTTPS.

We've come a long way since Chapter 3. With what we know about C library bindings and nonblocking I/O, we're now prepared to design and build an HTTP client with far greater power. Before we dive into implementation, though, let's take a step back and design our API. Having a clear goal in mind will help us as we integrate libcurl and libuv and deal with their various quirks and gotchas.

Designing an Asynchronous API

Fortunately, we've done a lot of the basic analysis of HTTP already. The fundamental structure of an HTTP Request and Response is unchanged:

---

1. https://curl.haxx.se/libcurl

HTTPClient/httpclient/HTTPClient.scala

```scala
case class HttpRequest(
  method:String,
  uri:String,
  headers:collection.Map[String, String],
  body:String)
case class HttpResponse(
  code:Int,
  headers:collection.Map[String, String],
  body:String)
```

However, the signature of our previous HTTP client methods is no longer appropriate. Have a look at the following function:

```scala
def send(request:Request):Response
```

A function like this will block the calling thread until send() returns. In the context of an asynchronous program, this can have many negative consequences. And on a single-threaded event loop such as what libuv provides, it can be catastrophic—a blocking function will prevent any new connections or requests from being handled until it returns! To get around this limitation, we need some way to rephrase the operation of the HTTP client so that it's compatible with an asynchronous event loop.

For the server we built in Chapter 5, Writing a Server the Old-Fashioned Way, on page 85, we defined handlers with callback functions that provided a way for us to say, "When this happens, do that." Although client APIs can be designed in this way as well, it's not always convenient, especially for a program that makes many different kinds of external requests. Instead, what you probably want is a way to tell your program, "Start doing this, and when it completes, then do that."

Although there are a variety of techniques to solve this kind of problem, the standard approach in Scala is the *future* pattern, as implemented by the class Future in Scala's standard library.

Introducing Futures

In Scala, values of type Future represent the result of an asynchronous computation that has not completed yet, but may either complete successfully or complete with an error in the future. (Other languages may use the term *promise* for very similar patterns). Futures provide us with a variety of useful methods that allow us to chain together operations, recover from errors, and take custom actions upon completion, all in a fully asynchronous, nonblocking fashion. For example, suppose we have a method, delay(duration:Duration):Future[Unit], that returns a future that will complete with the empty value Unit after duration has elapsed. If we wanted to print a message only after it completes, we could do this:

```
val delayed = delay(5 seconds)
delayed.onComplete {
  println("done after 5 seconds!")
}
```

Whereas if we want to wait again and print a second message, we can use flatMap to run futures one after another:

```
val delayed = delay(5 seconds)
delayed.flatMap {
  println("5 seconds elapsed, now waiting 10 seconds"
  delay(10 seconds)
}.onComplete {
  println("done after 15 seconds!"
}
```

This pattern is surprisingly common and useful in practice, appearing often in such domains as API clients, databases, and workload orchestration.

Keeping futures in mind, let's return to our HTTP API. If our fundamental model is now a function that transforms a HttpRequest into Future[HttpResponse], we might have an underlying method and a few wrappers like so:

LibUVFutures/api.scala
```
private def makeRequest(Request):Future[Response]

def get(uri:String, headers:Seq[String] = Seq()): Future[Response] =
  makeRequest(Request(GET,uri,headers,None)

def post(uri:String, headers:Seq[String] = Seq(),
         body:String): Future[Response] =
  makeRequest(Request(POST,uri,headers,Some(body))

def put(uri:String, headers:Seq[String] = Seq(),
        body:String): Future[Response] =
  makeRequest(Request(PUT,uri,headers,Some(body))
```

Then, we would be able to make asynchronous HTTP calls that look like this:

LibUVFutures/api.scala
```
val getRequest = get(some_uri)
getRequest.onComplete { response =>
  println(s"got back response code ${response.code}")
  println(s"response body: ${response.body}")
}
```

This design appears to strike a good balance between practicality and performance while remaining within the idioms that are familiar to Scala developers. But to implement this API and integrate it with our web server, we'll need to go deep into the guts of Scala concurrency.

Implementing Futures

In Scala, most asynchronous functions take an implicit parameter called ExecutionContext. ExecutionContext is a trait implemented by anything that can "run" futures.

Regular JVM Scala provides a global ExecutionContext backed by a thread pool, but there are many other implementations available, both in the standard library as well as in libraries like Akka[2] and Finagle,[3] and as you'll see shortly, you can even write your own. So how does it work?

Every asynchronous action we can define on a future needs an ExecutionContext as an implicit parameter. For example, when we invoke future.map(action)(ec), we are, in effect, registering that ec should perform action when future is complete; however, almost all of this logic is in the implementation of Future itself. The signature of the ExecutionContext, in comparison, is trivial:

LibUVFutures/ec.scala
```scala
trait ExecutionContext {

  /** Runs a block of code on this execution context. */
  def execute(runnable: Runnable): Unit

  /** Reports that an asynchronous computation failed. */
  def reportFailure(t: Throwable): Unit

}
```

This minimal interface is the key to Scala's flexible, modular concurrency support, and we'll make use of it to provide futures from our event loop. Although most Scala ExecutionContexts use some kind of thread pool for background processing, this isn't required; in fact, Scala Native has a built-in single-threaded ExecutionContext implementation that we can use for a model. Its major limitation is that it only starts processing futures once the main function of a program completes. This makes it unsuitable for working with libuv, but if we take a look at the code, there's a lot we can adapt:

LibUVFutures/ec.scala
```scala
object ExecutionContext {
  def global: ExecutionContextExecutor = QueueExecutionContext

  private object QueueExecutionContext extends ExecutionContextExecutor {
    def execute(runnable: Runnable): Unit = queue += runnable
    def reportFailure(t: Throwable): Unit = t.printStackTrace()
  }
```

---

2. https://akka.io
3. https://twitter.github.io/finagle

```scala
  private val queue: ListBuffer[Runnable] = new ListBuffer

  private def loop(): Unit = {
    while (queue.nonEmpty) {
      val runnable = queue.remove(0)
      try {
        runnable.run()
      } catch {
        case t: Throwable =>
          QueueExecutionContext.reportFailure(t)
      }
    }
  }
}
```

Essentially, this code keeps a queue containing Runnables for later execution. While the loop is processing, it continuously pulls items from the head of the queue until the queue is exhausted and there's no more work to perform. This is definitely a pattern we can adapt to our codebase; instead of running at the very end of our program, we'll just need some way to pull work from our queue as soon as it's available, but without interrupting or blocking during other operations.

Implementing an ExecutionContext

Fortunately, libuv provides us with exactly what we need to implement this sort of ExecutionContext in the form of the prepare_t handle. Unlike the other handles we've seen, such as the Timer and Socket handles, the prepare handle is fired on every iteration of the event loop, immediately before I/O actions are performed, and before any long sleeping/waiting actions. It just takes a few simple functions to set up:

LibUVFutures/simple_async/loop.scala
```scala
type PrepareHandle = Ptr[Byte]
type TimerHandle = Ptr[Byte]
type PrepareCB = CFuncPtr1[PrepareHandle, Unit]
type TimerCB = CFuncPtr1[TimerHandle,Unit]

def uv_prepare_init(loop:Loop, handle:PrepareHandle):Int = extern
def uv_prepare_start(handle:PrepareHandle, cb: PrepareCB):Int = extern
def uv_prepare_stop(handle:PrepareHandle):Unit = extern
```

So if we want to use the PrepareHandle to implement an ExecutionContext, we just need to create a queue, and then write a PrepareCB function that pulls work from the queue every time it's invoked, like this:

```
LibUVFutures/simple_async/loop.scala
object EventLoop extends ExecutionContextExecutor {
  val loop = uv_default_loop()
  private val taskQueue = ListBuffer[Runnable]()
  private val handle = stdlib.malloc(uv_handle_size(UV_PREPARE_T))
  check(uv_prepare_init(loop, handle), "uv_prepare_init")

  val prepareCallback = new PrepareCB {
    def apply(handle:PrepareHandle) = {
      while (taskQueue.nonEmpty) {
        val runnable = taskQueue.remove(0)
        try {
          runnable.run()
        } catch {
          case t: Throwable => reportFailure(t)
        }
      }
      if (taskQueue.isEmpty) {
        println("stopping dispatcher")
        uv_prepare_stop(handle)
      }
    }
  }

  def execute(runnable: Runnable): Unit = {
    taskQueue += runnable
    check(uv_prepare_start(handle, prepareCallback), "uv_prepare_start")
  }

  def reportFailure(t: Throwable): Unit = {
    println(s"Future failed with Throwable $t:")
    t.printStackTrace()
  }

  def run(mode:Int = UV_RUN_DEFAULT):Unit = {
    var continue = 1
    while (continue != 0) {
      continue = uv_run(loop, mode)
      println(s"uv_run returned $continue")
    }
  }

  private val bootstrapFuture = Future(run())(ExecutionContext.global)
}
```

Overall, that's less than 50 lines of code for a custom asynchronous scheduler! However, a few subtleties are worth calling attention to, because it's very important to ensure that this code does the following:

1. Runs every future that it can.
2. Completes and allows the program to exit when there's no more work.

We're assisted in this by libuv itself; the default behavior of uv_run is to complete when there are no more active handles and requests, which is exactly what we want. All we have to do is ensure that we manually stop and start the prepare handle as needed. The trick we can use here is calling uv_prepare_start() from the execute() method, which ensures that the loop is always running if there's work that it can do, even if it means we "start" the loop many times, harmlessly.

We also want to take care to ensure that our loop runs in the first place with uv_run; in our server program we invoked it manually, but here we instead use the bootstrapFuture to tell the built-in Scala Native ExecutionContext to immediately run our event loop, as soon as the main() function completes.

This is all much easier to follow if we run a very simple asynchronous program:

```
LibUVFutures/simple_async/main.scala
def main(args:Array[String]):Unit = {
  println("hello")
  implicit val loop = EventLoop
  println("setting up futures")
  Future {
    println("Future 1!")
  }.map { _ =>
    println("Future 2!")
  }
  println("main about to return...")
}
```

It produces output like this:

```
hello
uv_prepare_init returned 0
setting up futures
uv_prepare_start returned 0
main about to return...
Future 1!
uv_prepare_start returned 0
Future 2!
uv_prepare_stop returned 0
uv_run returned 0
```

Now, we've ensured that our ExecutionContext is working correctly; however, we're still missing one piece of the puzzle. In the last example, we used Future(0) to create a future with a precomputed value and verified that we could transform it in the ways we would expect. However, how do we create a Future that we can return immediately when we have *not* computed its value, such as a request that has not yet returned? For that, we'll need to use Future's lesser-known helper, Promise.

Futures and Promises

Basically, Promise is where Future comes from; it allows an API surface to provide an "empty" future that can be completed, behind the scenes, at some point in the future. The code that calls the API doesn't know, or need to know, when or how the future will be fulfilled. Likewise, the code that supplies the value doesn't need to track who is currently holding on to the future, which makes it mostly straightforward for us to use. Promise[T]() creates a new promise, and then promise.future, which returns a Future[T] that we can pass on to our caller. When we call promise.success or promise.failure, the Future will succeed or fail as well.

For example, we can use it, along with libuv's TimerHandle type we worked with in the previous chapter, to implement the delay() function.

```
LibUVFutures/timer_async/timer.scala
object Timer  {

  var serial = 0L
  var timers = mutable.HashMap[Long,Promise[Unit]]()

  def delay(dur:Duration):Future[Unit] = {
    val promise = Promise[Unit]()
    serial += 1
    val timer_id = serial
    timers(timer_id) = promise
    val millis = dur.toMillis

    val timer_handle = stdlib.malloc(uv_handle_size(UV_TIMER_T))
    uv_timer_init(EventLoop.loop,timer_handle)
    val timer_data = timer_handle.asInstanceOf[Ptr[Long]]
    !timer_data = timer_id
    uv_timer_start(timer_handle, timerCB, millis, 0)

    promise.future
  }
  val timerCB = new TimerCB {
    def apply(handle:TimerHandle):Unit = {
      println("callback fired!")
      val timer_data = handle.asInstanceOf[Ptr[Long]]
      val timer_id = !timer_data
      val timer_promise = timers(timer_id)
      timers.remove(timer_id)
      println(s"completing promise ${timer_id}")
      timer_promise.success(())
    }
  }
}
```

Here, much like in our web server, we're generating serial numbers for each active timer—because the serial numbers are plain integers, we can store them in the local storage of the TimerHandle, which we can look up in the callback. This allows us to work around a tricky limitation of C interoperability: since we cannot convert any Scala function that captures local state to a static CFuncPtr, we'll frequently use this technique to give callback functions access to higher-level Scala Promise and Map objects with an intermediate lookup.

Now, with the implementation out of the way, the actual main function to use our timers is remarkably streamlined:

LibUVFutures/timer_async/main.scala
```
def main(args:Array[String]):Unit = {
  println("hello")
  implicit val loop = EventLoop
  println("setting up timer")
  Timer.delay(2.seconds).map { _ =>
    println("timer done!")
  }
  println("about to invoke loop.run()")
  loop.run()
  println("done!")
}
```

Let's test it:

```
$ ./target/scala-2.11/async_timer-out
hello
setting up timer
about to invoke loop.run()
callback fired!
completing promise 1
adding task to queue
executing task
timer done!
task queue empty, stopping queue
done!
```

Looks good! This same implementation technique will serve us well throughout the book, even for much more powerful libraries.

Introducing libcurl

libcurl is a widely used and full-featured C library for file transfer. It's been in active development for over twenty years, and it supports not just plain HTTP, but also HTTPS, FTP, SCP, IMAP, SMTP, Gopher, LDAP, and many other protocols. Experienced UNIX console hackers probably know the main command-line utility, curl, but you may have just as likely used it via a binding to its underlying C library from one of dozens of other languages.

Much like libuv, libcurl is designed for convenient use from other programming languages, and as you'll see shortly, it even has hooks for integration with external event loops like libuv. In other words, it's perfect for our use case. Even more than libuv, libcurl relies on a small number of functions to do all its work; one consequence, however, is many of those functions have highly generic signatures and hundreds of possible options. Thankfully, libcurl is exceedingly well documented, and I'll provide definitions for the constants as we go.

The libcurl Easy API

libcurl's API has an elegant, layered design. Functions with easy in their names, like libcurl_easy_init, provide everything you need to make individual requests in a synchronous fashion, whereas the multi API calls build on top of that to coordinate multiple requests. This structure will allow us to focus on the basics before moving on to the more challenging concurrent use cases.

First, we have to initialize and configure an *easy request* handle, using the following functions and constants:

```
LibUVFutures/curl_sync/curl.scala
type Curl = Ptr[Byte]
type CurlOption = Int
type CurlInfo = CInt

@name("curl_global_init")
def global_init(flags:Long):Unit = extern

@name("curl_easy_init")
def easy_init():Curl = extern

@name("curl_easy_setopt")
def curl_easy_setopt(handle: Curl, option: CInt,
                     parameter: Ptr[Byte]): CInt = extern

@name("curl_easy_getinfo")
def easy_getinfo(handle: Curl, info: CInt,
                 parameter: Ptr[Byte]): CInt = extern

@name("curl_easy_perform")
def easy_perform(easy_handle: Curl): CInt = extern
```

libcurl itself needs to be initialized before making any requests, and its global_init() function can take several options; however, we'll only be using LIBCURL_ALL, which enables SSL and a few other useful options. Once libcurl is initialized, easy_init() creates and returns what libcurl calls an *easy handle*, which we'll model as an opaque Ptr[Byte] aliased as EasyCurl. Unlike our libuv handles, we aren't permitted to stash custom data inside of the EasyCurl handle; instead, we'll use easy_setopt to stash custom data as well as all kinds of important request metadata.

easy_setopt takes a lot of different options. Here are the ones we'll be using:

```
LibUVFutures/curl_sync/curl.scala
val URL:CurlOption = 10002
val PORT:CurlOption = 10003
val USERPASSWORD:CurlOption = 10005

val READDATA:CurlOption = 10009
val HEADERDATA:CurlOption = 10029
val WRITEDATA:CurlOption = 10001

val READCALLBACK:CurlOption = 20012
val HEADERCALLBACK:CurlOption = 20079
val WRITECALLBACK:CurlOption = 20011

val TIMEOUT:CurlOption = 13
val GET:CurlOption = 80
val POST:CurlOption = 47
val PUT:CurlOption = 54
val CONTENTLENGTHDOWNLOADT:CurlInfo = 0x300000 + 15
val HTTPHEADER:CurlOption = 10023

val PRIVATEDATA:CurlOption = 10103
val GET_PRIVATEDATA:CurlInfo = 0x100000 + 21
```

This can be a little overwhelming, but we can organize it if we work backward from the API we want to provide. First we need to set options for all the key fields on our HTTP Request object:

- The URL
- HTTP method
- Headers
- Body (if present)

URL is the most straightforward—we just convert our URL to a CString and pass it in to easy_setopt. The HTTP method is relatively easy as well—GET is the default, and anything else we can set with CUSTOMREQUEST. Likewise, we can set our request body with POSTFIELDS and a CString. We'll have to pay a little more attention to headers, though. Because libcurl has a special linked list struct for setting headers, we'll need to convert our Scala Seq using two utility functions provided by libcurl:

```
LibUVFutures/curl_sync/curl.scala
type CurlSList = CStruct2[Ptr[Byte],CString]

@name("curl_slist_append")
def slist_append(slist:Ptr[CurlSList], string:CString):Ptr[CurlSList] = extern

@name("curl_slist_free_all")
def slist_free_all(slist:Ptr[CurlSList]):Unit = extern
```

Fortunately, we don't have to concern ourselves with the layout of the list, but we will have to work out a way to keep a pointer to the linked list around for us to free after the request completes.

We're almost ready to tie together all of the request configuration, but if we want to actually use the data, we need to figure out the callbacks. Even if we're running libcurl in its easy, blocking mode, the only way we can get access to the results of our request is if we provide callbacks, as well as design and provide data structures for storage. If we were to model this as a C-level struct, we would need all of the following:

- A resizable byte array to store the response body.
- A pointer to a list of headers in the response.
- A request ID for simple tracking and bookkeeping.
- The numeric response code.

For now, however, we can instead define a simpler Scala-style case class like so:

LibUVFutures/curl_sync/curl.scala
```scala
case class ResponseState(
  var code:Int = 200,
  var headers:mutable.Map[String,String] = mutable.Map(),
  var body:String = ""
)
```

We can retrieve it by request serial number as needed. With that, we're ready to implement two callbacks—one for when we receive a line of header data and one for when we receive some chunk of body data:

LibUVFutures/curl_sync/main.scala
```scala
val statusLine =  raw".+? (\d+) (.+)\n".r
val headerLine = raw"([^:]+): (.*)\n".r
val headerCB = new CurlDataCallback {
  def apply(ptr: Ptr[Byte], size: CSize, nmemb: CSize,
            data: Ptr[Byte]): CSize = {
    val serial = !(data.asInstanceOf[Ptr[Long]])
    val len = stackalloc[Double]
    !len = 0
    val byteSize = size * nmemb
    val headerString = bufferToString(ptr,size,nmemb)
    headerString match {
        case statusLine(code, description) =>
            println(s"status code: $code $description")
        case headerLine(k, v) =>
            val resp = responses(serial)
            resp.headers(k) = v
            responses(serial) = resp
        case l =>
    }
```

```
      fwrite(ptr, size, nmemb, stdout)
      return byteSize
   }
}
```

LibUVFutures/curl_sync/main.scala
```
val writeCB = new CurlDataCallback {
  def apply(ptr: Ptr[Byte], size: CSize, nmemb: CSize,
            data: Ptr[Byte]): CSize = {
    val serial = !(data.asInstanceOf[Ptr[Long]])
    val len = stackalloc[Double]
    !len = 0
    val strData = bufferToString(ptr,size,nmemb)

    val resp = responses(serial)
    resp.body = resp.body + strData
    responses(serial) = resp

    return size * nmemb
  }
}
```

A Synchronous curl API

We're now ready to start putting the pieces together. We can write a getSync function that will initialize a request and set up all of its options, headers, and callbacks. We'll want to take extra care to create a unique serial number for our request and register it with libcurl so that our callbacks receive it:

LibUVFutures/curl_sync/main.scala
```
var request_serial = 0L
val responses = HashMap[Long,ResponseState]()

def getSync(url:String, headers:Seq[String] = Seq.empty):ResponseState = {
    val req_id_ptr = malloc(sizeof[Long]).asInstanceOf[Ptr[Long]]
    !req_id_ptr = 1 + request_serial
    request_serial += 1
    responses(request_serial) = ResponseState()
    val curl = easy_init()

    Zone { implicit z =>
        val url_str = toCString(url)
        println(curl_easy_setopt(curl, URL, url_str))
    }
    curl_easy_setopt(curl, WRITECALLBACK, Curl.func_to_ptr(writeCB))
    curl_easy_setopt(curl, WRITEDATA, req_id_ptr.asInstanceOf[Ptr[Byte]])
    curl_easy_setopt(curl, HEADERCALLBACK, Curl.func_to_ptr(headerCB))
    curl_easy_setopt(curl, HEADERDATA, req_id_ptr.asInstanceOf[Ptr[Byte]])
    val res = easy_perform(curl)
    easy_cleanup(curl)
    return responses(request_serial)
}
```

This functionality is, by itself, enough to write many useful programs. For example, we can write a utility that takes a URL from the command line and fetches it, like so:

```
LibUVFutures/curl_sync/main.scala
def main(args:Array[String]):Unit = {
    println("initializing")
    global_init(1)
    val resp = getSync(args(0))
    println(s"done.  got response: $resp")
    println("global cleanup...")
    global_cleanup()
    println("done")
}
```

And we can run it, like so:

```
$ ./target/scala-2.11/curl_sync-out
initializing
0
status code: 200 OK
HTTP/1.1 200 OK
Accept-Ranges: bytes
...
<html>
<head>
    <title>Example Domain</title>

    <meta charset="utf-8" />
    <meta http-equiv="Content-type" content="text/html; charset=utf-8" />
    <meta name="viewport" content="width=device-width, initial-scale=1" />
    <style type="text/css">
    body {
        background-color: #f0f0f2;
...
</body>
</html>
```

That sure looks like a web page! Now that we've looked at the fundamentals of libcurl, we're ready to adapt it to our libuv-backed ExecutionContext and see how much faster it can go.

Asynchronous curl

Despite its power, the libcurl code we've written so far still has some limitations. Most important, whenever we run doRequestSync, our program blocks until the HTTP request is completed, which prevents other work from happening in the meantime. This is just fine for a simple command-line program, but it prevents us from integrating it with our asynchronous server, which needs to ensure that the event loop never blocks. Likewise, if we want to provide an asynchronous API with futures, we'll also need some way to ensure that our program can continue while requests are in flight.

For the remainder of this chapter, we'll build a solution to both of these problems by fully integrating libcurl with the libuv event loop. Rather than driving libcurl with a blocking easy_perform call, we'll instead use additional callbacks to allow libuv to determine when to transfer data and complete requests, much like it did with our delay function.

This deep integration of the two libraries isn't trivial, but it's a well-documented and well-supported path. libcurl, in particular, provides a variety of API supports for integrating with external event loops.

Integrating with libuv

libcurl's extensive documentation contrasts the easy API we've looked at so far with the multi API. At its core, the multi API revolves around another opaque pointer—called a multi handle in C—as well as the curl_multi_add function that *associates* an easy handle with a multi handle. We'll model them in Scala like so, and call the multi handle MultiCurl for clarity:

```
LibUVFutures/curl_async/curl.scala
type MultiCurl = Ptr[Byte]

@name("curl_multi_init")
def multi_init():MultiCurl = extern

@name("curl_multi_add_handle")
def multi_add_handle(multi:MultiCurl, easy:Curl):Int = extern

@name("curl_multi_setopt")
def curl_multi_setopt(multi:MultiCurl, option:CInt,
                    parameter:CVarArg): CInt = extern

@name("curl_multi_setopt")
def multi_setopt_ptr(multi:MultiCurl, option:CInt,
                    parameter:Ptr[Byte]): CInt = extern

@name("curl_multi_assign")
def multi_assign(
  multi:MultiCurl,
  socket:Ptr[Byte],
  socket_data:Ptr[Byte]):Int = extern

@name("curl_multi_socket_action")
def multi_socket_action(
  multi:MultiCurl,
  socket:Ptr[Byte],
  events:Int,
  numhandles:Ptr[Int]):Int = extern
```

```
@name("curl_multi_info_read")
def multi_info_read(multi:MultiCurl,
                    message:Ptr[Int]): Ptr[CurlMessage] = extern

@name("curl_multi_perform")
def multi_perform(multi:MultiCurl, numhandles:Ptr[Int]):Int = extern

@name("curl_multi_cleanup")
def multi_cleanup(multi:MultiCurl):Int = extern
```

Once we have a multi handle, there are many different ways libcurl allows us to use it to perform multiple requests at once. We can use techniques for blocking on all of the requests at once or for poll/select-style handling, either of which would be appropriate for smaller numbers of requests or if we weren't interested in interleaving requests with other processes in a server program. But for truly fine-grained control, the multi API provides an additional set of callbacks on the multi handle itself, which can be used to control and coordinate interactions with an external event loop, such as libuv. Correct implementation of this API can be tricky, but with a little bit of planning and preparation, you'll see that it doesn't require that much more code than what we've already written.

On the libcurl side, we'll only need a few new type signatures and functions:

LibUVFutures/curl_async/curl.scala
```
val SOCKETFUNCTION = 20001
type SocketCallback = CFuncPtr5[Curl, Ptr[Byte], CInt, Ptr[Byte], Ptr[Byte],
                                CInt]
val TIMERFUNCTION = 20004
type TimerCallback = CFuncPtr3[MultiCurl, Long, Ptr[Byte], CInt]

type CurlAction = CInt
val POLL_NONE:CurlAction = 0
val POLL_IN:CurlAction = 1
val POLL_OUT:CurlAction = 2
val POLL_INOUT:CurlAction = 3
val POLL_REMOVE:CurlAction = 4
```

Likewise, on the libuv side, we'll need to use a new handle type, the poll handle, which can provide notifications of the *readiness* of an externally managed socket:

LibUVFutures/curl_async/loop.scala
```
def uv_poll_init_socket(loop:Loop, handle:PollHandle, socket:Ptr[Byte]):
  Int = extern
def uv_poll_start(handle:PollHandle, events:Int, cb: PollCB):Int = extern
def uv_poll_stop(handle:PollHandle):Int = extern
```

Rather than try to explain each of these components on their own, we can get a better sense of the big picture by first considering how libcurl and libuv will interact:

1. curl creates one or more sockets.

2. curl notifies libuv that it has created new sockets.

3. libuv starts watching the sockets.

4. libuv sees that a socket is readable or writable and notifies curl.

5. curl performs the appropriate transfer on the ready socket(s).

6. curl checks to see if the request is complete.

7. If the request is complete, curl completes the request and closes the socket.

8. When there are no more requests in flight, the loop terminates.

An interesting property of this algorithm is that the only time libcurl initiates an action is on request creation. All data transfer is initiated by libuv, which is watching the sockets libcurl creates. libcurl supports this workflow with the multi_socket_action function, which allows libuv code to briefly hand over the reins for curl's own callbacks:

```
@name("curl_multi_socket_action")
  def multi_socket_action(
    multi:MultiCurl,
    socket:Ptr[Byte],
    events:Int,
    numhandles:Ptr[Int]):Int = extern
```

multi_socket_action behaves differently based on the arguments it receives. If it's called with a running socket in its socket argument, it will work only on that socket, whereas if it's called with the constant SOCKET_TIMEOUT, it will check *every* socket for changes in state, including administrative functions such as timeouts. multi_socket_action also works closely with the two new callbacks that we'll define on our MultiCurl handle: the SOCKETFUNCTION and TIMERFUNCTION callback. Together, these two callback functions give libcurl "feedback" into libuv's control structures by creating and modifying new handles on the event loop. In particular, our TIMERFUNCTION, which we'll call set_timer, allows libcurl to create and adjust the delay on a libuv Timer handle, which will invoke multi_socket_action when it fires. Likewise, our SOCKETFUNCTION callback instructs libuv when to create a Poll handle for a new socket, and how to adjust.

All together, the whole network of callbacks looks like this:

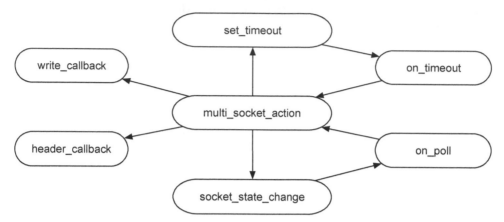

While I was researching this pattern, however, I was still puzzled by one thing: there isn't an obvious way to start the whole system! After a fair amount of experimentation, I discovered the answer: once the TIMERFUNCTION is set, it will be invoked not only during multi_socket_action but also during multi_add_handle! This makes bootstrapping much easier, but it does have some impact on the order in which we initialize things, so we'll need to be careful.

With this overall design in place, we can start implementing the individual callbacks one at a time.

Implementing the Callbacks

Let's start by implementing start_timer, which will be passed to libcurl as a TIMERFUNCTION, and control a libuv TimerHandle:

```
LibUVFutures/curl_async/curl.scala
val startTimerCB = new CurlTimerCallback {
  def apply(curl:MultiCurl, timeout_ms:Long, data:Ptr[Byte]):Int = {
    println(s"start_timer called with timeout ${timeout_ms} ms")
    val time = if (timeout_ms < 1) {
      println("setting effective timeout to 1")
      1
    } else timeout_ms
    println("starting timer")
    check(uv_timer_start(timerHandle, timeoutCB, time, 0), "uv_timer_start")
    cleanup_requests()
    0
  }
}
```

Essentially, libcurl uses set_timeout() in two different ways: either to tell libuv to call multi_socket_action *right away*, in which case we'll pass on a timeout of 1ms, or at some point in the future. When the timeout expires, libuv will invoke another callback, which is relatively simple because all it has to do is invoke multi_socket_action as instructed:

```
LibUVFutures/curl_async/curl.scala
val timeoutCB = new TimerCB {
  def apply(handle:TimerHandle):Unit = {
    println("in timeout callback")
    val running_handles = stackalloc[Int]
    multi_socket_action(multi,int_to_ptr(-1),0,running_handles)
    println(s"on_timer fired, ${!running_handles} sockets running")
  }
}
```

In contrast, the SOCKETFUNCTION callback will be more complex because it has to handle a variety of different cases:

- A totally new socket has been created, and needs to be registered with libuv.

- A socket has entered writable state, and we can start sending data to the remote server.

- The request has been sent, and the socket has switched to readable state, awaiting a response.

- The request has been completed, and the poll handle can be deactivated.

The good news is that setting up the local state of the socket is mostly simple; we can use the same RequestData struct that we used for our blocking implementation. There's one catch, though. We'll need to use a helper function called multi_socket_assign to associate that struct with a particular socket within the larger MultiCurl.

```
@name("curl_multi_assign")
def multi_assign(
  multi:MultiCurl,
  socket:Ptr[Byte],
  socket_data:Ptr[Byte]):Int = extern
```

Finally, we'll also need to translate between libcurl's flags for readability and writability to another set of flags that libuv can understand. Each library uses very similar encodings, but the binary logic is tricky to get right. All together, the handling code in the SOCKETFUNCTION callback looks like this:

LibUVFutures/curl_async/curl.scala

```scala
val socketCB = new CurlSocketCallback {
  def apply(curl:Curl, socket:Ptr[Byte], action:Int, data:Ptr[Byte],
            socket_data:Ptr[Byte]):Int = {
    println(s"socketCB called with action ${action}")
    val pollHandle = if (socket_data == null) {
      println(s"initializing handle for socket ${socket}")
      val buf = malloc(uv_handle_size(UV_POLL_T)).asInstanceOf[Ptr[Ptr[Byte]]]
      !buf = socket
      check(uv_poll_init_socket(loop, buf, socket), "uv_poll_init_socket")
      check(multi_assign(multi, socket, buf.asInstanceOf[Ptr[Byte]]),
            "multi_assign")
      buf
    } else {
      socket_data.asInstanceOf[Ptr[Ptr[Byte]]]
    }

    val events = action match {
      case POLL_NONE => None
      case POLL_IN => Some(UV_READABLE)
      case POLL_OUT => Some(UV_WRITABLE)
      case POLL_INOUT => Some(UV_READABLE | UV_WRITABLE)
      case POLL_REMOVE => None
    }

    events match {
      case Some(ev) =>
        println(s"starting poll with events $ev")
        uv_poll_start(pollHandle, ev, pollCB)
      case None =>
        println("stopping poll")
        uv_poll_stop(pollHandle)
        startTimerCB(multi, 1, null)
    }
    0
  }
}
```

But the actual libuv PollHandle callback is, once again, refreshingly concise:

LibUVFutures/curl_async/curl.scala

```scala
val pollCB = new PollCB {
  def apply(pollHandle:PollHandle, status:Int, events:Int):Unit = {
    println(s"""ready_for_curl fired with status ${status} and
            events ${events}""")
    val socket = !(pollHandle.asInstanceOf[Ptr[Ptr[Byte]]])
    val actions = (events & 1) | (events & 2)
    val running_handles = stackalloc[Int]
    val result = multi_socket_action(multi, socket, actions, running_handles)
    println("multi_socket_action",result)
  }
}
```

And now that on_poll is also calling back into multi_socket_action, we've completed the loop, and all of the control mechanisms are in place. Best of all, we don't even need to write new implementations for on_header and on_body—we can use our previous ones unchanged, so this code is almost ready to run! We just need to implement a beginRequestAsync and completeRequestAsync method corresponding to those we wrote before.

Again, like with our delay() function, we'll create a promise when our request starts and use a global Map[Int,Promise{Response}] to convert request ids back to promises. Creating the promises is relatively clean:

```scala
LibUVFutures/curl_async/curl.scala
def startRequest(method:Int, url:String,headers:Seq[String] =
 Seq.empty,body:String = ""):Future[ResponseState] = Zone { implicit z =>
  init()
  val curlHandle = easy_init()
  serial += 1
  val reqId = serial
  println(s"initializing handle $curlHandle for request $reqId")
  val req_id_ptr = malloc(sizeof[Long]).asInstanceOf[Ptr[Long]]
  !req_id_ptr = reqId
  requests(reqId) = ResponseState()
  val promise = Promise[ResponseState]()
  requestPromises(reqId) = promise

  method match {
    case GET =>
      check(curl_easy_setopt(curlHandle, URL, toCString(url)),
        "easy_setopt")
      check(curl_easy_setopt(curlHandle, WRITECALLBACK, func_to_ptr(dataCB)),
        "easy_setopt")
      check(curl_easy_setopt(curlHandle, WRITEDATA,
        req_id_ptr.asInstanceOf[Ptr[Byte]]), "easy_setopt")
      check(curl_easy_setopt(curlHandle, HEADERCALLBACK,
        func_to_ptr(headerCB)), "easy_setopt")
      check(curl_easy_setopt(curlHandle, HEADERDATA,
        req_id_ptr.asInstanceOf[Ptr[Byte]]), "easy_setopt")
      check(curl_easy_setopt(curlHandle, PRIVATEDATA,
        req_id_ptr.asInstanceOf[Ptr[Byte]]), "easy_setopt")
  }
  multi_add_handle(multi, curlHandle)

  println("request initialized")
  promise.future
}
```

Completing them is a little trickier. We don't get a callback that fires every time a request is done; instead, libcurl puts messages in a queue that we can handle with multi_info_read. We'll also need to use easy_getinfo with GET_PRIVATEDATA to get a pointer back to the response data we've been tracking all this time, which will allow us to construct a Response object and complete the Future successfully:

LibUVFutures/curl_async/curl.scala

```scala
def cleanup_requests():Unit = {
  val messages = stackalloc[Int]
  val privateDataPtr= stackalloc[Ptr[Long]]
  var message:Ptr[CurlMessage] = multi_info_read(multi,messages)
  while (message != null) {
    println(s"""Got a message ${message._1} from multi_info_read,
            ${!messages} left in queue""")
    val handle:Curl = message._2
    check(easy_getinfo(handle, GET_PRIVATEDATA,
        privateDataPtr.asInstanceOf[Ptr[Byte]]),"getinfo")
    val privateData = !privateDataPtr
    val reqId = !privateData
    val reqData = requests.remove(reqId).get
    val promise = Curl.requestPromises.remove(reqId).get
    promise.success(reqData)
    message = multi_info_read(multi,messages)
  }
  println("done handling messages")
}
```

With these methods in place, we can then adapt our command-line utility from before to make asynchronous requests, on a single libuv event loop:

LibUVFutures/curl_async/main.scala

```scala
def main(args:Array[String]):Unit = {
  if (args.length == 0) {
      println("usage: ./curl-out https://www.example.com")
      ???
  }

  println("initializing loop")
  implicit val loop = EventLoop
  val resp = Zone { implicit z =>
    for (arg <- args) {
      val url = arg
      val resp = Curl.startRequest(GET,url)

      resp.onComplete {
        case Success(data) =>
          println(s"got response for ${arg} - length ${data.body.size}")
          println(s"headers:")
```

```scala
        for (h <- data.headers) {
          println(s"request header: $h")
        }
        println(s"body: ${data.body}")
      case Failure(f) =>
        println("request failed",f)
    }
  }
}

loop.run()
println("done")
}
```

When run, it should behave like this:

```
$ ./target/scala-2.11/curl_async-out https://www.example.com
initializing loop
uv_prepare_init returned 0
...
got back response for https://www.example.com - body of length 1270
headers:
request header: (X-Cache,HIT)
request header: (Vary,Accept-Encoding)
...
body: <!doctype html>
<html>
<head>
    <title>Example Domain</title>
...
stopping dispatcher
on_timer fired, 0 sockets running
uv_run returned 0
loop done, cleaning up
cleaning up internals
done handling messages
done
```

This does, essentially, the same work as the blocking version, except it can perform all the requests *at the same time*. If we time it, we'll see that it can perform many requests at once without impacting its performance and vastly improve on the speed of the blocking version.

What's Next

In this chapter, you've taken a deep dive into the guts of Scala concurrency and learned how to use futures to orchestrate many concurrent computations.

You've also learned how to use libcurl, a powerful HTTP library, and integrate it with our fully asynchronous event loop.

In the next chapter, we'll close the loop and combine the client and server capabilities we've built around this asynchronous platform. But that's not all. You'll also learn how to build the quintessential asynchronous server-side function: database interaction. Together, these capabilities will allow you to build robust, practical services in Scala Native that will be compelling alternatives to the sort of programs typically created in vanilla Scala, Java, or Go.

CHAPTER 8

Streaming with Pipes and Files

In the last chapter, you learned about the guts of asynchronous programming, as we went deep into Scala's ExecutionContext and Future patterns. In this chapter, we'll investigate *streams*, another aspect of asynchronous programs, as we adapt libuv's facilities for terminal and file I/O to our rapidly growing framework.

Looking at Streams, Files, and Descriptors

So far, we've encountered a few different flavors of file-like objects. We've used the standard input, standard output, and anonymous pipes, as well as sockets. From an API perspective, we've worked with both the low-level int file descriptors used by the ANSI C core, as well as the higher-level Ptr[File] accepted by fgets, fprintf, and other standard POSIX I/O functions. All of these abstractions provide a notion of a *stream*: the plain int fd is an ordered series of bytes, retrieved with read(), whereas the Ptr[File] objects behave more like an ordered series of lines, retrieved by fgets().

Both of these abstraction layers try to abstract over the differences between sockets, pipes, and regular on-disk files, but not without a few pain points—after all, the underlying entities have fundamental differences. For example, pipes are unidirectional, meaning you can read from stdin, but not write, whereas you can write to stdin, but not read. Sockets, on the other hand, are bidirectional: once I have a TCP connection, I can read a request from it, and then write a response back on the same connection. Disk files behave differently still. Not only do they support simultaneous reads and writes, but files also have *seekable position*—I can rewind a file back to the beginning or jump ahead to any arbitrary byte.

All of which is to say that providing a safe, ergonomic interface over this functionality is difficult. The POSIX functions we used in the first half of the book are often awkward and prone to throw obscure errors. For example, what is the computer supposed to do if I ask it to seek() a socket back to its beginning? As Scala developers, we would hope, instead, to provide type-safe APIs that behave consistently, and catch misuse at compile time.

Fortunately, we don't have to be quite as general as POSIX. The model we developed in the last chapter using a Future[T] to model an asynchronous request-response cycle, takes care of the typical use of a bidirectional socket nicely. And likewise, fully read-write, freely seeking file I/O is unusual, and probably left to low-level POSIX wrangling. What we are left with, then, is bulk, unidirectional, typed I/O over pipes and files.

In Scala, the most popular idioms for this sort of problem has a distinctly functional flavor. Scala has a plethora of fine functional streaming libraries, including monix,[1] cats-effect,[2] fs2,[3] zio,[4] and others. This book isn't about functional programming, but even libuv biases us toward stateless, function-oriented processing. However, our focus will be on providing a natural, idiomatic wrapper for libuv's capabilities that we can compose into powerful programs that solve real-world problems.

Streaming Pipe Input in libuv

We'll start with our reliable favorite, the standard input pipe. libuv makes it much simpler to work with pipes than to work with files. True disk files don't natively support the same poll-based I/O techniques that pipes and sockets do, but we'll work around that a little later.

The PipeHandle provided by libuv, and its associated methods, aren't especially novel at this point:

```
LibUVPipes/simple_pipe/loop.scala
type PipeHandle = Ptr[Byte]
```

Despite adding a few new methods, we'll largely interact with pipe input like we did with sockets, via the read_start() function and its callbacks.

Before we start writing code, however, we should work out a clean, adaptable design for our data structure. Since Scala already has a standard library class called Stream, we'll just call ours Pipe. If we were only concerned with standard input, we could use a very simple design indeed:

---

1. https://monix.io
2. https://typelevel.org/cats-effect
3. https://fs2.io/guide.html
4. https://github.com/zio/zio

```scala
trait StandardInput[T] {
  def onInput[T](f:CString => T):Unit
}
```

But this wouldn't easily generalize to chains of processors, where values are transformed to different types. Further, in many cases it's useful for a pipe to "fan out" to multiple destinations, as well. A more general representation, then, would be a Pipe[I,O], which consumes values of type I and produces values of type O. Some more advanced streaming libraries, like Akka Streams, further distinguish Sources, which only produce values, and Sinks, which can only consume data.

This design has many benefits, but the complex trait mixtures and type parameters that result can be unwieldy to work with, and their implementation is outside the scope of this book. Instead, we can model a source like standard input as a Pipe[String]—this doesn't prevent all possible misuse, but should be sufficient for our purposes.

Our Pipe trait has three responsibilities:

1. It receives values of type I from somewhere, and transforms them to type O, by a user-supplied function.

2. It sends values of type O onward to any number of destinations or sub-scribers.

3. It correctly cleans up streams when done, including closing open files.

We can model these responsibilities in the following trait signature:

LibUVPipes/simple_pipe/main.scala
```scala
trait Pipe[T,U] {
  val handlers = mutable.Set[Pipe[U,_]]()

  def feed(input:T):Unit
  def done():Unit = {
    for (h <- handlers) {
      h.done()
    }
  }
  def addDestination[V](dest:Pipe[U,V]):Pipe[U,V] = {
    handlers += dest
    dest
  }
  // ...
```

With the overall design in mind, this won't be too hard to implement on top of libuv. In many ways, it's closer to the underlying patterns of libuv's API than our Future-based client in Chapter 7, Functions and Futures: Patterns for Distributed Services, on page 131.

LibUVPipes/simple_pipe/main.scala
```scala
case class SyncPipe[T,U](f:T => U) extends Pipe[T,U] {
  def feed(input:T):Unit = {
    val output = f(input)
    for (h <- handlers) {
      h.feed(output)
    }
  }
}
```

As before, we'll have a global object that holds a bit of state and allows our callbacks to distinguish a few different pipes. We'll set that state up when we initialize a new pipe, like so:

LibUVPipes/simple_pipe/main.scala
```scala
object SyncPipe {
  import LibUV._, LibUVConstants._

  var active_streams:mutable.Set[Int] = mutable.Set()
  var handlers = mutable.HashMap[Int,SyncPipe[String,String]]()
  var serial = 0

  def apply(fd:Int):SyncPipe[String,String] = {
    val handle = stdlib.malloc(uv_handle_size(UV_PIPE_T))
    uv_pipe_init(EventLoop.loop,handle,0)
    val pipe_data = handle.asInstanceOf[Ptr[Int]]
    !pipe_data = serial
    active_streams += serial
    val pipe = SyncPipe[String,String]{ s => s }
    handlers(serial) = pipe

    serial += 1
    uv_pipe_open(handle,fd)
    uv_read_start(handle,SyncPipe.allocCB,SyncPipe.readCB)
    pipe
  }
```

We simply take the fd integer file descriptor here to work easily with standard input (which always has the fd 0), but we could extend this to handle named pipes as well. Likewise, we will then need a handler for on_read:

LibUVPipes/simple_pipe/main.scala
```scala
val allocCB = new AllocCB {
  def apply(client:PipeHandle, size:CSize, buffer:Ptr[Buffer]):Unit = {
    val buf = stdlib.malloc(4096)
    buffer._1 = buf
    buffer._2 = 4096
  }
}
```

```scala
val readCB = new ReadCB {
  def apply(handle:PipeHandle,size:CSize,buffer:Ptr[Buffer]):Unit = {
    val pipe_data = handle.asInstanceOf[Ptr[Int]]
    val pipe_id = !pipe_data
    println(s"read $size bytes from pipe $pipe_id")
    if (size < 0) {
      println("size < 0, closing")
      active_streams -= pipe_id
      handlers.remove(pipe_id)
    } else {
      val data_buffer = stdlib.malloc(size + 1)
      string.strncpy(data_buffer, buffer._1, size + 1)
      val data_string = fromCString(data_buffer)
      stdlib.free(data_buffer)
      val pipe_destination = handlers(pipe_id)
      pipe_destination.feed(data_string.trim())
    }
  }
}
```

Since this code already detects when a file has finished, we don't need to manually close the file; however, we do need to signal to all downstream consumers that it's time for them to complete.

And just those few lines of code already make up a complete implementation of the Pipe trait! To write a meaningful program, though, we'll need to be able to transform these values. The most straightforward way to do this is with a map function that applies a function to each item passing through it. We can implement that as a full implementation of the Pipe trait, like so:

LibUVPipes/simple_pipe/main.scala
```scala
def map[V](g:U => V):Pipe[U,V] = {
  val destination = SyncPipe(g)
  handlers += destination
  destination
}
```

And with two pipe implementations in hand, we can compose them into a useful program like this:

LibUVPipes/simple_pipe/main.scala
```scala
object Main {
  import LibUV._, LibUVConstants._
  def main(args:Array[String]):Unit = {
    println("hello!")
    val p = SyncPipe(0)
```

```scala
    val q = p.map { d =>
      println(s"consumed $d")
      d
    }.map { d =>
      val parsed = Try {
        d.toInt
      }
      println(s"parsed: $parsed")
      parsed
    }.map {
      case Success(i) => println(s"saw number $i")
      case Failure(f) => println(s"error: $f")
    }
    uv_run(EventLoop.loop,UV_RUN_DEFAULT)
    println("done")
  }
}
```

And we can test it, too:

```
$ ./target/scala-2.11/simple_pipe-out
hello!
uv_prepare_init returned 0
uv_prepare_start returned 0
foo
read 4 bytes from pipe 0
consumed foo
parsed: Failure(java.lang.NumberFormatException: foo)
error: java.lang.NumberFormatException: foo
1
read 2 bytes from pipe 0
consumed 1
parsed: Success(1)
saw number 1
2
read 2 bytes from pipe 0
consumed 2
parsed: Success(2)
saw number 2
read -4095 bytes from pipe 0
size < 0, closing
stopping dispatcher
done
```

Looks good! Everything we do in the rest of this chapter will elaborate upon this single, elegant Pipe trait.

Streaming File Input in libuv

In the POSIX model, we could treat pipes and files more or less interchangeably and use the same blocking I/O patterns, such as fgets and println, with either one. But in libuv, files are a totally different beast from anything else we've encountered. Because ordinary disk files are *not pollable* for readiness in Linux, there's no way to read or write from a file without the risk of blocking.

libuv provides an alternative: a background *thread pool* for running UNIX-style system calls, where blocking calls can run without interfering with our event loop. These system calls are *not* modeled as streams, though. Each call is one-off, which means we'll need to do a little extra work to create something that fits our Pipe interface.

The tricky part is that there are quite a few of these calls, but they all take the same callback type, uv_fs_cb, which only returns the uv_fs_t request handle that originated it. However, we'll only need a few actual syscalls to implement streaming file I/O. All we need to do is open files, read from them, write from them, and close them:

```
LibUVPipes/file_pipe/loop.scala
type FSReq = Ptr[Ptr[Byte]]
type FSCB = CFuncPtr1[FSReq,Unit]

def uv_fs_open(loop:Loop, req:FSReq, path:CString, flags:Int, mode:Int,
  cb:FSCB):Int = extern
def uv_fs_read(loop:Loop, req:FSReq, fd:Int, bufs:Ptr[Buffer], numBufs:Int,
  offset:Long, fsCB:FSCB):Int = extern
def uv_fs_write(loop:Loop, req:FSReq, fd:Int, bufs:Ptr[Buffer], numBufs:Int,
  offset:Long, fsCB:FSCB):Int = extern
def uv_fs_close(loop:Loop, req:FSReq, fd:Int, fsCB:FSCB):Int = extern
def uv_req_cleanup(req:FSReq):Unit = extern
def uv_fs_get_result(req:FSReq):Int = extern
def uv_fs_get_ptr(req:FSReq):Ptr[Byte] = extern
```

As before, we'll need a small case class to instantiate our actual Pipe object:

```
LibUVPipes/file_pipe_out/main.scala
case class FilePipe(serial:Long) extends Pipe[String,String] {
  override def feed(input:String):Unit = {
    for (h <- handlers) {
      h.feed(input)
    }
  }
}
```

But most of the implementation will be in the companion object. We'll keep our global state there as before:

LibUVPipes/file_pipe_out/main.scala
```
object FilePipe {
  import LibUV._, LibUVConstants._
  type FilePipeState = CStruct3[Int,Ptr[Buffer],Long] // fd, buffer, offset

  var active_streams:mutable.Set[Int] = mutable.Set()
  var handlers = mutable.HashMap[Int,Pipe[String,String]]()
  var serial = 0
```

And we'll use the following block of code to open new files for reading, instantiate a FilePipe object, and make an initial call to uv_fs_read:

LibUVPipes/file_pipe_out/main.scala
```
def apply(path:CString):Pipe[String,String] = {
  val req = stdlib.malloc(uv_req_size(UV_FS_REQ_T)).asInstanceOf[FSReq]
  println("opening file")
  val fd = util.open(path,0,0)
  stdio.printf(c"open file at %s returned %d\n", path, fd)

  val state = stdlib.malloc(sizeof[FilePipeState])
    .asInstanceOf[Ptr[FilePipeState]]
  val buf = stdlib.malloc(sizeof[Buffer]).asInstanceOf[Ptr[Buffer]]
  buf._1 = stdlib.malloc(4096)
  buf._2 = 4095
  state._1 = fd
  state._2 = buf
  state._3 = 0L
  !req = state.asInstanceOf[Ptr[Byte]]

  println("about to read")
  uv_fs_read(EventLoop.loop,req,fd,buf,1,-1,readCB)
  println("read started")
  val pipe = Pipe.source[String]
  handlers(fd) = pipe
  println("about to return")
  active_streams += fd
  pipe
}
```

So far, this has been pretty similar to other code we've written. The difference, however, is that uv_fs_read will only execute and return one time. As a result, if we want to read a file until we're done, we need to add logic to the corresponding handler function so that we continue issuing read requests whenever we need more data:

LibUVPipes/file_pipe_out/main.scala
```scala
val readCB:FSCB = new FSCB {
  def apply(req:FSReq):Unit = {
    println("read callback fired!")
    val res = uv_fs_get_result(req)
    println(s"got result: $res")
    val state_ptr = (!req).asInstanceOf[Ptr[FilePipeState]]
    println("inspecting state")
    val fd = state_ptr._1
    val buf = state_ptr._2
    val offset = state_ptr._3
    printf("state: fd %d, offset %d\n", fd, offset.toInt)

    if (res > 0) {
      println("producing string")
      (buf._1)(res) = 0
      val output = fromCString(buf._1)
      val pipe = handlers(fd)
      pipe.feed(output)
      println("continuing")
      state_ptr._3 = state_ptr._3 + res
      uv_fs_read(EventLoop.loop,req,fd,state_ptr._2,1,state_ptr._3,readCB)
    } else if (res == 0) {
      println("done")
      val pipe = handlers(fd)
      pipe.done()
      active_streams -= fd
    } else {
      println("error")
      active_streams -= fd
    }
  }
}
```

And with the Pipe trait fully implemented, we can now swap a file in for standard input easily:

LibUVPipes/examples.scala
```scala
object FileInputPipeExample {
  import LibUV._, LibUVConstants._
  def main(args:Array[String]):Unit = {
    val p = FilePipe(c"./data.txt")
    .map { d =>
      println(s"consumed $d")
      d
    }.map { d =>
      val parsed = Try {
        d.toInt
      }
```

```
      println(s"parsed: $parsed")
      parsed
    }
    .addDestination(FileOutputPipe(c"./output.txt", false))
    uv_run(EventLoop.loop,UV_RUN_DEFAULT)
    println("done")
  }
}
```

When you run this, you should see output like this:

```
$ ./target/scala-2.11/file_input-out
uv_prepare_init returned 0
uv_prepare_start returned 0
read 4 bytes from pipe 0
consumed foo
parsed: Failure(java.lang.NumberFormatException: foo)
error: java.lang.NumberFormatException: foo
read 2 bytes from pipe 0
consumed 1
parsed: Success(1)
saw number 1
read 2 bytes from pipe 0
consumed 2
parsed: Success(2)
saw number 2
read -4095 bytes from pipe 0
size < 0, closing
stopping dispatcher
done
```

But what's next? We could write many interesting transformation stages, but the most pressing need now is a similar way to handle output so that we don't have to rely on the blocking println any longer.

Streaming File Output in libuv

As you saw in the last two chapters, output in libuv works differently than input. Where input events originate from outside our program, and can happen at any time and in any number, output always initiates from our own code. Although this slightly complicates our implementation, the good news is that we won't need to introduce any new library or system calls. But we will want to think hard about the consequences of our design for performance.

Streaming Output and Performance

Consider the cases where input and output run at different rates. If a standard input produces data more slowly than standard output has the capacity to receive it, there's no problem; output is perfectly happy to run below peak capacity. But if standard input runs faster than standard output, we have a problem. Because we allocate memory for each item we write, if those writeRequest and buffer objects are allowed to pile up, they'll eventually exhaust our memory and take down the program.

The preferred solution to this problem is *backpressure*—some way for a downstream processor, like standard output, to tell standard input to *slow down* until it can work through its backlog. (In some circles, the term *backpressure* can be used to refer to the backlog itself, rather than the mechanism for dealing with it. For clarity, I'm following the terminology of the Java/Scala Reactive Streams community[5] and will use *backpressure* to refer to control mechanism that *pushes back* against excess throughput.)

One way to implement backpressure is to add a method, such as demand(n:Int), to our Pipe trait that a destination pipe would call on the pipe that feeds it to signal how many items it can accept. But that would substantially complicate our code, since the current design doesn't require a pipe to know where its input comes from. A simpler design that could work well for a single-threaded system like this is to add an Int return value to feed(), or even a Bool, to indicate our ability to consume more items. But even a minimal design for backpressure raises more questions: we then need to actually implement our "slow-down" logic and decide whether to drop elements, buffer them, or somehow control the rate of data upstream.

An alternative approach is to rely on the rate-control mechanisms provided by the operating system, which we've already used in other contexts. For example, in Chapter 6, Doing I/O Right, with Event Loops, on page 103, the system's TCP connection queue allowed us to buffer incoming connections in a backlog, which can smooth out bursts, and then dump excess connections when the queue is full. Likewise, for straightforward I/O cases, in which reading is usually faster than writing, the blocking I/O functions we've used since Chapter 1 provide a natural limit—they prevent us from handling a new line of input until the previous one is done.

Implementing Optional Backpressure

Fortunately, libuv allows us to exploit these patterns, all while maintaining a consistent, high-level API. All uv_fs_* functions have the ability to complete the underlying syscall synchronously on the main thread if we pass them null for their callback argument. In other words, we're saying "don't bother with the callback, just do this right away and return a value." And with a careful

---

5. http://www.reactive-streams.org

design, we can create a Pipe implementation where this functionality is *optional*, allowing us to choose blocking or nonblocking characteristics as needed, without modifying our code otherwise.

The implementation will follow the same pattern: a case class that overrides the key Pipe trait methods, and a companion object that contains a helper to construct new pipes, as well as all the callback requests. One thing that helps us is that—unlike the file input pipe—we don't have to chain together asynchronous calls; all of the output will be initiated by a call to feed(), so we only need to handle the sync/async switch in that one spot. With this design, the case class will look something like this:

LibUVPipes/file_pipe_out/main.scala
```scala
case class FileOutputPipe(fd:Int, serial:Int, async:Boolean)
  extends Pipe[String,Unit] {
  import LibUV._, LibUVConstants._
  import stdlib._, string._
  var offset = 0L

  val writeCB = if (async) { FileOutputPipe.writeCB } else null

  override def feed(input:String):Unit = {
    val output_size = input.size
    val req = stdlib.malloc(uv_req_size(UV_FS_REQ_T)).asInstanceOf[FSReq]

    val output_buffer = malloc(sizeof[Buffer]).asInstanceOf[Ptr[Buffer]]
    output_buffer._1 = malloc(output_size)
    Zone { implicit z =>
      val output_string = toCString(input)
      strncpy(output_buffer._1, output_string, output_size)
    }
    output_buffer._2 = output_size
    !req = output_buffer.asInstanceOf[Ptr[Byte]]

    uv_fs_write(EventLoop.loop,req,fd,output_buffer,1,offset,writeCB)
    offset += output_size
  }
  override def done():Unit = {
    val req = stdlib.malloc(uv_req_size(UV_FS_REQ_T)).asInstanceOf[FSReq]
    uv_fs_close(EventLoop.loop,req,fd,null)
    FileOutputPipe.active_streams -= serial
  }
}
```

Whereas the initialization code in the companion object is mostly standard—the only difference here is that we choose whether to set the async flag to true or false:

LibUVPipes/file_pipe_out/main.scala
```scala
object FileOutputPipe {
  import LibUV._, LibUVConstants._
  import stdlib._

  var active_streams:mutable.Set[Int] = mutable.Set()
  var serial = 0

  def apply(path:CString, async:Boolean = true):FileOutputPipe = {
    active_streams += serial

    stdio.printf(c"opening %s for writing..\n", path)
    val fd = util.open(path,O_RDWR + O_CREAT,default_permissions)
    println(s"got back fd: $fd")

    val pipe = FileOutputPipe(fd,serial,async)
    serial += 1
    println(s"initialized $pipe")
    pipe
  }
```

And then the on_write callback is routine:

LibUVPipes/file_pipe_out/main.scala
```scala
val writeCB = new FSCB {
  def apply(req:FSReq):Unit = {
    println("write completed")
    val resp_buffer = (!req).asInstanceOf[Ptr[Buffer]]
    stdlib.free(resp_buffer._1)
    stdlib.free(resp_buffer.asInstanceOf[Ptr[Byte]])
    stdlib.free(req.asInstanceOf[Ptr[Byte]])
  }
}
```

That's it! Now, we can plug in this FileOutputPipe at the end of a pipeline by passing to addDestination, like so:

LibUVPipes/examples.scala
```scala
object FileOutputPipeExample {
  import LibUV._, LibUVConstants._
  def main(args:Array[String]):Unit = {
    println("hello!")
    val p = SyncPipe(0)
    val p = FilePipe(c"./data.txt")

    val q = p.map { d =>
      println(s"consumed $d")
      d
    }.map { d =>
      val parsed = Try {
        d.toInt
      }
```

```
        println(s"parsed: $parsed")
        parsed.toString
      }
      .addDestination(FileOutputPipe(c"./output.txt", false))
      uv_run(EventLoop.loop,UV_RUN_DEFAULT)
      println("done")
    }
}
```

This should produce about the same output as our previous program, when run:

```
$ ./target/scala-2.11/file_output-out
uv_prepare_init returned 0
uv_prepare_start returned 0
read 4 bytes from pipe 0
consumed foo
parsed: Failure(java.lang.NumberFormatException: foo)
error: java.lang.NumberFormatException: foo
read 2 bytes from pipe 0
consumed 1
parsed: Success(1)
saw number 1
read 2 bytes from pipe 0
consumed 2
parsed: Success(2)
saw number 2
read -4095 bytes from pipe 0
size < 0, closing
stopping dispatcher
done
```

This looks good so far, but let's look at the contents of the file we wrote:

```
Failure(java.lang.NumberFormatException: foo)
Success(1)
Success(2)
```

Looks good! With standard input and output both taken care of, we can move on to some trickier cases.

Stream Processors

With input and output taken care of, we can fill in the gaps with more stream processors. The MapPipe we already wrote is pretty generic and modular, and in theory, the signature O => T can do a huge range of tasks, but it's less ergonomic for functions that produce lists, options, or futures, all of which are better handled by specialized implementations. We can also work with custom stateful components and look at a few ways to get values out of them.

One of the most useful would be a component to take a value of type I, apply
a function that produces an Option[O], and only pass the inner O on to destination pipes if the Option isn't None. We can implement it with just a few lines of
code, like this:

LibUVPipes/file_pipe/main.scala
```
case class OptionPipe[T,U](f:T => Option[U]) extends Pipe[T,U] {
  override def feed(input:T):Unit = {
    val output = f(input)
    for (h <- handlers;
         o <- output) {
      h.feed(o)
    }
  }
}
```

And although we could use addDestination to add it to a chain of pipes, it's more
convenient if we add a method to the Pipe trait itself to construct it for us:

LibUVPipes/file_pipe/main.scala
```
def mapOption[V](g:U => Option[V]):Pipe[U,V] = {
  addDestination(OptionPipe(g))
}
```

While we're at it, we can construct a .map method to do the same thing with
our MapPipe:

LibUVPipes/file_pipe_out/main.scala
```
def map[V](g:U => V):Pipe[U,V] = {
  addDestination(SyncPipe(g))
}
```

We can even construct a .filter method, which takes any true/false function
with the type signature I -> Bool and removes elements from the stream that
return false:

LibUVPipes/examples.scala
```
def filter(f:T => Boolean):Pipe[T] = {
  addDestination(mapOption { t =>
    f(t) match {
      case true => Some(t)
      case false => None
    }
  }
}
```

This technique allows us to chain simple functions, one after the other, without
accumulating increasingly complex types as we proceed, as in this example:

LibUVPipes/examples.scala

```scala
SyncPipe(0)
.map { d =>
  println(s"consumed $d")
  d
}.map { d =>
  val parsed = Try {
    d.toInt
  }
}.filter {
  case Success(i) =>
    println(s"saw number $i")
    true
  case Failure(f) =>
    println(s"error: $f")
    false
}
// ...
```

But that's just the start.

MapConcat

Another extremely useful family of functions are those that take a value of type I and output a Seq[O]—for example, methods like String.split()—and output each item to the destination individually. Not only does this handle functions that transform one output into many, but it can also critically transform one value into nothing at all—meaning it can actually provide filtering functionality as well.

Much like with Option, an empty Seq() produces no output:

LibUVPipes/file_pipe/main.scala

```scala
case class ConcatPipe[T,U](f:T => Seq[U]) extends Pipe[T,U] {
  override def feed(input:T):Unit = {
    val output = f(input)
    for (h <- handlers;
         o <- output) {
      h.feed(o)
    }
  }
}
```

And again, we wrap it in the Pipe trait for convenience:

LibUVPipes/file_pipe/main.scala

```scala
def mapConcat[V](g:U => Seq[V]):Pipe[U,V] = {
  addDestination(ConcatPipe(g))
}
```

This allows us to chain together many more kinds of processes without accumulating deeply nested sequence types. Even if we've repeatedly split large buffers of text into smaller pieces, we can still process individual chunks one at a time downstream.

Asynchronous Transformations

So far, everything we've added to the chain has been a synchronous transformation. But what if we try to add asynchronous functions, of the signature I => Function[O], to our chain? It turns out that they aren't much harder to implement than the handlers for Option and Seq:

```
LibUVPipes/file_pipe/main.scala
case class AsyncPipe[T,U](f:T => Future[U])
  (implicit ec:ExecutionContext) extends Pipe[T,U] {

  override def feed(input:T):Unit = {
    f(input).map { o =>
      for (h <- handlers) {
        h.feed(o)
      }
    }
  }
}
```

And we can wrap it as .mapAsync for all pipe instances:

```
LibUVPipes/file_pipe/main.scala
def mapAsync[V](g:U => Future[V])(implicit ec:ExecutionContext):Pipe[U,V] = {
  addDestination(AsyncPipe(g))
}
```

This code comes with the same concerns and caveats about backpressure that our output pipes have; without any kind of throttling mechanism we could easily overwhelm our system with a fast, unbounded input. But for limited inputs, like command-line input, this is incredibly useful. It would let us, for example, add HTTP client requests to a pipeline; supposing we have a Pipe[String], that contains URLs to fetch, we could then just do this:

```
LibUVPipes/examples.scala
val p:Pipe[String] = ???
p.mapAsync { url =>
  Curl.get(url)
}.map { response =>
  println(s"got back result: $response")
}
```

Stateful Processors

Finally, it's time to add state to our streaming processors. We'll work through a few different use cases and implementation techniques before we arrive at the most general and powerful cases.

To start, it would be nice to have a simple counter. Suppose we want to count the number of lines in a file. If we already have a Pipe[String] containing each line, we could do something like this:

```
LibUVPipes/examples.scala
val p:Pipe[String,String] = ???
var counter = 0
p.map { i =>
  counter += 1
  i
}
// ...
uv_run(EventLoop.loop,UV_RUN_DEFAULT)
println(s"saw $counter elements")
```

This is reasonably idiomatic Scala, and easy enough to follow, but in most Scala streaming libraries, it's strongly discouraged or forbidden. Due to some particularities of the JVM's memory model, sharing mutable state across threads can result in a wide variety of unintended behaviors. However, in our single-threaded, event-loop runtime, this is perfectly safe, just like using a var in a for loop! But if we want to, we can still package this up as a self-contained Pipe class:

```
LibUVPipes/file_pipe/main.scala
case class CounterSink[T]() extends Pipe[T,Nothing] {
  var counter = 0
  override def feed(input:T) = {
    counter += 1
  }
}
```

We can then instantiate it, and extract the value at the end, like so:

```
LibUVPipes/examples.scala
val p:Pipe[String] = ???
val c = p.addDestination(Counter())
uv_run(EventLoop.loop,UV_RUN_DEFAULT)
println(s"saw ${c.counter} elements")
```

With that basic pattern in place, we can treat some more complex cases. Perhaps the most relevant one is *tokenization*. This is what we would use to take the buffer-sized strings that we get from our STDIN pipe, and transform them into proper line-terminated strings. One could make a rough attempt at implementing it like so:

```
LibUVPipes/examples.scala
val p:Pipe[String] = ???
p.mapConcat { content =>
  content.split("\n")
}.mapConcat { line =>
  line.split(" ")
}.map { word =>
  println(s"saw word: ${word}")
}
uv_run(EventLoop.loop,UV_RUN_DEFAULT)
println(s"saw ${c.counter} elements")
```

But this has a serious flaw. This code will badly malfunction if a buffer boundary doesn't fall precisely on a line-ending character, which is going to be the case almost all of the time. To implement this properly, we need to maintain a buffer containing any "leftover" string content so that we can wait for the next line-ending character to come through. We also need special handling of the end of a stream so that we remember to emit any remaining contents of the buffer before we signal done() to downstream consumers.

```
LibUVPipes/file_pipe/main.scala
case class Tokenizer(separator:String) extends Pipe[String,String] {
  var buffer = " "

  def scan(input:String):Seq[String] = {
    println(s"scanning: '$input'")
    buffer = buffer + input
    var o:Seq[String] = Seq()
    while (buffer.contains(separator)) {
      val space_position = buffer.indexOf(separator)
      val word = buffer.substring(0,space_position)
      o = o :+ word
      buffer = buffer.substring(space_position + 1)
    }
    o
  }
  override def feed(input:String):Unit = {
    for (h       <- handlers;
         word <- scan(input)) {
           h.feed(word)
    }
  }
}
```

```
  override def done():Unit = {
    println(s"done!  current buffer: $buffer")
    for (h <- handlers) {
        h.feed(buffer)
        h.done()
    }
  }
}
```

We could even generalize this further in a more functional style, by accepting a fold function and an initial value in the style of Scala's powerful foldLeft method:

LibUVPipes/file_pipe/main.scala
```
case class FoldPipe[I,O](init:O)(f:(O,I) => O) extends Pipe[I,O] {
  var accum = init

  override def feed(input:I):Unit = {
    accum = f(accum,input)
    for (h <- handlers) {
      h.feed(accum)
    }
  }

  override def done():Unit = {
    for (h <- handlers) {
      h.done()
    }
  }
}
```

In some ways, however, the more direct implementation style may be preferable; the subtleties of how to handle state, and what to do with accumulated state in done(), tend to either resist easy generalization, or produce a large number of slight variations with confusing names. So for now, we'll stick with our tokenizers.

You may also observed how similar the tokenization-buffer problem is to the problem of HTTP requests that took up more than one buffer in our async HTTP server, back in Chapter 6, Doing I/O Right, with Event Loops, on page 103. Indeed, treating an HTTP request as a pipe-like stream object will point a way forward as we come closer to the end of this book.

What's Next

Before we return to our server framework, we have one more topic left to cover: storage. Without the ability to reliably store data between requests, it's going to be hard for our code to be much of actual use to anyone; however, integrating with databases can be one of the most complex aspects of programming, typically requiring large codebases and ecosystems for basic functionality. In the next chapter, we'll take a different approach to storage and see how Scala Native can provide a new, fresh approach to durable, transactional storage.

CHAPTER 9

Durability: An Embedded Key-Value Database with LMDB

If you've previously worked with databases like MySQL, Postgres, or SQL Server—especially in Scala—you may expect working with storage to involve many hassles and headaches, including these:

- Asynchronous calls for storage operations.
- Obscure maintenance and setup operations.
- Persistent sluggishness and resource limitations.
- Arcane bindings between the contents of storage and Scala data types.

Indeed, in many real-world programs, storage becomes both a site of enormous complexity as well as a performance bottleneck for the whole system. That said, a well-configured database provides benefits as well:

- *Durability.* Once a storage operation succeeds, we can rely on it being kept around until we say otherwise.

- *Transactionality.* We can be guaranteed that a set of operations happen all at once, or don't happen at all.

If we were so inclined, we could use a traditional database system with Scala Native. Just about every database under the sun, including Postgres and MySQL, as well as newer options like Redis, have excellent C client libraries we could use, just like we used libcurl for our asynchronous HTTP client in Chapter 7, Functions and Futures: Patterns for Distributed Services, on page 131. But if you've read the rest of this book, you already know how to do that, and the bulk of the implementation will be tied to the patterns and idiosyncrasies of whichever database you choose, rather than anything particular or special about Scala Native.

Instead, in this chapter, we'll explore a different strategy, one that's familiar to C programmers but few others: *embedded storage*. And you'll learn how to use a recent and very exciting embedded data store called the Lightning Memory-Mapped Database, or LMDB. Let's first see what embedded storage is all about.

Introducing Embedded Storage

The key factor that distinguishes an embedded database from those you may be used to is that an embedded database *lives entirely in your program*. There's no remote server, no connection pool, no login credentials. Data is stored on the filesystem of the machine that runs the host process. Because of this, embedded databases will have very different properties than traditional databases.

Since access to local storage, especially local memory, is much faster than network access, embedded databases can be accessed synchronously, without blocking. However, this often places limitations on the query capabilities, especially for bulk queries that can return hundreds or thousands of objects. Thus, instead of providing a traditional query language like SQL, many embedded stores provide variations of the *key-value lookup* data storage paradigm.

In a key-value store, all data has a *primary key*, which uniquely identifies it, allowing us to store, update, or retrieve that item. In many ways, a key-value store functions quite a bit like Scala's Map data type, with the constraint that keys must be strings. What's missing is the notion of a *secondary index*, which would allow us to retrieve items by values other than the primary key. Instead, it falls on us to design data structures that will serve the needs of our application. However, if we accept this requirement, it's often possible to write much more efficient, custom designs than what a general-purpose database would provide. And indeed, modern key-value stores like LevelDB[1] and RocksDB[2] are often internal components of relational and other databases; all of the higher-level operations can be implemented as a series of operations on a reliable key-value store.

Defining LMDB Concepts

LMDB's design provides extraordinarily fast access to data by mapping file-based storage directly into process memory, avoiding the cost of intermediate

---

1. https://github.com/google/leveldb
2. https://rocksdb.org

copies. Although that does generally limit us to an amount of data we can fit into working memory, it provides many other benefits, including transactionality. And as you'll see, the fast, synchronous data access patterns LMDB provides are an exceedingly good fit for the nonblocking libuv server we've constructed over the last several chapters. Compared to libuv or libcurl, LMDB's API surface is refreshingly compact, consisting of a handful of functions and types. That said, it does introduce a few concepts that are worth defining before we get into the weeds.

Environment

In LMDB, an *environment* is the global, top-level object, corresponding to a directory somewhere on the filesystem. LMDB will not create a directory for us, and trying to open a directory that doesn't yet exist is a common error for beginners.

Databases

Inside a directory there are one or many *databases*. If an environment contains a single database, it may be anonymous, otherwise each database is distinguished by name.

Keys

Each database contains *keys*. Keys are unique within a single database, but the same key may exist in multiple databases in a single environment. Keys are shortish bytestrings—the default upper limit on length is 512 bytes.

Values

In a default configuration, each key has exactly one *value*, which may be a bytestring of variable length. However, there are ways to configure LMDB to allow a single key to have multiple distinct values; in this case, the values are *sorted* in some deterministic order, which is defined by a user-supplied function pointer. Multiple values may be traversed one at a time by a *cursor*, as can ranges of keys.

Cursors, multiple values, and custom sorting are incredibly powerful techniques for designing custom data structures, but they are outside of the scope of this book. Instead, we'll focus on simple, transactional updates of a few straightforward data structures, and you'll discover just how powerful these simple techniques can be when integrated with what we've already built.

Working with the LMDB API

To get started with LMDB, we need to perform three tasks, usually in this order:

1. Create a new environment object.
2. Store data.
3. Retrieve data.

Fortunately, the LMDB API makes it straightforward to do each of these tasks and wrap them in idiomatic Scala functions.

To open an environment, we'll use the following functions and data structures:

LMDB/lmdb_simple/main.scala
```
type Env = Ptr[Byte]
type DB = UInt
def mdb_env_create(env:Ptr[Env]):Int = extern
def mdb_env_open(env:Env, path:CString, flags:Int, mode:Int):Int = extern
```

Env here is an opaque pointer, and we have a convenient helper function mdb_env_create to allocate it for us. Once initialized, we use mdb_env_open to open an actual directory path. We can pass it a set of option flags packed into an integer (which we won't be using), and we also need to provide a UNIX file permissions flag (we'll only be using read-write permissions, represented as 0600 in octal notation, or 384 as a Scala integer literal). A helper function to do all this will look like so:

LMDB/lmdb_simple/main.scala
```
def open(path:CString):Env = {
  val env_ptr = stackalloc[Env]
  check(mdb_env_create(env_ptr), "mdb_env_create")
  val env = !env_ptr
  // Unix permissions for octal 0644 (read/write)
  check(mdb_env_open(env, path, 0, 420), "mdb_env_open")
  env
}
```

Likewise, to store data, we need to first allocate a Transaction object—again, an opaque pointer—with mdb_txn_begin.

Once we have a transaction object, we "open" a database within our environment with mdb_dbi_open. Once the transaction is begun and the database is opened, we're ensured a consistent view of the database's contents, without the risk of modification by other processes.

Now, we can call `mdb_put` to store data. This function takes the Transaction object as well as a Key and a Value; but, the key and value structs are simple and almost identical to libuv's Buffer. Here are all the definitions:

LMDB/lmdb_simple/main.scala
```
type Transaction = Ptr[Byte]
type Key = CStruct2[Long,Ptr[Byte]]
type Value = CStruct2[Long,Ptr[Byte]]
def mdb_txn_begin(env:Env, parent:Ptr[Byte], flags:Int,
  tx:Ptr[Transaction]):Int = extern
def mdb_dbi_open(tx:Transaction, name:CString, flags:Int,
  db:Ptr[DB]):Int = extern
def mdb_put(tx:Transaction, db:DB, key:Ptr[Key], value:Ptr[Value],
  flags:Int):Int = extern
def mdb_txn_commit(tx:Transaction):Int = extern
```

A straightforward Scala wrapper might work like this:

LMDB/lmdb_simple/main.scala
```
def get(env:Env,key:CString):CString = {
  val db_ptr = stackalloc[DB]
  val tx_ptr = stackalloc[Transaction]

  check(mdb_txn_begin(env, null, 0, tx_ptr), "mdb_txn_begin")
  val tx = !tx_ptr

  check(mdb_dbi_open(tx,null,0,db_ptr), "mdb_dbi_open")
  val db = !db_ptr

  val rk = stackalloc[Key]
  rk._1 = string.strlen(key) + 1
  rk._2 = key
  val rv = stackalloc[Value]

  check(mdb_get(tx,db, rk, rv), "mdb_get")

  stdio.printf(c"key: %s value: %s\n", rk._2, rv._2)
  val output = stdlib.malloc(rv._1)
  string.strncpy(output,rv._2,rv._1)
  check(mdb_txn_abort(tx), "mdb_txn_abort")
  return output
}
```

Finally, we can retrieve back the data we've written. The steps to reading data are similar to writing data: we still have to create a transaction, and are still ensured a consistent view of all data. However, if we specify that this will be a read-only transaction with a special flag, we can do so without blocking other readers. The signature of `mdb_get` is straightforward:

LMDB/lmdb_simple/main.scala
```
def mdb_get(tx:Transaction, db:DB, key:Ptr[Key],
  value:Ptr[Value]):Int = extern
```

And we can wrap it in much the same way as mdb_put:

LMDB/lmdb_simple/main.scala
```
def put(env:Env,key:CString,value:CString):Unit = {
  val db_ptr = stackalloc[DB]
  val tx_ptr = stackalloc[Transaction]

  check(mdb_txn_begin(env, null, 0, tx_ptr), "mdb_txn_begin")
  val tx = !tx_ptr
  check(mdb_dbi_open(tx,null,0,db_ptr), "mdb_dbi_open")
  val db = !db_ptr

  val k = stackalloc[Key]
  k._1 = string.strlen(key) + 1
  k._2 = key
  val v = stackalloc[Value]
  v._1 = string.strlen(value) + 1
  v._2 = value

  check(mdb_put(tx, db, k,v,0), "mdb_put")
  check(mdb_txn_commit(tx), "mdb_txn_commit")
}
```

Although there are quite a few more functions and capabilities in the full LMDB API, this is enough for us to write many useful programs!

Before we integrate with our HTTP server framework, let's write a simple command-line utility to interact with a database. Since LMDB is a library, and not an application, it doesn't include a command-line toolkit. This means we'll need to use this kind of tool for database testing and maintenance, even after we've completed the HTTP integration. To keep the design simple, we'll parse lines of input into two types of commands to store and lookup data:

```
put $key $value
get $key
```

With the Scala wrapper functions we've already prepared, this is just a few lines of code to implement:

LMDB/lmdb_simple/main.scala
```
val line_buffer = stdlib.malloc(1024)
val get_key_buffer = stdlib.malloc(512)
val put_key_buffer = stdlib.malloc(512)
val value_buffer = stdlib.malloc(512)

def main(args:Array[String]):Unit = {
  val env = LMDB.open(c"./db")
  stdio.printf(c"opened db %p\n", env)
  stdio.printf(c"> ")

  while (stdio.fgets(line_buffer, 1024, stdio.stdin) != null) {
    val put_scan_result = stdio.sscanf(line_buffer,c"put %s %s",
      put_key_buffer, value_buffer)
```

```
    val get_scan_result = stdio.sscanf(line_buffer,c"get %s",
      get_key_buffer)

    if (put_scan_result == 2) {
      stdio.printf(c"storing value %s into key %s\n",
          put_key_buffer, value_buffer)
      LMDB.put(env,put_key_buffer,value_buffer)
      stdio.printf(c"saved key: %s value: %s\n", put_key_buffer, value_buffer)
    } else if (get_scan_result == 1) {
      stdio.printf(c"looking up key %s\n", get_key_buffer)
      val lookup = LMDB.get(env,get_key_buffer)
      stdio.printf(c"retrieved key: %s value: %s\n", get_key_buffer,lookup)
    } else {
      println("didn't understand input")
    }
    stdio.printf(c"> ")
  }
  println("done")
}
```

Now let's test it out. First, we'll need to create an empty directory to serve as our database with mkdir, then we can store and retrieve some data:

```
$ ./target/scala-2.11/lmdb_simple-out
mdb_env_create returned 0
mdb_env_open returned 0
opened db 0x7fa0e6500000
> put foo bar
storing value foo into key bar for db 0x7fab02d00000
mdb_txn_begin returned 0
mdb_dbi_open returned 0
mdb_put returned 0
mdb_txn_commit returned 0
saved key: foo value: bar
> get foo
looking up key foo for db 0x7fab02d00000
mdb_txn_begin returned 0
mdb_dbi_open returned 0
mdb_get returned 0
key: foo value: bar
mdb_txn_abort returned 0
retrieved key: foo value: bar
> done
```

Now, if you exit the program, you can observe that two files have been created in ./db:

```
$ ls -al db/*
-rw-r--r--  1 rwhaling  staff  32768 Mar  2 12:10 db/data.mdb
-rw-r--r--  1 rwhaling  staff   8192 Mar  2 12:07 db/lock.mdb
```

That's our data! Now, if you run the program again, you can query for the key we set before:

```
$ ./target/scala-2.11/lmdb_simple-out
mdb_env_create returned 0
mdb_env_open returned 0
opened db 0x7fa0e6500000
> get foo
looking up key foo for db 0x7ffa20c03070
mdb_txn_begin returned 0
mdb_dbi_open returned 0
mdb_get returned 0
key: foo value: bar
mdb_txn_abort returned 0
retrieved key: foo value: bar
> done
```

And you get back exactly what we stored previously. However, we're still only storing and retrieving plain strings. Next, we'll extend what we've built to handle other kinds of data.

Serialization and Deserialization with JSON

If you've ever worked on a large Java codebase, you've no doubt seen huge class files for serializing and deserializing objects, often hundreds of lines of highly repetitive code, *per class*. In contrast, Scala is rightly famous for its capabilities for safe, boilerplate-free serialization. Indeed, Scala's ability to transparently serialize and transport most data has been a huge factor in the success of frameworks like Akka and Spark. Although Scala has strong support for most serialization formats, including some extremely powerful ones such as Protobufs, msgpack, and Avro, we're going to use JSON for now.

JSON (JavaScript Object Notation) is almost universally supported, human-readable, and easy to understand. Best of all, there are many high-quality JSON libraries available in Scala, and one of them—Argonaut[3]—has strong Scala Native support.

Adding Argonaut to a Scala Native project is straightforward; just add this to your build.sbt:

libraryDependencies += "io.argonaut" % "argonaut_native0.3_2.11" % "6.2.3-SNAPSHOT"

With Argonaut and Scala Native, you can easily read and write regular Scala case classes, as well as generic data structures like Lists and Maps. Argonaut does this by relying on *implicit parameters*. Just like we used an

---

3.   http://argonaut.io/doc

implicit ExecutionContext to let Scala's Future implementation utilize our event loop, Argonaut lets us supply EncodeJson[T] and DecodeJson[T] instances to our functions to define the transformation of any type T to and from JSON. Best of all, Argonaut provides default encoder and decoder instances for us, so we don't have to write any boilerplate:

```
LMDB/json_simple/main.scala
def main(args:Array[String]):Unit = {
  import argonaut._, Argonaut._
  val l:List[String] = List("list","of","strings")
  println(l.asJson.spaces2)
// ...
```

By importing argonaut._, we've already brought all of the implicits we need into scope to convert JSON to strings in our main routine. But for a general-purpose tool or library, we wouldn't want to hard-code in the default encoder; instead, we can abstract over a user-supplied encoder for more flexibility. For example, we can write a function to make any type T with a decoder into a CString, and print it with printf():

```
LMDB/json_simple/main.scala
def printfJson[T](data:T)(implicit e:EncodeJson[T]):Unit =
  Zone { implicit z =>
    val stringData = data.asJson.spaces2
    val cstring = toCString(stringData)
    stdio.printf(c"rendered json: %s\n", cstring)
  }
```

We can invoke it like this:

```
LMDB/json_simple/main.scala
val m:Map[String,String] = Map(
  "key1" -> "value1",
  "key2" -> "value2"
)

printfJson(m)
```

If we run this whole program, we'll see both the list and map outputs, like so:

```
$ ./target/scala-2.11/json_simple-out
[
  "list",
  "of",
  "strings"
]
rendered json: {
  "key1" : "value1",
  "key2" : "value2"
}
```

With this pattern, we can send, receive, and transform all kinds of data, both on the internal, LMDB-based parts of our application, as well as the web-facing components.

Putting LMDB on the Web

Although we won't be introducing any new LMDB functions as we integrate with our libuv-based framework, we should review a few fine points of the API before we start writing code. In particular, we need to know in what circumstances LMDB will block; if we inadvertently block the event loop, a single bad or expensive input can cause our whole server to stop processing requests.

Essentially, the only time we have to worry about LMDB blocking is when we create a transaction and open a database. If another transaction has locked that database, mdb_dbi_open won't return until the lock is released. And because transactions can run as much Scala Native code as they like, this would have the potential to block our program more or less indefinitely.

However, we have a major architectural benefit in this case: libuv and Scala Native are both single-threaded. As a result, we can be assured that we'll only ever run a single transaction at a time. We'll need to be particularly careful about exception handling to ensure we don't unintentionally leave "dangling" transactions, but so long as we maintain that discipline, we don't need to worry about blocking at all. We can even relax some of our requirements for transactionality. Grouping sequences of get() and put() operations together into a single transaction would require a substantially more complex API, but so long as we're assured that our code will run uninterrupted, we can safely perform these actions with the current API.

Wrappers and Serialization

We can also take this opportunity to wrap the low-level API we've already provided to make it more ergonomic for high-level application programming. The JSON serialization code from Serialization and Deserialization with JSON, on page 184, provides a solid foundation; we just need to adapt it to LMDB's interfaces and provide an ergonomic wrapper. We'll start with get/put wrappers for String:

LMDB/lmdb_web/lmdb.scala
```
def getString(env:Env, key:String):String = {
  Zone { implicit z =>
    val k = toCString(key)
    fromCString(get(env,k))
  }
}
```

```
def putString(env:Env, key:String, value:String):Unit = {
  Zone { implicit z =>
    val k = toCString(key)
    val v = toCString(value)
    put(env,k,v)
  }
}
```

Then, we can add encoders and decoders for different kinds of objects easily enough:

LMDB/lmdb_web/lmdb.scala
```
def getJson[T](env:Env, key:String)(implicit dec:DecodeJson[T]):T = {
  val value = getString(env,key)
  value.decodeOption[T].get
}

def putJson[T](env:Env, key:String, value:T)
              (implicit enc:EncodeJson[T]):Unit = {
  val valueString = value.asJson.nospaces
  putString(env,key,valueString)
}
```

Note that we do use some methods that may through exceptions, and that these functions rely on having robust error-catching higher up the stack. Since we'll catch all nonfatal exceptions outside of our HTTP router function, we should be just fine.

Designing a REST API

Now we can design a simple HTTP-based server as a front end for our LMDB database. We'll use the exact same server code and framework from Chapter 6, Doing I/O Right, with Event Loops, on page 103. The only difference is that we'll add a different implementation of the router. Since we've already learned how to store and retrieve plain keys and values, we'll try to model a more complex data structure.

This program will store lists of items. Each item is a Map[String,String] with arbitrary keys, and each list has a unique name. Every item belongs to exactly one list, but it can be retrieved on its own as well. We'll provide three HTTP endpoints for manipulating this data structure:

- /add/$list_key/$item_key takes a Map[String,String] as its body, and adds it onto the front of the named list.

- /fetch/$item_key retrieves an item by its key.

- /list/$list_key retrieves a list as a List[String] containing only the keys of all contained items, in order.

Although this is a deeply minimal set of capabilities, it resembles the fundamental structure of many common applications like chat, message boards, content-management systems, and others, and is a great way to work through some of the key basic patterns.

First, we'll need to devise a way to distinguish the three different kinds of requests that could be present in an HttpRequest object. For now, we'll use standard Scala regular expressions to match on the patterns and extract their component values, with the following pattern definitions:

LMDB/lmdb_web/main.scala
```scala
val addPatn = raw"/add/([^/]+)/([^/]+)".r
val fetchPatn = raw"/fetch/([^/]+)".r
val listPatn = raw"/list/([^/]+)".r
```

Then we can use them in a match/case statement, along with our actual request handlers, like so:

LMDB/lmdb_web/main.scala
```scala
def main(args:Array[String]):Unit = {
  val env = LMDB.open(c"./db")
  Server.serve_http(8080, request => request.uri match {
    case addPatn(set_key,key) =>
      val data = parseBody[Map[String,String]](request)
      val set = LMDB.getJson[List[String]](env,set_key)
      val new_set = key :: set
      LMDB.putJson(env, set_key, new_set)
      LMDB.putJson(env, key, data)
      makeResponse("OK")
    case fetchPatn(key) =>
      val item = LMDB.getJson[Map[String,String]](env,key)
      makeResponse(item)
    case listPatn(set_key) =>
      val set = LMDB.getJson[List[String]](env,set_key)
      makeResponse(set)
    case _ =>
      makeResponse("no route match\n")
  })
}
```

And that's all it takes: less than twenty lines of code. The fetch and list handlers are especially simple, and even the add handler isn't very bad. All of the serialization/deserialization is handled by our wrappers, and updating both the item and the list containing it is two calls to putJson. We do have to provide a type parameter to our call to getJson, which is somewhat inconvenient. With a more complex API design, we could probably eliminate that by providing a typed view of LMDB databases, but at the cost of flexibility.

However, there's still a big gap that we have to think hard about. As I've noted before, our API doesn't let us group operations into a single transaction, and it doesn't let us distinguish read-only from read-write transactions. Since this program contains only synchronous operations, and no async or Future calls, we don't need to worry about race conditions. But, if we extended our HTTP framework to allow for asynchronous response handlers—of the signature HttpRequest => Future[HttpResponse]—we could get into trouble. For example, if we put a get() and a put() operation on different sides of an asynchronous boundary, they could become inconsistent. Whereas if we tried to keep a single transaction open across an asynchronous boundary, we could easily lock up the whole server.

Coming up with a good solution to that design problem isn't easy. We'll need to use a variety of techniques from all over this book, as well as making some hard architectural decisions about how to design networked services.

What's Next

In the next and final chapter, I'll tie together the themes we explored throughout the book as we extend our HTTP framework one final time to encompass a wider variety of synchronous and asynchronous styles. In doing so, we'll open up the possibility of designing services that call other services—so-called microservice architecture. However, the unusual properties and performance of LMDB challenge many of the assumptions made by other Scala microservice patterns, and as we follow these techniques through to their conclusion, we'll arrive at a promising and novel approach to distributed systems as a whole.

CHAPTER 10

Services: Encapsulation and Abstraction for Modern Designs

Over the last four chapters, we've applied a variety of different capabilities of the libuv, libcurl, and LMDB libraries to some of the core capabilities of a modern computer system: a web server, futures, a web client, streams, and persistence. Now, we'll "zoom out" to think about how these capabilities relate to one another and what kind of systems we can build with them.

Services and Distributed Systems

The concept of a *service* is indisputably among the most influential guiding design principles to modern, distributed computer systems. Just as an object encapsulates the details of its implementation with a program, a *service* encapsulates the implementation of a much broader subset of functionality. And by decomposing a complex system into services, a hard problem can be divided into more manageable chunks.

A lot of great books have been written about such microservices, such as *Practical Microservices*[1] by Ethan Garofolo and *Microservices Patterns*[2] by Chris Richardson. Although the design of a large-scale distributed system is outside the scope of this book, these trends do have an impact on the way we design the kind of programs we've been writing for the last few chapters.

In particular, it's common for services in this style to share some or all of the following characteristics:

- They are written in a modern, typed programming language.

---

1. https://pragprog.com/book/egmicro/practical-microservices
2. https://www.manning.com/books/microservices-patterns

- They are fully asynchronous and nonblocking in nature.
- They rely upon a load-balancer or other gateway middleware for routing.
- They permit services to call one another more or less freely.
- They consume streams of events from other systems.

One of the most influential designs in this space is the Scala library, Finagle,[3] which was developed at Twitter in 2011. The success of Finagle at handling Twitter's enormous scale and workload was, in turn, a huge factor in more broadly popularizing Scala as a language. Other popular frameworks include Google's gRPC[4] and a broad portfolio of open-source libraries from Netflix, notably Ribbon.[5]

In other words, Scala is already a great language for writing microservices; and for the rest of this chapter, we'll explore how to adapt our asynchronous framework to this modern environment.

Service Calls, HTTP, and JSON

The two most essential aspects of a service framework are the *endpoint* and the *service call*. An *endpoint* is a particular functionality provided by a service, analogous to a method on an object. For example, suppose we have an Authentication service. It might have a login endpoint, a getUserDetails endpoint, and so on, each with typed arguments and return values—just like a regular Scala function.

Accordingly, a *service call* is what happens when some other service *invokes* another service remotely. For example, if we had a Widget service, it might call getUserDetails on the user service. And one of the fundamental insights of modern distributed systems is that service calls are *fundamentally asynchronous*. Even if the Authentication service itself doesn't block at any point in generating the result of getUserDetails, the call is asynchronous from the point of view of the Widget service because the request and response must both be routed over a network, which brings with it any number of possible failure and delay scenarios.

Finally, we're also going to orient the services described in this chapter toward HTTP and JSON. Although it's becoming more and more common to use other protocols for messaging and serialization, HTTP and JSON are still suitable for many real-world workloads and can be much easier to implement and debug than more efficient binary protocols. If you're interested in learning about

---

3.   https://twitter.github.io/finagle

4.   https://grpc.io

5.   https://github.com/Netflix/ribbon

alternatives, however, the gRPC stack of Protocol Buffers[6] for serialization and HTTP/2[7] or QUIC[8] for transport are widely adopted and well documented.

Service APIs and DSLs

It's common for microservice frameworks in Scala to follow one of two patterns for the high-level design of a microservice API:

- A DSL design, often with macros to transform elegant code into a more sophisticated representation.

- A trait-based design, where a base trait is extended with application-specific methods.

Both have their respective pros and cons, and unfortunately, both tend to demand more specialized Scala techniques that are outside the scope of this book. What we'll do instead is design a framework from the bottom up, beginning with HTTP parsing and basic web serving, while relying on more or less ordinary Scala techniques, thoughtfully applied.

The basic requirements are these:

1. A service needs to be able to declare any number of endpoints by HTTP method and URL.

2. A service needs to declare a regular Scala type for endpoint requests and responses.

3. A service needs to be able to read HTTP headers on requests, and set them on response.

4. A service needs to be able to provide some results asynchronously, while still supporting synchronous endpoints as well.

All of these capabilities are well within reach for us, simply by applying the techniques we've developed over the last few chapters. I'll introduce one new capability to support the design, though: a proper HTTP parser.

Parsing, Revisited

We relied on the C standard library functions fgets() and scanf() for HTTP parsing in Chapter 5, Writing a Server the Old-Fashioned Way, on page 85, and in Chapter 6, Doing I/O Right, with Event Loops, on page 103, we still

---

6. https://developers.google.com/protocol-buffers
7. https://en.wikipedia.org/wiki/HTTP/2
8. https://en.wikipedia.org/wiki/QUIC

relied on scanf. However, these began to feel increasingly clunky when driven by libuv's asynchronous, buffer-based I/O design. Although the code we wrote performed reasonably well, it did so at the expense of handling certain real-world edge cases.

We'll solve these problems by introducing another external C library: the node.js http-parser library,[9] which is a low-level C library that is tightly integrated with libuv in the node.js core.

The http-parser API

http-parser and libuv really do go together like peanut butter and jelly; the parser API has just a handful of methods we'll need to call, and two structs. Unlike with our libuv and libcurl bindings, we won't be able to model these as opaque pointers. Instead, we'll need to correctly model all of the external-facing fields of the parser object so we can pull out its state when needed.

The parser struct itself looks like this:

```
LibUVService/parsing.scala
type Parser = CStruct8[
  Long,   // private data
  Long,   // private data
  UShort, // major version
  UShort, // minor version
  UShort, // status (request only)
  CChar, // method
  CChar, // Error (last bit upgrade)
  Ptr[Byte] // user data
]
```

This is a little unwieldy, but we'll only need to access fields number six (http method) and eight (the custom user data field). The actual library functions we'll use are as follows:

```
LibUVService/parsing.scala
def http_parser_init(p:Ptr[Parser],parser_type:Int):Unit = extern
def http_parser_settings_init(s:Ptr[ParserSettings]):Unit = extern
def http_parser_execute(p:Ptr[Parser],s:Ptr[ParserSettings],
    data:Ptr[Byte],len:Long):Long = extern
def http_method_str(method:CChar):CString = extern
```

This sets up and executes parsing when we have data available; the trick is all in the ParserSettings struct, which holds two kinds of callbacks:

---

9.   https://github.com/nodejs/http-parser

```
LibUVService/parsing.scala
type HttpCB = CFuncPtr1[Ptr[Parser],Int]
type HttpDataCB = CFuncPtr3[Ptr[Parser],CString,Long,Int]

type ParserSettings = CStruct8[
  HttpCB, // on_message_begin
  HttpDataCB, // on_url
  HttpDataCB, // on_status
  HttpDataCB, // on_header_field
  HttpDataCB, // on_header_value
  HttpCB, // on_headers_complete
  HttpDataCB, // on_body
  HttpCB  // on_message_complete
]
```

In short, we'll supply a HttpCB for a notification, where something has occurred but no new data is present, and HttpDataCB for data callbacks, where there's a new buffer of data for us. We also won't necessarily need to handle all of these. If we leave any null, they simply won't get called. Otherwise, all of these are called by http_parser_execute when we pass it a buffer of data, and all of the callbacks will receive pointers and offsets into the same data, without intermediate copies.

In other words, this parser maintains state but doesn't accumulate data, leaving us free to do so ourselves.

Parsing Requests

We can design a simple mutable RequestState case class that we can use to accumulate values as they become available:

```
LibUVService/parsing.scala
case class RequestState(
  url:String,
  method:String,
  var lastHeader:String = "None",
  headerMap:mutable.Map[String,String] = mutable.Map[String,String](),
  var body:String = "")
```

We'll also need to design some kind of struct that we can store in the eighth field of Parser to identify requests and responses. For this design to work, we'll need to closely coordinate the functionality of libuv's TCP I/O callbacks and handles with a Parser instance per connection, as well as a RequestState per request, although we'll only have one active RequestState at a time per connection.

If we design a simple, three-field struct containing the connection ID, the TCPHandle, and the Parser struct, we can share it between the libuv and parser aspects of our codebase. In fact, we can structure all the parsing components into a trait that we can mix into our server implementation, allowing for a cleaner design. We just need to require that the server allows us to look up RequestStates by id and provide a handleRequest function for us to call (from the onComplete parser callback) when a request is fully parsed.

The basic interface looks like this:

```
LibUVService/parsing.scala
trait Parsing {
  import LibUV._,HttpParser._
  val requests:mutable.Map[Long,RequestState]

  def handleRequest(id:Long,handle:TCPHandle,request:RequestState):Unit

  type ConnectionState = CStruct3[Long,TCPHandle,Parser]

  val HTTP_REQUEST = 0
  val HTTP_RESPONSE = 1
  val HTTP_BOTH = 2
```

Now, we just need to implement the actual callbacks. The first callback to be executed for any request is the onURL callback. We'll use that to initialize the RequestState with its method and URL (since these will be called from a libuv on_read callback, we can rely on the ConnectionState already being populated).

```
LibUVService/parsing.scala
def onURL(p:Ptr[Parser],data:CString,len:Long):Int = {
  val state = (p._8).asInstanceOf[Ptr[ConnectionState]]
  val message_id = state._1
  val url = bytesToString(data,len)
  println(s"got url: $url")
  val m = p._6
  val method = fromCString(http_method_str(m))
  println(s"method: $method ($m)")
  requests(message_id) = RequestState(url,method)
  0
}
```

The tricky part is header parsing. We can receive any number of headers, but we'll always alternate between keys and values. But http-parser can call onValue twice in a row in some circumstances, such as when a buffer boundary falls in the middle of a header line. As a result, we'll need to keep track of whether we last saw a header key or value, and what that value was, so we can know how to update our Map of headers as we receive each component, like so:

```
LibUVService/parsing.scala
def onHeaderKey(p:Ptr[Parser],data:CString,len:Long):Int = {
  val state = (p._8).asInstanceOf[Ptr[ConnectionState]]
  val message_id = state._1
  val request = requests(message_id)
```

```
    val k = bytesToString(data,len)
    request.lastHeader = k
    requests(message_id) = request
    0
}
def onHeaderValue(p:Ptr[Parser],data:CString,len:Long):Int = {
  val state = (p._8).asInstanceOf[Ptr[ConnectionState]]
  val message_id = state._1
  val request = requests(message_id)

  val v = bytesToString(data,len)
  request.headerMap(request.lastHeader) = v
  requests(message_id) = request
  0
}
```

And likewise, if we have a POST, PUT, or other HTTP request with a body, we can append that content to our state like so:

LibUVService/parsing.scala
```
def onBody(p:Ptr[Parser],data:CString,len:Long):Int = {
  val state = (p._8).asInstanceOf[Ptr[ConnectionState]]
  val message_id = state._1
  val request = requests(message_id)

  val b = bytesToString(data,len)
  request.body += b
  requests(message_id) = request
  0
}
```

Finally, once the method is complete, we can finalize it and pass it on to the actual server implementation via the handleRequest interface (which we'll implement shortly):

LibUVService/parsing.scala
```
  def onMessageComplete(p:Ptr[Parser]):Int = {
    val state = (p._8).asInstanceOf[Ptr[ConnectionState]]
    val message_id = state._1
    val tcpHandle = state._2
    val request = requests(message_id)
    handleRequest(message_id,tcpHandle,request)
    0
  }
}

@link("http_parser")
@extern
object HttpParser {
  type Parser = CStruct8[
    Long,    // private data
    Long,    // private data
```

```
    UShort, // major version
    UShort, // minor version
    UShort, // status (request only)
    CChar, // method
    CChar, // Error (last bit upgrade)
    Ptr[Byte] // user data
  ]

  type HttpCB = CFuncPtr1[Ptr[Parser],Int]
  type HttpDataCB = CFuncPtr3[Ptr[Parser],CString,Long,Int]

  type ParserSettings = CStruct8[
    HttpCB, // on_message_begin
    HttpDataCB, // on_url
    HttpDataCB, // on_status
    HttpDataCB, // on_header_field
    HttpDataCB, // on_header_value
    HttpCB, // on_headers_complete
    HttpDataCB, // on_body
    HttpCB  // on_message_complete
  ]
  def http_parser_init(p:Ptr[Parser],parser_type:Int):Unit = extern
  def http_parser_settings_init(s:Ptr[ParserSettings]):Unit = extern
  def http_parser_execute(p:Ptr[Parser],s:Ptr[ParserSettings],
      data:Ptr[Byte],len:Long):Long = extern
  def http_method_str(method:CChar):CString = extern
}
```

That's it! With the skills we've developed over the course of this book, we can now integrate an external HTTP parser in less code that it took us to build one ourselves.

Moving from Server to Service

Now, we're ready to implement the Server layer and lay the foundation for a service DSL. This will largely follow the pattern of the server we implemented in Chapter 6, Doing I/O Right, with Event Loops, on page 103, but will be more oriented toward supporting typed messages and responses rather than free-form strings. However, we'll try to isolate the server from some of the subtleties of the actual DSL to control the complexity and allow for alternative designs.

Basic Definitions

First, the core data structures we need to define are the Request and Response types—the core accommodation we need to make is to parameterize both over some Scala type T. By design, the actual server will only receive Request[String] and Response[String] (it will fall upon the Service layer to translate other types while still allowing them to set headers freely):

LibUVService/server.scala
```scala
case class Request[T](method:String, url:String, headers:Map[String,String],
                      body:T)
case class Response[T](code:Int, description:String,
                       headers:Map[String,String],body:T)
```

The other critical data structure is the Route—a way to map incoming requests to a particular handler function according to some combination of request method and URL. We'll also need a way to distinguish synchronous from asynchronous routes, so we know whether to send them back immediately or wait for a Future to complete:

LibUVService/server.scala
```scala
sealed trait Route {
  val method:String
  val path:String
}
case class SyncRoute(method:String, path:String, handler:Request[String] =>
  Response[String]) extends Route
case class AsyncRoute(method:String, path:String, handler:Request[String] =>
  Future[Response[String]]) extends Route
```

Again, our Server layer doesn't need to know what to do with the routes, just how to handle their results.

Now, we're ready to write the server code itself, starting with the mostly routine setup and initialization:

LibUVService/server.scala
```scala
object Server extends Parsing {
  import LibUVConstants._, LibUV._,HttpParser._
  implicit val ec = EventLoop
  val loop = EventLoop.loop
  var serial = 1L
  override val requests = mutable.Map[Long,RequestState]()
  var activeRequests = 0

  val urlCB:HttpDataCB = new HttpDataCB {
    def apply(p:Ptr[Parser],data:CString,len:Long):Int = onURL(p,data,len)
  }
  val onKeyCB:HttpDataCB = new HttpDataCB {
    def apply(p:Ptr[Parser],data:CString,len:Long):Int =
      onHeaderKey(p,data,len)
  }
  val onValueCB:HttpDataCB = new HttpDataCB {
    def apply(p:Ptr[Parser],data:CString,len:Long):Int =
      onHeaderValue(p,data,len)
  }
  val onBodyCB:HttpDataCB = new HttpDataCB {
    def apply(p:Ptr[Parser],data:CString,len:Long):Int = onBody(p,data,len)
  }
```

```scala
  val completeCB:HttpCB = new HttpCB {
    def apply(p:Ptr[Parser]):Int = onMessageComplete(p)
  }
  val parserSettings = malloc(sizeof[ParserSettings])
    .asInstanceOf[Ptr[ParserSettings]]
  http_parser_settings_init(parserSettings)
  parserSettings._2 = urlCB
  parserSettings._4 = onKeyCB
  parserSettings._5 = onValueCB
  parserSettings._7 = onBodyCB
  parserSettings._8 = completeCB

  var router:Function1[Request[String],Route] = null
```

Note that we mix in the Parsing trait here, and also declare the CFunctionPtr callbacks, because CFunctionPtrs cannot be declared in traits, only static objects.

We'll also declare a router, the service-supplied function to resolve an incoming URL to its appropriate handler, which we'll initialize shortly thereafter:

LibUVService/server.scala
```scala
def init(port:Int, f:Request[String] => Route):Unit = {
  router = f
  val addr = malloc(64)
  check(uv_ip4_addr(c"0.0.0.0", 9999, addr),"uv_ip4_addr")
  val server = malloc(uv_handle_size(UV_TCP_T)).asInstanceOf[TCPHandle]
  check(uv_tcp_init(loop, server), "uv_tcp_init")
  check(uv_tcp_bind(server, addr, 0), "uv_tcp_bind")
  check(uv_listen(server, 4096, connectCB), "uv_listen")
  this.activeRequests = 1
  println("running")
}
```

Unlike our other asynchronous components, this one basically runs forever, so we don't need to count individual connections. We can just set activeRequests to 1 for now, although this could be modified to allow for multiple services running on different ports.

Handling I/O

The basic libuv callback functions are all similar to what we used before in Chapter 6. Some of them won't be changed at all, but we'll need to make a few adjustments to work with the HTTP parser. First, we'll need to initialize everything when a new connection comes in:

LibUVService/server.scala
```scala
val connectCB = new ConnectionCB {
  def apply(server:TCPHandle, status:Int):Unit = {
    println(s"connection incoming with status $status")
    val client = malloc(uv_handle_size(UV_TCP_T)).asInstanceOf[TCPHandle]
```

```
      val id = serial
      serial += 1

      val state = malloc(sizeof[ConnectionState])
        .asInstanceOf[Ptr[ConnectionState]]
      state._1 = serial
      state._2 = client
      http_parser_init(state.at3,HTTP_REQUEST)
      (state.at3)._8 = state.asInstanceOf[Ptr[Byte]]
      !(client.asInstanceOf[Ptr[Ptr[Byte]]]) = state.asInstanceOf[Ptr[Byte]]

      stdio.printf(c"initialized handle at %x, parser at %x\n", client, state)

      check(uv_tcp_init(loop, client), "uv_tcp_init (client)")
      check(uv_accept(server, client), "uv_accept")
      check(uv_read_start(client, allocCB, readCB), "uv_read_start")
    }
}
```

And then, whenever we receive data, we will pass it on to the parser with http_parser_execute():

```
LibUVService/server.scala
val readCB = new ReadCB {
  def apply(handle:TCPHandle, size:CSize, buffer:Ptr[Buffer]):Unit = {
    val state_ptr = handle.asInstanceOf[Ptr[Ptr[ConnectionState]]]
    val parser = (!state_ptr).at3
    val message_id = (!state_ptr)._1
    println(s"conn $message_id: read message of size $size")

    if (size < 0) {
      uv_close(handle, null)
      stdlib.free(buffer._1)
    } else {
      http_parser_execute(parser,parserSettings,buffer._1,size)
      stdlib.free(buffer._1)
    }
  }
}
```

Writing data becomes a bit more complex because we have to handle a few new situations: when a request is complete, we invoke the router to determine how to handle the request, then we check whether the matched route is a SyncRoute or AsyncRoute. If it's a SyncRoute, we can send the response immediately, but if it's an AsyncRoute, we can get a Future[Response[String]] and send a response when it completes.

We'll provide a helper method for each of the two basic cases. sendResponse will handle all of the complex string-manipulation logic in synchronous cases:

```
LibUVService/server.scala
def sendResponse(id:Long,client:TCPHandle, resp:Response[String]):Unit = {
  var respString = s"HTTP/1.1 ${resp.code} ${resp.description}\r\n"
  val headers = if (!resp.headers.contains("Content-Length")) {
    resp.headers + ("Content-Length" -> resp.body.size)
  } else { resp.headers }

  for ( (k,v) <- headers) {
    respString += s"${k}: $v\r\n"
  }
  respString += s"\r\n${resp.body}"

  val buffer = malloc(sizeof[Buffer]).asInstanceOf[Ptr[Buffer]]
  Zone { implicit z =>
    val temp_resp = toCString(respString)
    val resp_len = strlen(temp_resp) + 1
    buffer._1 = malloc(resp_len)
    buffer._2 = resp_len
    strncpy(buffer._1, temp_resp, resp_len)
  }
  stdio.printf(c"response buffer:\n%s\n",buffer._1)

  val writeReq = malloc(uv_req_size(UV_WRITE_REQ_T)).asInstanceOf[WriteReq]
  !writeReq = buffer.asInstanceOf[Ptr[Byte]]
  check(uv_write(writeReq, client,buffer,1,writeCB),"uv_write")
}
```

And sendResponseAsync simply wraps sendResponse within a Future.map handler:

```
LibUVService/server.scala
def sendResponseAsync(id:Long,client:TCPHandle,
                        resp:Future[Response[String]]):Unit = {
  resp.map { r =>
    println("async?")
    sendResponse(id,client,r)
  }
}
```

With those helpers in place, we can finally write the handleRequest method, which completes our interface with the parser. All we need to do is convert the parser's RequestState into a Request[String], pass it to the router, and then decide how to handle the result:

```
LibUVService/server.scala
override def handleRequest(id:Long,client:TCPHandle, r:RequestState):Unit = {
  println(s"got complete request $id: $r\r\n")
  val request = Request(r.method,r.url,r.headerMap.toMap,r.body)
  val route = router(request)
```

```scala
    route match {
      case SyncRoute(_,_,handler) =>
        val resp = handler(request)
        println("sending sync response")
        sendResponse(id,client,resp)
      case AsyncRoute(_,_,handler) =>
        val resp = handler(request)
        resp.map { r =>
          println("about to send async response")
          sendResponse(id,client,r)
        }
        println("returning immediately, async handler invoked")
    }
  }
}
```

The rest is up to the service layer, which we're now prepared to implement!

Implementing an Idiomatic Service DSL

With the solid foundation we created, it shouldn't be too hard to implement a straightforward DSL for services; however, in many ways the design of the API is a harder problem, and much more a matter of taste than engineering. In this case our limitations can guide us. Since our limited space and scope prevent us from pursuing more elaborate options like macros and complex base traits, we can instead focus on a thoughtful arrangement of basic Scala patterns: case classes, method chaining, and implicits.

Designing a Service

We'll again rely on Argonaut for serialization and deserialization. As you saw in the previous section, our Response class can hold any kind of value, but we need a good way to transform it into a String for our Server to transmit. We can do this with a little shorthand helper method that will make it simple for us to generate normal successful HTTP responses:

```scala
LibUVService/service.scala
object ServiceHelpers {
  def OK[T](body:T, headers:Map[String,String] = Map.empty)
           (implicit e:EncodeJson[T]):Response[String] = {
    val b = body.asJson.nospaces
    Response(200,"OK",headers,b)
  }
}
```

The Service class itself is also mostly straightforward: it's initialized with a sequence of routes, and its dispatch method matches them by looking for a full prefix match on the incoming URL. Although this is a minimalistic design for a URL router, the implementation, by design, would allow a much more sophisticated design with named URL components, and so on, to be supplied. We'll also provide a small helper method to start the Service and attach it to a Server:

LibUVService/service.scala
```scala
case class Service(routes:Seq[Route] = Seq.empty)
                  (implicit ec:ExecutionContext) {
  def dispatch(req:Request[String]):Route = {
    for (route <- routes) {
      if (req.method == route.method && req.url.startsWith(route.path)) {
        println(s"matched route ($route)")
        return route
      }
    }
    throw new Exception("no match!")
  }

  def run(port:Int) = {
    Server.init(port, this.dispatch)
  }
}
```

Now, all that's left is the actual DSL.

Implementing a Router DSL

We'll implement our router DSL by appending additional routes onto the Service's (initially empty) list. Since the OK helper already does the hard work, the GET method handlers are very straightforward:

LibUVService/service.scala
```scala
def get(path:String)(h:Request[String] => Response[String]):Service = {
  return Service(this.routes :+ SyncRoute("GET",path,h))
}
def getAsync(path:String)(h:Request[String] => Future[Response[String]]):
  Service = {
  return Service(this.routes :+ AsyncRoute("GET",path,h))
}
```

The POST handlers are just a bit trickier, since they need to decode a request body:

LibUVService/service.scala
```scala
def post[I,O](path:String)(h:Request[I] => Response[O])
    (implicit d:DecodeJson[I], e:EncodeJson[O]):Service = {
  val handler = (r:Request[String]) => {
    val parsedRequest = Parse.decodeOption[I](r.body) match {
      case Some(i) =>
        Request[I](r.method,r.url,r.headers,i)
    }
```

```scala
      val resp = h(parsedRequest)
      Response[String](resp.code, resp.description,
                      resp.headers, resp.body.asJson.nospaces)
    }
    return Service(this.routes :+ SyncRoute("POST",path,handler))
}
def postAsync[I,O](path:String)(h:Request[I] => Future[Response[O]])
    (implicit d:DecodeJson[I], e:EncodeJson[O]):Service = {
  val handler = (r:Request[String]) => {
    val parsedRequest = Parse.decodeOption[I](r.body) match {
      case Some(i) =>
        Request[I](r.method,r.url,r.headers,i)
    }
    h(parsedRequest).map { resp =>
      Response[String](resp.code, resp.description,
                      resp.headers, resp.body.asJson.nospaces)
    }
  }
  return Service(this.routes :+ AsyncRoute("POST",path,handler))
}
```

With that, we can put together a true microservice composed of synchronous and asynchronous routes:

```scala
LibUVService/service.scala
object Main {
  import LibUVConstants._, LibUV.uv_run, ServiceHelpers._
  implicit val ec = EventLoop

  def main(args:Array[String]):Unit = {
    Service()
      .getAsync("/async/") { r => Future(OK(
        Map("asyncMessage" -> s"got (async routed) request $r")
      ))}
      .get("/") { r => OK(
        Map("message" -> s"got (routed) request $r")
      )}
      .run(9999)
    uv_run(EventLoop.loop, UV_RUN_DEFAULT)
    println("done")
  }
}
```

You can test this out with curl, or a browser, and get a sense of it's flexibility and power. Argonaut's JSON codecs, in particular, are flexible enough to handle lists, maps, case classes, and many other common data structures without boilerplate, which can make our services as compact as you might write in a scripting language, like Python or JavaScript, but with all the power and type-safety of Scala.

Integrations and Ecosystems

Now, we finally have all the pieces of the puzzle. Over the last several chapters, we've accumulated a wide range of capabilities based around libuv's event loop for a full asynchronous programming environment.

curl

Since our curl client provides results as a Future[HttpResponse], it's straightforward to plug in to our async request handler pattern:

```
def main(args:Array[String]):Unit = {
  Service()
    .getAsync("/fetch/example") { r =>
      Curl.get(c"https://www.example.com").map { response =>
        Response(200,"OK",Map(),response.body)
      }
    }
  uv_run(EventLoop.loop, UV_RUN_DEFAULT)
}
```

This makes writing a straightforward proxy server trivial. But we can make it even cleaner if we write some boilerplate to convert the ResponseState class used by our curl binding to the Response[String] that our server API expects:

```
def makeResponse(responseState:ResponseState):Response[String] = {
  Response(200,"OK",responseState.headers,responseState.body)
}
```

And we can also, again, use Argonaut to parse a curl response as any Scala class:

```
def makeJsonResponse[T](responseState:ResponseState)
                       (implict d:DecodeJson[T]):Response[T] = {
  Parse.decodeOption[T](responseState.body) match {
    case Some(t) =>
      Response(200,"OK",responseState.headers,t)
    case None =>
      throw new Exception(s"parse error: couldn't decode {responseState.body}")
  }
}
```

This close integration makes it easy to provide a curl-based client for any service we write. If we were to revisit our curl client, in fact, we could probably adjust the API to consolidate on Response[String] as a result type and add JSON support directly to the library.

LMDB

LMDB integration is a trickier case. As you may recollect from Chapter 9, Durability: An Embedded Key-Value Database with LMDB, on page 177, our LMDB binding is synchronous, since it generally returns instantaneously, and single-threaded operation means that we don't have to worry about simultaneous writes locking each other out. Although in theory, that does mean that an LMDB operation can block the event loop, LMDB's latency in practical usage is much faster than any network operation, so it can be better thought of as "effectively synchronous." This means we can use it with a simple synchronous handler, like this:

```
val fetchPatn = raw"/fetch/([^/]+)".r
def main(args:Array[String]):Unit = {
  val env = LMDB.open(c"./db")

  Service()
    .get("/fetch/") { r =>
      val key = r.url match {
        case fetchPatn(key) => key
        case _ => "route error; couldn't find key to lookup"
      }
      val data = LMDB.getJson[Map[String,String]](env,key)
      OK(data)
    }
    .run(9999)
  uv_run(EventLoop.loop, UV_RUN_DEFAULT)
}
```

This code is pretty minimally modified from the minimal web app we wrote in Chapter 9. One pain point here is that we have to inspect the request route twice, once to match the URL for the handler, and a second time to extract the key to look up. Many popular URL routers solve this by allowing URL patterns to contain wildcard or placeholder expressions for routing. In this case, something like /fetch/:key could extract the key for us and somehow pass it into the handler function.

However, this approach raises even more questions: how do we pass named parameters into functions in a typed, safe way? As an alternative approach, our HTTP POST handler can accept and parse any kind of JSON-structured data as a case class with validation and typed fields. Generally speaking, JSON-based patterns lend themselves to the sort of interservice communication scenarios we've been working with.

As such, we could rework the previous example to look like this:

```
case class FetchRequest(key:String)
case class SetRequest(key:String,value:Map[String,String])

def main(args:Array[String]):Unit = {
  val env = LMDB.open(c"./db")

  Service()
    .post[FetchRequest,Map[String,String]]("/fetch/") { r =>
      val data = LMDB.getJson[Map[String,String]](env,key)
      OK(data)
    .post[SetRequest,Map[String,String]]("/set/") { r =>
      LMDB.putJson(env,r.body.key,r.body.value)
      OK(r.body.value)
    }
  // ...
}
```

This seems both simpler and more robust than a URL-based approach. That said, a robust URL matcher is still useful for many common use cases and would be a great addition to our framework.

Other Integrations

We could integrate many more additional C libraries with our event loop for connectivity with real-world systems. For example, Redis[10] is a high-performance key-value store, popular for use as a persistent caching layer. It doesn't offer the same level of durability or transaction support as LMDB, but it has great support for a wide variety of data structures and is widely used in cloud environments. Its official C library, hiredis,[11] has excellent synchronous and asynchronous APIs, and includes example C code[12] for libuv integration.

Postgres,[13] a full-featured relational database, is one of the most widely used database engines available and is always being updated with new features like JSON support and clustering. Its C client library, libpq,[14] likewise has thorough support for asynchronous processing. Although it's somewhat more complex to use than hiredis, open-source projects do exist that demonstrate a full integration with libuv,[15] following an implementation style similar to our libcurl client.

---

10. https://redis.io
11. https://github.com/redis/hiredis
12. https://github.com/redis/hiredis/blob/master/examples/example-libuv.c
13. https://www.postgresql.org
14. https://www.postgresql.org/docs/9.5/libpq.html
15. https://github.com/rootmos/libpquv

Sqlite[16] is another popular relational database that has the benefit of running as a daemonless library, embedded in your application code. David Bouyssié has contributed a Scala Native binding for Sqlite[17] that can replace a traditional database for many common use cases.

In short, any C library that supports asynchronous, callback-based processing is a great candidate for integration with our event loop framework. And there are high-quality C libraries available for just about every problem domain under the sun.[18]

The Way Forward

Traditionally, one of the key selling points of Scala has been its close integration with the broader JVM ecosystem. However, I believe that this book has demonstrated that the native ecosystem of C libraries is just as rich a resource, if not richer. And if you've read this far, I hope you've seen that systems programming doesn't have to be an obscure art! With the techniques you've learned here, you're ready to take part in the growing community of Scala Native developers. So many tools and technologies and libraries are there to explore, and I can't wait to see what you'll accomplish.

---

16. https://www.sqlite.org/index.html
17. https://github.com/david-bouyssie/sqlite4s
18. https://notabug.org/koz.ross/awesome-c

Setting Up the Environment

Setting up a local development environment has traditionally been the Achilles' heel of native software development—even in sophisticated technical organizations, getting a large C++ project to compile on a new developer's machine can take days of work. Fortunately, getting up and running with Scala Native isn't quite as challenging, even among different operating systems and all the subtle differences between machines. Scala Native has fewer dependencies than most C++ projects, and the instructions for getting Mac OS X or Linux systems set up properly are straightforward. However, if you want to sidestep the environment setup problem entirely (or if you're using Windows OS), the easiest way to get up and running quickly is to use Docker containers.

In this Appendix, I'll first run through instructions for getting Scala Native set up on Mac OS X. I'll then explore using containers, which may be the best course of action for everyone.

Whichever way you go, don't forget that there's also a community chat room for the book on Gitter,[1] where you can get help and connect with other readers.

Running Scala Native on Mac OS

Scala Native runs well on modern versions of Mac OS (10.12 or newer), and it only takes a few steps to install. If something goes wrong in the installation, however, it can be tricky to troubleshoot. But if all goes well, installing on Mac OS is probably the easiest way to get started with Scala Native.

First, you'll need the same basic components as for any Scala project:

- Java 8
- sbt 0.13.15 (the Scala build tool)

---

1.   https://gitter.im/scala-native-book/community

To install sbt, follow the instructions in the sbt release docs.[2] You can install any version; sbt can bootstrap an earlier or later version of itself as needed.

Once sbt is installed, you'll need the following C/C++ dependencies for the Scala Native compiler and runtime, plus a few others we'll use in the book:

- LLVM/Clang 3.7 or newer
- re2
- libuv
- libcurl

These you can install with Homebrew,[3] the Mac OS package manager. Once brew is installed, run brew install llvm re2 libuv curl curl-openssl and you should be good to go. To test it out, try to set up and build the sample code in the Systems Programming in the Twenty-First Century, on page xix. You can also download all of the code used in this book from the book's web page at pragprog.com.[4]

While getting started with Scala Native might be easy to do on Mac OS, if things go wrong, it can be very tricky to debug. If you'd rather forgo the potential headaches, containers may be the way to go.

Why Use Containers?

Properly speaking, a *container* in this context is a reproducible disk image of a Linux-based environment that contains all the files and dependencies necessary to run some piece of software. Container technology is built into all modern Linux OS kernels and supports projects like Docker, Kubernetes, rkt, among others.

Even though container technology is 100% Linux, Docker distributes a Toolbox that contains everything you need to run a container image on any Mac, Linux, or Windows system. With a well-assembled container image, we can package up all the code in this book and all of its dependencies so that any reader, anywhere, can have a perfectly configured development environment. (Under the hood, the Docker Toolbox runs a tiny Linux Virtual Machine, on which the containers will actually run. But it's almost 100% transparent for ordinary use.)

For all these reasons, I recommend using Docker to work through the exercises in this book; however, there are a few wrinkles we'll have to work through also. In particular, many of Docker's excellent security features, which provide

---

2. https://www.scala-sbt.org/release/docs/Setup.html
3. https://brew.sh
4. https://pragprog.com/titles/rwscala/source_code

total isolation between the running container and the host machine's network and filesystem, can cause problems when we want to interact with a running program. But we'll see how to resolve these issues shortly.

Installing and Configuring Docker

First, you need to get Docker.[5] If you're on Linux, you'll be running the Docker daemon and CLI directly on your machine, whereas if you're using Windows or Mac, you'll download an application that will manage a VM for you. For Scala Native, I recommend configuring the VM with at least 4GB of RAM for fast build times.

Once Docker is installed and running, we can start creating containers. We can go to a terminal and execute this:

```
$ docker run -it nginx
```

Docker will download an image and run the nginx web server in an isolated container.

Elsewhere in the book, I'll use command prompts like this, beginning with a bare $, to indicate Docker or networking-related commands to be run outside of the container environment.

If we then switch to another terminal, we can use docker ps to check on it:

```
$ docker ps
CONTAINER ID    IMAGE     COMMAND               CREATED
dd95c11bd40e    nginx     "nginx -g 'daemon of…"    Less than a second ago
STATUS          PORTS             NAMES
Up 1 second     443/tcp, 80/tcp   inspiring_ramanujan
```

This tells us that the nginx process is running and is listening on ports 443 and 80; however, if we try to connect to localhost:80 with a web browser, we won't be able to connect because *Docker containers are isolated by default.* If we want this web server to be accessible, even from our own machine, we need to *map* the port on the container to one that's available on our host machine. We can map the port by passing additional arguments to docker run: if we do docker run -p 80 -it nginx, Docker will map port 80 to a random, free port on our host:

```
CONTAINER ID    IMAGE     COMMAND               CREATED
e6ef6a3f55d8    nginx     "nginx -g 'daemon of…"    Less than a second ago
STATUS              PORTS                       NAMES
Up 1 second         443/tcp, 0.0.0.0:32770->80/tcp   thirsty_bassi
```

---

5. https://docs.docker.com/install

This tells us the port 32770 on our host (0.0.0.0 or 127.0.0.1 or localhost) is mapped to port 80 on the container. However, note that the assigned port is *random* and you may have a different port on your system. Now, we can point a browser at localhost:32770 (or whichever port you've been assigned) and we should see a Welcome to nginx! page, as well some log lines in our docker run terminal, indicating that it has received HTTP requests and served a successful response.

Running Scala Native in Docker

Now that we've established that Docker is running and properly configured, we can hit Ctrl + C in the docker run terminal to shut down our nginx container. Running Scala Native in Docker is just as easy: I've published an image called rwhaling/scala-native-book with a full Scala Native installation and all of the code in the book on Docker Hub, so let's run it like this:

```
$ docker run -it -p 8080:8080 rwhaling/scala-native-book
:scala-native:~ $ ~/book-code #
```

Unlike nginx, which started the nginx server immediately, this container opens up a shell. In this Appendix, you'll know you're in the container environment when you see a prompt like :scala-native:some_directory $, whereas a prompt on your host machine will be indicated with a plain $.

You'll also note that we've changed the form of the port argument—by specifying -p 8080:8080 we tell Docker to use the same port number, both inside and outside of the container, so you can reach it at localhost:8080 in a web browser or other utility.

Let's take a look around:

```
:scala-native:~ $ ls -al
total 221632
drwxr-xr-x  11 root      root            4096 Jan 12 15:54 .
drwx------   9 root      root            4096 Jan 12 17:45 ..
-rw-r--r--   1 root      root            6148 Jan 12 15:32 .DS_Store
-rw-r--r--   1 root      root             107 Jan 12 15:29 .dockerignore
-rw-r--r--   1 root      root            1352 Jan 12 15:53 Dockerfile
drwxr-xr-x   2 root      root            4096 Dec 16 19:19 ForkWaitShell
drwxr-xr-x   3 root      root            4096 Mar 21  2018 HTTPClient
drwxr-xr-x   3 root      root            4096 Mar 21  2018 HTTPServer
drwxr-xr-x   8 root      root            4096 Jan 12 15:54 InputAndOutput
drwxr-xr-x   2 root      root            4096 Sep  7 02:23 LibUVFutures
drwxr-xr-x   2 root      root            4096 Jul 23 00:27 LibUVServer
drwxr-xr-x   2 root      root            4096 Jul 10  2018 MapReduce
drwxr-xr-x   9 root      root            4096 Jul 10  2018 MemoryManagement
-rw-r--r--   1 root      root            1246 Dec 16 19:40 build.sbt
-rw-r--r--   1 root      root       226885816 May  2  2018 googlebooks-eng-all...
-rwxr-xr-x   1 root      root               0 Jan 12 15:25 start_docker.sh
```

Here, we have a directory for each chapter in the book, as well as some data to work with. We can build and run a Hello, World program like this:

```
~ $ cd InputAndOutput/hello_native/
~/book-code/InputAndOutput/hello_native $ sbt run
[warn] Executing in batch mode.
...
[info] Compiling 1 Scala source to /...
[info] Linking (2671 ms)
[info] Discovered 1275 classes and 9462 methods
[info] Optimizing (debug mode) (4288 ms)
[info] Generating intermediate code (1258 ms)
[info] Produced 37 files
[info] Compiling to native code (2504 ms)
[info] Linking native code (immix gc) (202 ms)
hello, world
[success] Total time: 22 s, completed Jan 12, 2019 5:47:48 PM
```

Success! And since we have port 8080 mapped, even the HTTP servers we write later will work just fine inside this Docker container.

There's one catch, though. Because Docker containers are immutable, if we change any files, these changes will be lost if we terminate and restart the container. If you intend to play with the code or write new Scala Native programs, you'll want to create a directory on your host system to hold your files and then *mount* it into the container with an extra argument. You can do this by passing an extra argument to docker run in the form -v source_directory_path:target_container_path. First, let's create a directory on our host system, like this:

```
$ mkdir ~/my_code
```

Then we can mount our local my_code directory to the path /root/my_code in the container filesystem like this:

```
$ docker run -it -p 8080:8080 -v ~/my_code:/root/my_code \
  rwhaling/scala-native-book
scala-native> ~/book-code # ls ..
book-code   my_code
```

Now, the my_code directory is visible from within the container, and any changes made will persist.

I *highly recommend* testing this out, making a few changes from both inside and outside the container, and verifying that changes are visible and persistent across container restarts. Docker is a robust and proven technology, but it's easy to make a mistake with some of the more complicated commands we're using. I also suggest creating a local shell script to launch the container just the way you prefer. You can save a lot of typing with a simple two-line file like this:

```
#!/bin/bash
docker run -it -p 8080:8080 -v ~/my_code:/root/my_code \
  rwhaling/scala-native-book
```

Caveats aside, you're good to go! If you came to this Appendix from the Introduction, you can go back and resume the sample project.

Index

Thank you!

How did you enjoy this book? Please let us know. Take a moment and email us at support@pragprog.com with your feedback. Tell us your story and you could win free ebooks. Please use the subject line "Book Feedback."

Ready for your next great Pragmatic Bookshelf book? Come on over to https://pragprog.com and use the coupon code BUYANOTHER2020 to save 30% on your next ebook.

Void where prohibited, restricted, or otherwise unwelcome. Do not use ebooks near water. If rash persists, see a doctor. Doesn't apply to *The Pragmatic Programmer* ebook because it's older than the Pragmatic Bookshelf itself. Side effects may include increased knowledge and skill, increased marketability, and deep satisfaction. Increase dosage regularly.

And thank you for your continued support,

Andy Hunt, Publisher

SAVE 30%!
Use coupon code
BUYANOTHER2020

Designing Elixir Systems with OTP

You know how to code in Elixir; now learn to think in it. Learn to design libraries with intelligent layers that shape the right data structures, flow from one function into the next, and present the right APIs. Embrace the same OTP that's kept our telephone systems reliable and fast for over 30 years. Move beyond understanding the OTP functions to knowing what's happening under the hood, and why that matters. Using that knowledge, instinctively know how to design systems that deliver fast and resilient services to your users, all with an Elixir focus.

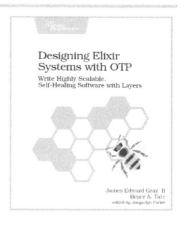

James Edward Gray, II and Bruce A. Tate
(246 pages) ISBN: 9781680506617. $41.95
https://pragprog.com/book/jgotp

Software Estimation Without Guessing

Developers hate estimation, and most managers fear disappointment with the results, but there is hope for both. You'll have to give up some widely held misconceptions: let go of the notion that "an estimate is an estimate," and estimate for your particular need. Realize that estimates have a limited shelf-life, and re-estimate frequently as needed. When reality differs from your estimate, don't lament; mine that disappointment for the gold that can be the longer-term jackpot. We'll show you how.

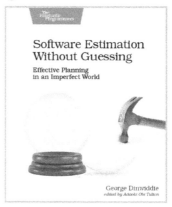

George Dinwiddie
(246 pages) ISBN: 9781680506983. $29.95
https://pragprog.com/book/gdestimate

Programming Phoenix 1.4

Don't accept the compromise between fast and beautiful: you can have it all. Phoenix creator Chris McCord, Elixir creator José Valim, and award-winning author Bruce Tate walk you through building an application that's fast and reliable. At every step, you'll learn from the Phoenix creators not just what to do, but why. Packed with insider insights and completely updated for Phoenix 1.4, this definitive guide will be your constant companion in your journey from Phoenix novice to expert as you build the next generation of web applications.

Chris McCord, Bruce Tate and José Valim
(356 pages) ISBN: 9781680502268. $45.95
https://pragprog.com/book/phoenix14

Programming Kotlin

Programmers don't just use Kotlin, they love it. Even Google has adopted it as a first-class language for Android development. With Kotlin, you can intermix imperative, functional, and object-oriented styles of programming and benefit from the approach that's most suitable for the problem at hand. Learn to use the many features of this highly concise, fluent, elegant, and expressive statically typed language with easy-to-understand examples. Learn to write maintainable, high-performing JVM and Android applications, create DSLs, program asynchronously, and much more.

Venkat Subramaniam
(460 pages) ISBN: 9781680506358. $51.95
https://pragprog.com/book/vskotlin

Programming Elm

Elm brings the safety and stability of functional programing to front-end development, making it one of the most popular new languages. Elm's functional nature and static typing means that runtime errors are nearly impossible, and it compiles to JavaScript for easy web deployment. This book helps you take advantage of this new language in your web site development. Learn how the Elm Architecture will help you create fast applications. Discover how to integrate Elm with JavaScript so you can update legacy applications. See how Elm tooling makes deployment quicker and easier.

Jeremy Fairbank
(308 pages) ISBN: 9781680502855. $40.95
https://pragprog.com/book/jfelm

Technical Blogging, Second Edition

Successful technical blogging is not easy but it's also not magic. Use these techniques to attract and keep an audience of loyal, regular readers. Leverage this popularity to reach your goals and amplify your influence in your field. Get more users for your startup or open source project, or simply find an outlet to share your expertise. This book is your blueprint, with step-by-step instructions that leave no stone unturned. Plan, create, maintain, and promote a successful blog that will have remarkable effects on your career or business.

Antonio Cangiano
(336 pages) ISBN: 9781680506471. $47.95
https://pragprog.com/book/actb2

Build Chatbot Interactions

The next step in the evolution of user interfaces is here. Chatbots let your users interact with your service in their own natural language. Use free and open source tools along with Ruby to build creative, useful, and unexpected interactions for users. Take advantage of the Lita framework's step-by-step implementation strategy to simplify bot development and testing. From novices to experts, chatbots are an area in which everyone can participate. Exercise your creativity by creating chatbot skills for communicating, information, and fun.

Daniel Pritchett
(206 pages) ISBN: 9781680506327. $35.95
https://pragprog.com/book/dpchat

Test-Driven React

You work in a loop: write code, get feedback, iterate. The faster you get feedback, the faster you can learn and become a more effective developer. Test-Driven React helps you refine your React workflow to give you the feedback you need as quickly as possible. Write strong tests and run them continuously as you work, split complex code up into manageable pieces, and stay focused on what's important by automating away mundane, trivial tasks. Adopt these techniques and you'll be able to avoid productivity traps and start building React components at a stunning pace!

Trevor Burnham
(190 pages) ISBN: 9781680506464. $45.95
https://pragprog.com/book/tbreact

Small, Sharp Software Tools

The command-line interface is making a comeback.
That's because developers know that all the best features of your operating system are hidden behind a
user interface designed to help average people use the
computer. But you're not the average user, and the
CLI is the most efficient way to get work done fast.
Turn tedious chores into quick tasks: read and write
files, manage complex directory hierarchies, perform
network diagnostics, download files, work with APIs,
and combine individual programs to create your own
workflows. Put down that mouse, open the CLI, and
take control of your software development environment.

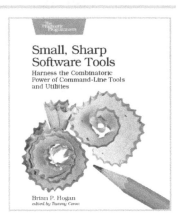

Brian P. Hogan
(326 pages) ISBN: 9781680502961. $38.95
https://pragprog.com/book/bhcldev

Programming Ecto

Languages may come and go, but the relational
database endures. Learn how to use Ecto, the premier
database library for Elixir, to connect your Elixir and
Phoenix apps to databases. Get a firm handle on Ecto
fundamentals with a module-by-module tour of the
critical parts of Ecto. Then move on to more advanced
topics and advice on best practices with a series of
recipes that provide clear, step-by-step instructions
on scenarios commonly encountered by app developers.
Co-authored by the creator of Ecto, this title provides
all the essentials you need to use Ecto effectively.

Darin Wilson and Eric Meadows-Jönsson
(242 pages) ISBN: 9781680502824. $45.95
https://pragprog.com/book/wmecto

Web Development with ReasonML

ReasonML is a new, type-safe, functional language that compiles to efficient, readable JavaScript. ReasonML interoperates with existing JavaScript libraries and works especially well with React, one of the most popular front-end frameworks. Learn how to take advantage of the power of a functional language while keeping the flexibility of the whole JavaScript ecosystem. Move beyond theory and get things done faster and more reliably with ReasonML today.

J. David Eisenberg
(208 pages) ISBN: 9781680506334. $45.95
https://pragprog.com/book/reasonml

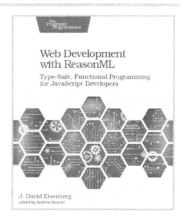

Programming WebAssembly with Rust

WebAssembly fulfills the long-awaited promise of web technologies: fast code, type-safe at compile time, execution in the browser, on embedded devices, or anywhere else. Rust delivers the power of C in a language that strictly enforces type safety. Combine both languages and you can write for the web like never before! Learn how to integrate with JavaScript, run code on platforms other than the browser, and take a step into IoT. Discover the easy way to build cross-platform applications without sacrificing power, and change the way you write code for the web.

Kevin Hoffman
(238 pages) ISBN: 9781680506365. $45.95
https://pragprog.com/book/khrust

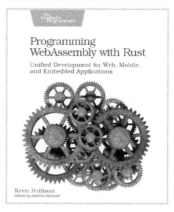

The Pragmatic Bookshelf

The Pragmatic Bookshelf features books written by professional developers for professional developers. The titles continue the well-known Pragmatic Programmer style and continue to garner awards and rave reviews. As development gets more and more difficult, the Pragmatic Programmers will be there with more titles and products to help you stay on top of your game.

Visit Us Online

This Book's Home Page
https://pragprog.com/book/rwscala
Source code from this book, errata, and other resources. Come give us feedback, too!

Keep Up to Date
https://pragprog.com
Join our announcement mailing list (low volume) or follow us on twitter @pragprog for new titles, sales, coupons, hot tips, and more.

New and Noteworthy
https://pragprog.com/news
Check out the latest pragmatic developments, new titles and other offerings.

Save on the ebook

Save on the ebook versions of this title. Owning the paper version of this book entitles you to purchase the electronic versions at a terrific discount.

PDFs are great for carrying around on your laptop—they are hyperlinked, have color, and are fully searchable. Most titles are also available for the iPhone and iPod touch, Amazon Kindle, and other popular e-book readers.

Buy now at *https://pragprog.com/coupon*

Contact Us

Online Orders:	*https://pragprog.com/catalog*
Customer Service:	*support@pragprog.com*
International Rights:	*translations@pragprog.com*
Academic Use:	*academic@pragprog.com*
Write for Us:	*http://write-for-us.pragprog.com*
Or Call:	+1 800-699-7764